Businesswise

Financial Planning for the Small and Medium-sized Enterprise

First Edition

by

Peter Lyons

Tolley Publishing

United Kingdom	Butterworths, a Division of Reed Elsevier (UK) Ltd, Halsbury House, 35 Chancery Lane, LONDON WC2A 1EL and 4 Hill Street, EDINBURGH EH2 3JZ
Australia	Butterworths, a Division of Reed International Books Australia Pty Ltd, CHATSWOOD, New South Wales
Canada	Butterworths Canada Ltd, MARKHAM, Ontario
Hong Kong	Butterworths Hong Kong, a division of Reed Elsevier (Greater China) Ltd, HONG KONG
India	Butterworths India, NEW DELHI
Ireland	Butterworth (Ireland) Ltd, DUBLIN
Malaysia	Malayan Law Journal Sdn Bhd, KUALA LUMPUR
New Zealand	Butterworths of New Zealand Ltd, WELLINGTON
Singapore	Butterworths Asia, SINGAPORE
South Africa	Butterworths Publishers (Pty) Ltd, DURBAN
USA	Lexis Law Publishing, CHARLOTTESVILLE, Virginia

© Reed Elsevier (UK) Ltd 2001

A CIP Catalogue record for this book is available from the British Library.

ISBN 0 75450 534 0

Typeset in Great Britain by Action Publishing Technology Ltd, Gloucester, GL1 5SR

Printed and bound in Great Britain by Hobbs the Printers Ltd, Totton, Hampshire

Visit Butterworths LEXIS *direct* at www.butterworths.com

Preface

The European Union defines Small and Medium-sized Enterprises, or SMEs for short, as businesses having no more than 250 employees or a turnover not greater than ECU 40 million. The exchange rate with sterling fluctuates and a generally prevalent turnover figure taken has been £25 million unless accuracy is demanded. There are approximately 3.7 million businesses operating in the United Kingdom, of which some 99% fall within the SME definition, employing for the most part less than 20 workers. They contribute 43% of the Gross National Product and employ half the number of workers in the private sector. Within this definition lie very many micro-organisations having, say, up to 8 to 10 employees on their books (Source: Federation of Small Businesses).

It is vital, therefore, that this very important sector of business has the capability of optimising its business returns and does not succumb to failure. This book has as its principal aims to encourage better financial management and to stave off business failure. Although aimed primarily to assist the owner-manager of an SME to make his business more profitable and more efficient from a financial aspect, it should also be of interest to business students and aspiring managers of larger enterprises and service providers generally who wish for a practical grounding in financial management and have to evaluate the financial health of SMEs or new projects in the course of their work. It encompasses:

- The basic tenets of managing a business;
- Start-up situations and the assessment of new projects;
- Financial pre-planning to account for future trading variations;
- Reasons why small businesses do not survive;
- What to do when things go wrong.

Related topics that are covered include:

- Business strategy;
- Introducing a Business Plan;
- The efficient use of business assets;
- Financial forecasting;
- Operational management;
- Raising finance;
- Trading under difficulties.

Throughout, an endeavour has been made to make the reader equally at home whether a particular topic is required to be studied in depth or whether only a brief referral is needed. Recognition is given that the available time of a working owner in a small business is valuable and that 'financial issues' are often not accorded a top management priority. Summaries of the text are therefore given at the end of each chapter and a composite example of an operating SME is provided in Appendix A.

About the Author

Most people are content with just one career in their working lives. Peter Lyons decided to benefit from the experience of having four before the idea of this book became fact. He commenced by qualifying as an accountant and, like many in the profession, decided to concentrate on future trends rather than historic records through writing company investment reviews for various stockbrokers. After having first-hand experience of the 1974 recession and how it affected businesses he then commenced on what was to be a fourteen-year career in banking.

During this period, as a lending and account relationship banker, the senior management of hundreds of companies were visited throughout the United Kingdom on behalf of British and German banks. As Peter says, he never quite finished his avocation in banking before being persuaded to become a funding adviser and procurer for a consultancy group specialising in Public Sector clients. By this time he had commenced his own accountancy practice that continues to this day. Most recently a period was spent as a financial appraiser for a Government Agency then dealing in grants and loan assistance for small businesses. Peter's practice now concentrates on offering a financial business advisory service to Small and Medium-sized Enterprises, frequently in conjunction with the services provided by Business Links.

Having written a number of articles for various publications in the past, the idea of collecting into one volume this wide diversity of financial experience met in practice was borne. It offers advice to the reader on how best to be prepared for the pitfalls met by the smaller business and how better to understand the views of banks and those to whom financial assistance is requested.

Peter is currently a Fellow of the Institute of Chartered Accountants in England and Wales; Fellow of the Institute of Management; Fellow of the Institute of Financial Professional Managers; Member of the Chartered Institute of Bankers; Member of the Institute of Business Advisers; Member of the Institute of Management Consultants; and Member of the Association for Investment Management and Research.

Contents

Contents

Contents

Chapter 1

The Business – an Overview

1.1   Every owner-manager should ask themselves the question: 'what do I want to get out of the business and over what period of time?' Perhaps the answer to the first question appears obvious: many would answer 'profit', when in reality they should be thinking of 'cash flow'. A business may make a profit and yet still fail if the profit is unrealised and locked up in assets or is spirited away in excessive drawings.

The second answer may invoke a more vague response: 'a better living until I retire' or 'higher profits for years to come'. This infers that no specific trading target has been set within a given timescale, let alone how that target is to be attained whether, for example, through indigenous expansion or by acquisition. It will be difficult to manage the business in the most effective manner and optimise its returns if no strategic goal is in place. On the other hand time may not be critical for the business if, for example, it is to be passed down within the family, in which case operating continuity and the enjoyment of a minimum level of profitability are likely to be the most important goals.

1.2   Years of operating experience allied with technical skills give the owner-manager an edge in being able to judge how the business is trading. At any one time answers should be at hand to these questions:

Question	Translation
What is my 'break-even' point?	What weekly average sales do I need to start earning a profit?
What is my average gross profit margin?	What is my average profit per £1 of sales?
What will be my cash flow over the next three months?	Will I be generating sufficient cash to continue to trade?
What profit am I expecting to earn in the current trading year?	What sales target am I working to?

1.3   Different types of business will require different levels of sophistication of financial reporting to be able properly to answer some of these questions. Take the retailer with multiple stock lines; he can work out an average gross profit margin by taking past years overall results or, better still, calculate different margins for the major sales lines. A contractor or manufacturer will have the problem of estimating the value of stocks of raw materials in hand if a proper stock take or on-going records are not maintained.

Break-even point

1.4   Each type of business will incur a mixture of costs, *fixed* or *variable*, according to the level of turnover being achieved. Whether one is considering an established or a start-up business, or just a new project, the viability of the business or project must be tested at outset and its break-even point calculated and checked at regular intervals thereafter. A broad example is shown in the following table:

Turnover: (£'000)			**2,000**	
To base 100				*100*
Direct Costs	Variable	Fixed		
Labour		1,284	1,284	
Materials	198		198	
Sub-contractors	51		51	
Transport	9		9	
Total Direct Costs	**258**	**1,284**	**1,542**	*77*
Gross Profit			**458**	*23*
Indirect Costs				
Wages		98	98	
Establishment overheads		61	61	
Other–travel/marketing etc		30	30	
Finance–short term	27		27	
–long term		4	4	
Proprietors' drawings		79	79	
Total Indirect Costs	**27**	**272**	**299**	*15*
Total Costs	**285**	**1,556**	**1,841**	*92*
Net Profit before tax			**159**	*8*
As a percentage of Turnover	*14*	*78*	*8*	*(profit)*

The table is set out abbreviated in standard accounts form but the example of costs have been analysed showing their fixed or variable nature relative to the turnover achieved. The company examined is involved in the service industry and is heavily labour intensive.

1.5   The **break-even point** for profit is at a turnover figure calculated by 1,556/(1-0.14) where 14 is the percentage of variable costs shown above. This resolves to £1,809. As a check, 14% of £1,809 = £253 added to the fixed costs of £1,556 makes the same turnover figure of £1,809.

In the example the work force is fully trained and its size is permanent. The cost of short-term finance comprises interest on a bank overdraft that fluctuates with cash flow and the level of turnover. The proprietors are working in the business and the drawings shown are their minimum salaries as living requirements excluding any share of profits earned. Non-cash costs such as depreciation of assets are excluded although they would be allowed for when projecting overall profitability and operating margins in tendering for job contracts.

The average Gross Profit Margin

1.6   In the example above the Gross Profit (£458,000) on Turnover (£2 million) shows an average margin of 23% (i.e. an average profit of 23 pence per £1 of sales). This is based on the actual but historic position and must be adjusted to allow for any subsequent events or deviations expected in the future. For instance, the current year may demand a wage rise of 3% p.a. for staff. This will put another £42,000 on to fixed costs and by itself would have dropped the gross profit margin to 21% in a full year.

1.7   Businesses should, wherever possible, try and recover any downturn in sales through increasing gross selling margins. This is not often possible midway through completing an order or where the contract is worked on a fixed price with or without set price escalation clauses. It may also be difficult if one is dealing with a long-standing customer. However, new customers will be less inconvenienced, it is less painful for the business than laying off workers if the downturn is likely to be short-term and it will be quicker to recover profits than trying to reduce indirect operating costs. It is more beneficial to cloak a small profit margin increase on a high turnover (by number) product line than to invoke a large increase on products with a relatively small number of sales. If competition prevents an increase in selling margins there are other choices available to management to help offset lower earnings when sales fall or are expected to fall, and these are analysed in the table following:

3

1.8 The Business – an Overview

£'000	Base case	Case A Sales fall	Case B GP% maintained	Case C Gross Profit maintained	Case D Changes in Direct Costs	
Turnover	2,000	1,800	1,800	1,800	1,800	
Direct costs:					*10.6% or*	*12.9%*
Variable	*12.9%* 258	*12.9%* 232	*12.9%* 232	*12.9%* 232	192	232
Fixed	1,284	1,284	1,156	1,110	1,284	1,244
Total	1,542	1,516	1,388	1,342	1,476	1,476
Gross Profit	458	284	412	458	324	324
GP%	*22.9%*	*15.8%*	*22.9%*	*25.4%*	*18.0%*	*18.0%*
reduction in		Gross Profit	Fixed Direct	Fixed Direct		

Case A shows the effect of the drop in turnover without any remedial measures. There is a 38% drop in Gross Profit.

Case B indicates what would occur were the gross profit margin to be maintained. The fall in Gross Profit is reduced to 10% but there would need to be a similar reduction in fixed direct costs, which may not be possible.

Case C assumes that Gross Profit must be maintained, but it would mean that the average profit margin would have to increase to 25.4% and Fixed Direct Costs fall by 13.5%.

Case D assumes that some gross profit margin increases can be implemented, with the average margin for the year coming out at 18%. Management also managed to curb a modest amount of fixed costs during the year. The fall in gross profit, although still high at 29%, was not as large as the situation when no remedial measures were undertaken.

1.8   These are theoretical examples but they do show the nature and extent of a fall in turnover, if only to underline how difficult it can be, particularly during a trading year, to maintain earnings. If the business had planned to trade and spend within the expectation of a reasonable turnover range, thereby allowing for any unexpected shortfall in sales giving rise to a lower profit, the effect on cash flow would be potentially far less dramatic.

The Cash Flow of the business

1.9   Maintenance of adequate cash flow is the single most important objective for any business. In importance it outweighs the growth of turnover; the adequacy of capital maintained in the business; and the extent of borrowings. A business can earn more profits while being less profitable *providing* turnover is increasing fast enough *and* an increase in commercial borrowings compensates for any reduction in the proprietors' capital employed in the business due to their wish to try and maintain their annual drawings. A typical example of how this could be accomplished to great effect would be a Factoring or Invoice Discounting facility based on financing debtor balances as turnover expands.

1.10   There are limitations as to how far this strategy can be invoked, notably depending on the particular mix of the sales debts and the limit that is put on the size of the credit facility made available by the borrower. Consider the following trading record of a proprietorial business. The figures have been rounded for illustration purposes.

Trading years	**1**	**2**	**3**	**4**
Turnover (£'000)	2,000	2,000	2,400	2,800
Net Profit margin	*6.35%*	*5.5%*	*5.2%*	*4.8%*
Net Profit (£'000)	127	110	125	134
Less Borrowing costs (10% p.a.)	20	23	25	27
Depreciation	27	40	45	50
Adjusted Net Profit	80	47	55	57
Cash Flow (adjusted Net Profit + Depreciation)	107	87	100	107
Less Assets acquired in year	70	80	60	65
Proprietors' drawings	64	66	67	68
Proprietors' tax payable	17	10	11	12
Cash left in the Business	– 44	– 69	– 38	– 38
Proprietors' Capital Accounts (end of year)	200	170	147	124
Borrowings (on-going)	200	230	253	276
Total Capital Employed in the Business	400	400	400	400
Trade Debtors (3 months turnover)	500	500	600	700
Borrowings as % of Trade Debts	*40%*	*46%*	*42%*	*39%*

1.11   The picture shows a business gearing itself up for future growth through a programme of asset re-equipment (high compared with past profits) and expecting to achieve this through higher turnover and profits to enable proprietors' drawings to remain broadly unchanged.

In the event, it is shown that turnover did improve but at the cost of lower profit margins. The resulting lower profits were insufficient to sustain the level of the capital re-equipping and the rate of proprietors' drawings. The business was able to continue up to the end of year 4 because borrowings were tied to the increasing level of trade debts and were still a relatively low proportion thereof.

1.12   There are several pointers to come from this scenario:

1.   The proprietors should have considered in advance whether the business's average profit margin would suffer in the dash for growth.

2.   The viability of the cost of the asset re-equipping programme should have been measured in advance with the profit return from the additional turnover expected to be won. If this was to occur over the medium term, then financing of the new assets should have been put in place at the point of purchase.

3.   The negative cash flow overall of the business should have led to immediate remedial action. Future asset purchases could have been stopped in favour of leasing. Proprietors' drawings should have been curbed. The future profitability of trading should have been examined to try and improve margins.

4.   As it now stands the business is at a critical trading phase. An additional borrowing request to the bank at a time when borrowings are already two and a quarter times the proprietors' total capital left in the business suggests an emphatic refusal. Equipment now purchased could only be sold at a loss and jeopardise future production levels. A cost paring review would be unlikely to raise sufficient savings to improve cash flow significantly. A capital injection from the proprietors is looking increasingly imminent to enable trading to continue. Turnover may or may not continue to expand and an immediate appraisal of prospects should be made.

1.13   A financial review of the business is overdue. When the Balance Sheet is examined this may highlight other beneficial actions for the business to pursue. The improving trend in Net Profit is an encouraging sign. There may be surplus assets to sell or rent out to boost income. The management should have planned its expansion better and reacted earlier to the adverse cash flow situation.

The Balance Sheet

1.14   For many small businesses the time of the annual accounts will be the only occasion when the *past* health of the business (its profit or loss) will be judged and little close scrutiny will be given to the Balance Sheet. This is unfortunate, since the figures portray to some degree the expected *future* health of the business. It will inform the reviewer of the net position of the debtors and creditors, not to forget the make up of the figures and the ages of the debts on the books.

1.15   A comparison of the overall **Cash** position will show how the cash management of the business has progressed. **Stocks** should be analysed: are the raw materials excessive bearing in mind the order position and the time needed to receive new supplies? What is the composition of the value of Work-in-Progress and what profit element is being carried forward? Are Finished Goods representative of delivery schedules or has too much been produced 'on speculation' to satisfy future orders?

1.16   The make-up and size of **Fixed Assets** should not be overlooked. Has a programme of Plant replacements been put in train, new or second-hand? Are there Freehold assets displayed on the Balance Sheet – if so, is this tax efficient? If earnings are more important to the proprietors than capital gains, should the property be rented rather than owned? Is it more efficient to own motor vehicles rather than lease? Indeed, is there a need for delivery vehicles rather than to outsource this component of the customer service?

1.17   **Borrowings** should be especially examined very carefully. Is there an approximate match between longer term assets and liabilities as against shorter term assets and liabilities (say, within one year ahead)? Most financial observers know the prime crime of the borrower in investing 'long' (term) through borrowing 'short'. If the former is based on variable interest rates and the latter is at fixed interest rates, were interest rates to rise excessively and wipe out the borrower's profit margin a (increasing?) loss will ensue. For a business, the risk is no less traumatic: to finance the purchase of fixed assets with short-term credit facilities raises the risk of the short-term borrowing increasing in cost or to be withdrawn by the borrower at their discretion. The business should always try to match the purchase and use of long-term assets with long-term borrowings.

1.18   What may be termed **Latent Assets** are a special case for businesses. These may comprise Goodwill purchased; Brand Names capitalised values; deferred Research Expenditure and similar costs carried forward until the project comes to fruition. In all these cases it is prudent to remove their so-called present day asset value off the capital employed in the business by deducting their values off the appropriate Proprietors' Capital Accounts or Shareholders' Capital and Reserves. By way of explanation, Goodwill may have been the money tendered historically for the business but it will bear no resemblance to the value that may ensue on any future sale. The capitalisation of Brand Names assumes that future use of the brand will accord a future super-value to trading.

1.18   *The Business – an Overview*

This does not equate in practice to situations such as when bottled mineral water suffers contamination and a loss of selling credibility; or when tyres are found to have production discrepancies leading to adverse publicity, replacement losses and lawsuits; or when fashion simply dictates a change in consumers' preferences.

Chapter 2

Business Strategy – the Objectives

2.1   Before a start is made to raise any Business Plan, which principally sets out how the business is to be run, there must be laid down a strategy for the future on which to base the Plan.

Start-up ventures with no track record are likely to have formulated an operating strategy at outset, probably strongly biased in favour of marketing and its potential rewards from the use of limited resources and showing a probable financial 'gap' that will be required to be funded at some stage in the trading cycle.

Established businesses, unless they are very conscientious, will tend to 'lose' their initial strategy after a period of time due to familiarity, or through not taking account of a changing trading scene, or simply because operational pressures prevent time being spent on revising the original strategy. A regular review should become a priority, say, at periods no longer than at the time the annual Accounts are drafted. The strategy can then be discussed with the firm's accountants and the Business Plan updated when finalising the results for the year.

2.2   There are three strategies that should be considered: Business, Personal and Operational.

Business strategy

2.3   A list should be made of the following characteristics of the business:

- The strengths of the business.

- What aspects should be improved.

- What changes have been made in the past three years and why.

- Have the changes been voluntary or involuntary.

- What new expectations are in the offing over the next two years.

- What assumptions underline these expectations.

- How do the expectations compare with current market trends.

- Will competitors allow these expectations to succeed.

- What change of direction (strategy) is necessary for the business.

2.4   It is much easier to build on the existing strengths of a business than to start to build a niche area from scratch. Often the proprietor takes for granted the strengths inherent in the business and does not capitalise more on the opportunities. Take the example of an engineering firm that is expert in renovating one line of machines that are being replaced by newer computer-driven models. To train and equip to service the new generation of machines will cost time and money and disrupt the existing business. Instead, as larger competitors change this will leave more opportunities for the smaller business to become better known; gain a greater share of the gradually shrinking market; offer a wider geographic service and have a better chance to raise customer charges and profit margin. There could also be the opportunity to act as a dealer rather than just a service provider for the equipment.

2.5   Once the strengths of the business have been listed, there should remain those parts that might be considered 'weak' in trading terms. There may be diverse reasons for this. It may be due to sub-standard profit margins, or because a part of the business has been carried on 'by tradition' for many years. Sentiment carries little weight in the competitive atmosphere of business nowadays. A critical review of all 'weak' trading areas or products should be made and a strategic decision taken whether the resources tied up in this area may beneficially be employed in other sections of the business.

2.6   It may seem retrograde why one should look at the changes made over the past three years, but it will indicate:

- The significant events that affected the business over that time.

- How they were combated and solved (or otherwise).

- Whether they are likely to recur, in which case remedial measures can be considered in advance now and implemented or retained for use at some future date.

- Whether the solution adopted, in retrospect, was the best one.

- If not, what strategy would be best in the future.

2.7   An example met in the printing industry showed that a majority of business was emanating from one major customer on a short-term but renewable contract. The business was peremptorily lost without any immediate replacement. The company procrastinated over a long-term strategic solution and adopted a crash programme to increase turnover. This had the effect of promoting the second most important customer as sales leader. This customer was then unexpectedly taken over and contractual changes were made by the new owner, effectively putting the printing business in terms of turnover growth back to square one.

2.8   It is very much preferred for a business voluntarily to make a change in its strategy rather than be forced to do so. It may entail re-training employees in new concepts and raising finance to re-equip the factory. These changes may disrupt existing production and will take time to show the best results. Unfortunately many micro-businesses operate with no plan to fall back to in case of need should they run short of working capital. They involuntarily have to ask their bank for a 'rescue' lending facility that may, or may not, be forthcoming on terms that may be unpalatable to the borrower.

2.9   Considering changes that may affect the business over the next two years should be constantly at the back of the owner-manager's mind. Frequently the timing of the change and positioning of the business to meet this change are wrongly judged. This can be particularly so where the business is seasonal by nature. The important strategy must be to operate conservatively during times of low trading activity, so that business continuity is maintained and is well placed to benefit from the expected period of high activity. The danger for the business is that it may over-reach itself financially and run out of working capital before the improvement in turnover is felt.

2.10   A service utility unfortunately succumbed to this trap when it over-spent re-equipping its business during the previous peak in turnover that arose out of expected legislative changes. Unfortunately it had insufficient liquid funds to ride out the subsequent drop in activity before benefiting from greater activity preparatory to the next period of legislative change.

2.11   In the last case the legislative change was forewarned. In practice many changes have to be assumed from market intelligence and other sources. A pertinent example would be the mobile telephone market. The public was informed well in advance that mobile telephones would be on sale and many manufacturers geared themselves up to attend to the expected demand. The retailer already with a high street outlet selling electrical goods might consider this a good opportunity to expand his business. Initially this was so, but the mushrooming of outlets soon led to intense competition, largely model preference and price-based, with a consequent drop in reward expectations. If this diversification had been financed by borrowings or through reducing the funds made available to sustain the traditional trading lines, the additional cost could be unsustainable and, in retrospect, inadequate planning had supported a poor strategic choice.

2.12   Compare this planning decision with that of a packaging manufacturer, long-established but who had outgrown the premises and had the opportunity to relocate, either by site acquisition or rental, a short distance away. Marketing and financial consultants were called in to advise whether increased sales could be won to support larger premises and whether the business would remain financially sound. The financier put a figure on future sales that were needed to generate a suitable net profit following the relocation. The marketeer then advised on the reality of this sales target. In this case the possible change of direction was rejected as unsound in the circumstances since the cost of change was greater than the expected reward of higher business to be won.

Personal strategy

2.13   For owner-managed businesses there are additional considerations that must be taken into account:

- What are the personal requirements of the owner; now, over the next two years, and for the long term.

- These requirements should be translated into financial and non-financial goals.

- Is the business set up to deliver these goals.

- In what areas is it not so set up.

- What changes should be made and when to achieve these goals.

- What problems are likely to be encountered.

- Can these problems be overcome.

- What change of direction for the business is called for.

2.14   The owner may be contemplating retirement or a sale of the business. If the business is family run then retirement may be in the form of taking a pension from the business and, therefore, ensuring its future good health. Drawings in the meantime may be muted or dictated by profits to achieve this end.

2.15   On the other hand, a sale to third parties calls for a different approach. The prime aim in this case will be to build up profits to gain the best sale price. Advising accountants usually examine at least three years financial records to evaluate the performance of the business and to put a 'goodwill' element on the business value. The two or three years trading results prior to sale will be crucial to the business's value and the proprietor should be looking to maximise profits over this period. The strategic decision time to commence this build-up could be five or six years in advance of the proposed sale.

2.16   If neither goal is closer than six years the owner may wish to defer a decision to commence planning for a future realisation of his business interest. There will still be the question of whether the business should in the meantime adopt a policy of controlled expansion or whether the owner should withdraw his capital that is surplus to the present requirements of the business and invest this money elsewhere. It is particularly true in large service industries that are price or competition controlled, that entrepreneur chairmen aim to maximise earnings and sell the company while it is at its most profitable stage of development.

2.17   The personal grounds for making a strategic decision when and how to address the future direction of the business may not depend primarily on financial reward. The owner may not wish to retire but continue with a personal interest in the business. This must not conflict with maintaining the day-to-day management of the firm in the most efficient way. Many cases have been met, however, where succeeding family generations with new ideas have been stifled to act through a refusal to submit to change by the patriarch. This may be the time to split responsibilities within the firm or to separate them into autonomous divisions.

Operational strategy

2.18   Management delegation and succession questions should be taken as early as possible when the situation first arises and then be monitored regularly: at least annually for the larger concerns and every year or so for the smaller businesses. When to delegate or change management must be specific to the individual business, but a general guide may be obtained by asking the question: 'Will the business continue to operate at least as efficiently and profitably on the new management basis as it has under the old?'.

2.19   Every business reflects many trading facets and nuances. Together they describe its character and standing and can be split into past, present and future responsibilities. If the past and present responsibilities are inadequately laid down, then the future returns for the business may well prove sub-standard. Experience of visiting very many smaller businesses has shown that the greatest amount of time is spent on production and selling. Accounting is left to the year-end figures with a monthly eye kept on sales results and cash. Marketing frequently is restricted to keeping existing customers happy and dealing with new enquiries. Intelligence is achieved through buyer visits and the 'grapevine'. Other activities of management are mostly internal and subject to time and staff constraints. Compare these observations with the chart following which sets out the principal timing of each activity.

Activity Timespan	*Past*	*Present*	*Future*
Accounting	= = = = = = = = = = =		
Reporting	= = = = = = = = = = =		
Production	= = = = = = = = = = =		
Intelligence	= = = = = = = = = = =		
Selling		= = = = = = = = = = = = =	
Marketing		= = = = = = = = = = = = =	
Planning		= = = = = = = = = = = = =	
Risk and Reward		= = = = = = = = = = = = =	

Relatively little financial Reporting is done by small businesses on a strict and regular schedule. There is little or no Planning with regular reviews and even less calculation of the future Risk and Reward to the business.

2.20   Faced with these comments the manager may say that business sales depend on the frequency of customers through the door or orders that may arise at any time. How can one plan ahead when the future is so unknown? The answer lies in part on gaining orders in advance and ensuring that production capacity is available to meet this demand. If the business is dependent on retail sales, reliance has to be placed on past experience and the assumption that the skill of the proprietor can sustain his customers to shop there. Greater importance in this instance should be placed on future influences affecting the business, such as the extent of competition; seasonal shopping; fashion buying; agency stocking enabling competitive pricing to be achieved; the stocking of specific product lines; and the quality of goods and service.

2.21   Managing a small staff, the proprietor of a modestly-sized manufacturing or finishing business is likely to have a 'hands-on' attitude to staff activity. There will be little time for voluntary slack periods and it is often a full-time job to gain sufficient orders in hand to ensure full-time production work. The order book in hand is not often equivalent to more than two or three months work unless the type of business concentrates on long term contracts. The employment of a specialist sales manager can be a real risk and reward decision: a successful manager will greatly improve the business's turnover and profits, but a poor manager could be costly to keep and then to sack. Prior to hiring an expensive executive the proprietor should ask questions such as: 'Realistically, by how much will sales improve?'; 'Will I be able to deliver the extra orders in good time?'; 'Can I lower the fixed salary cost by paying commission by results?'.

2.22   Reverting to the chart earlier and the timing of future activities of the business, a regular on-going analysis of sales enquiries, their conversion into firm orders; their delivery dates and their values should be conducted each week. A pattern of expected sales receipts can then be built up, regularly updated, that will comprise the base figures for future cash flow and profit projections and production schedules. Quick recourse to targeted marketing promotions may be made if certain areas of sales activity decline. Where new investment is called for, such as for additional plant, risk and reward calculations should be made to see whether the expenditure is likely to prove viable or not.

Chapter 3

Existing Products and their Costing

3.1   The philosophy of many small businesses is to try and sell as much as possible at the highest price possible and they tend to forget to keep a watch on the cost to them of producing/stocking the products. Making a profit is about selling and pricing, but it is also about the relative profitability of individual products, the overheads they incur and how those overheads can be minimised.

Why the costs of trading each product should be monitored

3.2   Different types of business will view the costs of trading differently. A retail organisation will offer customers many different product lines, partly to encourage customers to spend and partly to provide a service to customers through the comprehensive range of products on sale.

3.3   Consider two examples, on the next page, where the turnover and indirect costs are identical, but the sales mix and profit margins are different. In each case the two products share the floor area of the shop equally. The costs of each product vary greatly and so does the Net Profit. In both examples it has been assumed that the trader has received the benefit of not paying for stock until two months after receiving the cash sales. In terms of operating efficiency, the trader should attempt to minimise the stock tied up in high value goods and concentrate on low value products.

3.3 Existing Products and their Costing

Example 1:	Product range A	Product range B	Combined
Sales margin	5%	50%	
Sales value	High	Low	
Turnover	£150,000	£50,000	£200,000
Cost of sales	£142,500	£25,000	£167,500
Gross profit	£7,500	£25,000	£32,500
Trade credit	2 months	2 months	
Borrowing cost	10% p.a.	10% p.a.	
Interest saving	£2,375	£416.66	£2,791.66
Gross trading cost	£9,875	£25,416.66	£35,291.66
Indirect costs, say	£12,500	£12,500	£25,000
Net Profit/Loss (–)	– £5,000	+ £12,500	+ £7,500

Example 2:	Product range A	Product range B	Combined
Sales margin	5%	50%	
Sales value	High	Low	
Turnover	£50,000	£150,000	£200,000
Cost of sales	£47,500	£75,000	£122,500
Gross profit	£2,500	£75,000	£77,500
Trade credit	2 months	2 months	
Borrowing cost	10% p.a.	10% p.a.	
Interest saving	£791.66	£1,250	£2,041.66
Gross trading cost	£3,291.66	£76,250	£79,541.66
Indirect costs, say	£12,500	£12,500	£25,000
Net Profit/Loss (–)	– £10,000	+ £62,500	+ £52,500

The results of the exercise may alter if the high value goods are of low bulk and take little floor space. The effect is shown in table Example 3.

Example 3:	*Product range A*	*Product range B*	*Combined*
Floor area	10%	90%	100%
Example 1:			
Indirect costs	£2,500	£22,500	£25,000
Net Profit/Loss (–)	+ £5,000	+ £2,500	+ £7,500
Example 2:			
Indirect costs	£2,500	£22,500	£25,000
Net Profit/Loss (–)	Nil	+ £52,500	+ £52,500

3.4   In practice there may be only a limited demand for one product (or similar group of products) and the trader will always have an in-built tendency to over-stock if finances permit. Example 4 shows the effect on cash flow for different stock turnover levels.

Example 4a:	*Stock range C*	*Stock range D*
Turnover	£240,000	£240,000
Stock movement	4 times p.a.	12 times p.a.
Stock to finance	£60,000	£20,000
Effect on cash flow:		
Maximum liability, in a month	£40,000	Nil
Maximum benefit, in a month	£20,000	£20,000

Continued on next page

17

3.5 Existing Products and their Costing

Example 4b:	Month 1	Month 2	Month 3	Month 4	Month 5	Month 6	etc	Month 12	YEAR
Sales	20,000	20,000	20,000	20,000	20,000	20,000		20,000	240,000
Stocking 'C'	60,000	0	0	60,000	0	0		0	240,000
Payment	0	0	60,000	0	0	60,000		60,000	240,000
Cash Flow	**20,000**	**20,000**	**–40,000**	**20,000**	**20,000**	**–40,000**		**–40,000**	**0**
Sales	20,000	20,000	20,000	20,000	20,000	20,000		20,000	240,000
Stocking 'D'	20,000	20,000	20,000	20,000	20,000	20,000		20,000	20,000
Payment	0	0	20,000	20,000	20,000	20,000		20,000	200,000
Cash Flow (a)	**20,000**	**20,000**	**0**	**0**	**0**	**0**		**0**	**40,000**
Cash Flow (b)	**0**	**0**	**0**	**0**	**0**	**0**		**0**	**0**

Note: Cash Flow (a) assumes a start trading date in month 1, whereas Cash Flow (b) assumes a continuing business at month 1.

On the figures presented the higher stock turnover shown in respect of products 'D' indicates a neutral cash flow situation, whereas the lower stock turnover with products 'C' indicates swings in cash flow as much as one-sixth of the annual turnover. The cost to the business of stocking and trading in products 'C' will require a much higher level of capital than products 'D'.

3.5   Another factor when considering stock levels is the possible loss of goods through deterioration or pilferage. Example 1 gave a modest net profit of £7,500 on sales of £200,000. If it is assumed that 2% of high value products and 5% of low value products are lost, the trading position and the effective loss on potential return for the business may be calculated as in Example 5:

Example 5:	*Product range A*	*Product range B*	*Combined*
Cost of stock	£142,500	£25,000	£167,500
Loss as assumed	£2,850	£1,250	£4,100
Revised Net Profit	– £7,850	+ £11,250	+ £3,400
Loss of potential sales	£2,992.50	£2,500	£5,492.50
Loss of potential profit	£149.62	£1,250	£1,399.62
Potential effect on the business	– £2,999.62	– £2,500	– £5,499.62

Although the actual cash loss suffered has been £4,100, this increases to £5,499.62 if loss of potential profit is included. A similar exercise on Example 2 shows the following revised figures:

18

Example 6:	Product range A	Product range B	Combined
Cost of stock	£47,500	£75,000	£122,500
Loss as assumed	£950	£3,750	£4,700
Revised Net Profit	– £10,950	+ £58,750	+ £47,800
Loss of potential sales	£997.50	£7,500	£8,497.50
Loss of potential profit	£49.87	£3,750	£3,799.87
Potential effect on the business	– £999.87	– £7,500	– £8,499.87

The potential cost of stocking high margin products (Product range B) to sell (Example 6) will result in a greater loss on the assumptions made. The trader can evaluate whether to change the mix of products to emphasise future trading of lower margin goods at a higher annual turnover if the risk of losses of stock are likely to persist.

Costing overheads

3.6   It will be important for the trader to know the break-even point for sales after which a profit can be earned on additional turnover. The calculation of this is given in table Example 7 (see next page):

3.6 Existing Products and their Costing

Example 7a: (retail)	Product range E	Product range F	Combined	Basis of calculation
Indirect costs:				
Admin wages	30,000	20,000	50,000	Time/job basis
Utilities	15,000	15,000	30,000	Floor area
Motor/travel	6,000	8,000	14,000	Usage
Office overheads	8,000	3,000	11,000	Usage/floor area
Marketing/advertising	12,000	4,000	16,000	Per product
Finance	2,000	2,000	4,000	Non-specific
Totals	73,000	52,000	125,000	
Direct Stocking costs:				
Purchases (30% of sales)	0.3 'X'		31,286	Average profit margin
Purchases (40% of sales)		0.4 'Y'	34,667	Average profit margin
Forecast Sales	'X'	'Y'		
Sales calculated	104,286	86,667	190,953	(1-0.3)'X' =73,000 etc

Example 7b: (manufacturing)	Product range E	Product range F	Combined	Basis of calculation
Indirect costs totals	73,000	52,000	125,000	As above
Direct production costs:				
Materials/Labour (40%)	0.4 'Pp'		48,667	Average profit margin
Materials/Labour (50%)		0.5 'Qq'	52,000	Average profit margin
Forecast units produced	'P'	'Q'		
Sales price per unit	'p'	'q'		
Sales calculated	121,667	104,000	225,667	As above

3.7   Taking Example 7b a stage further, the manufacturer may wish to discover whether product range 'E' or 'F', bearing in mind their costs, should be concentrated on in future to expand turnover more profitably. Example 8 provides the key calculations and shows production rising in approximate steps of 5%. For the same increase in production (and sales) product range E offers better scope for gaining more profit and the break-even sales point is lower than for product range F.

Example 8: **Product range E**	*Output*	*Output*	*Output*	*Output*	*Output*
Production (units)	190,000	200,000	210,000	220,000	230,000
Indirect costs (£)	73,000	73,000	73,000	73,000	73,000
Direct costs tied to prod'n (£)	48,667	51,228	53,790	56,351	58,913
Total costs (£)	121,667	124,228	126,790	129,351	131,913
Sales at unit price of 64p (£)	121,667	128,000	134,400	140,800	147,200
Net Profit (£)	nil	3,772	7,610	11,449	15,287
Break-even sales price per unit	*64.0p*	*62.1p*	*60.4p*	*58.8p*	*57.4p*
Unit sales price reduction					*–10.3%*
Product range F					
Production (units)	400,000	420,000	440,000	460,000	480,000
Indirect costs (£)	52,000	52,000	52,000	52,000	52,000
Direct costs tied to prod'n (£)	52,000	54,600	57,200	59,800	62,400
Total costs(£)	104,000	106,600	109,200	111,800	114,400
Sales at unit price of 26p (£)	104,000	109,200	114,400	119,600	124,800
Net profit(£)	nil	2,600	5,200	7,800	10,400
Break-even sales price per unit	*26.0p*	*25.4p*	*24.8p*	*24.3p*	*23.8p*
Unit sales price reduction					*–8.5%*

Considering the cost of divisional activities

3.8   The business to appraise is a printers and publishers and recent years' trading results have shown the following trends:

3.9 Existing Products and their Costing

£'000	1996	1997	1998	1999	2000
Printing Turnover	900	950	970	980	1,020
Costs	820	920	920	920	980
Net Profit	70	30	50	60	40
Net assets employed (average)	145	160	190	160	150
Net Profit return percent on net assets	*48%*	*19%*	*26%*	*37%*	*26%*
Net Profit return percent on turnover	*7.8%*	*3.2%*	*5.2%*	*6.1%*	*3.9%*
Costs as percent of turnover	*91%*	*97%*	*95%*	*94%*	*96%*
Staff costs (average)	*550*	*560*	*570*	*580*	*610*
Publishing Turnover	2,000	1,970	2,030	2,020	2,090
Costs	1,970	1,940	2,000	1,990	2,060
Net Profit	30	30	30	30	30
Net assets employed (average)	420	350	370	480	520
Net Profit return percent on net assets	*7.1%*	*8.6%*	*8.1%*	*6.3%*	*5.8%*
Costs as percent of turnover	*99%*	*98%*	*99%*	*99%*	*99%*

3.9   In both divisions profits are low and the incidence of costs is high relative to turnover. The company should have been looking at reducing costs to improve profitability some years earlier. New management has just been appointed and they would like to expand the business, but which division should it be?

3.10   Leaving aside the pertinent questions of relative external competitiveness and the portents for growth in these activities as well as other local business factors, there has been a much higher return on net assets employed in printing than in publishing although there have been some fluctuations in earnings for the former division over the period under review. Publishing, on the other hand, potentially holds greater scope to expand through increasing the range of publications unless printing can win some large and regular commissions and improve turnover while retaining approximately the present cost base. Staff costs for printing have been steady and those attributable to publishing are not significant due to the sub-contracted labour force.

3.11   In this case, the costs of both the printing and the publishing divisions should be carefully examined not only for cost savings but to see how an increase in either division would be affected by future costs. Once this is completed, and subject to its findings, the review can move on to the sales prospects for each division and what amount of new capital would be required for investment. Finally, the net asset base of each division should be analysed: are there assets employed that are no longer required (capital surplus to needs) and, conversely, what assets require to be replaced in order to support an expansion of either division?

How to cost a product

3.12 This may seem to be a simple exercise, and in most cases it is, but there are always some problems that can arise in practice. The general rule is to approach the problem as follows:

- Raise a best quotation in-house for supplying a service/product;
- Discern what input will be necessary to provide the service/product;
- Place a cost on the supply of direct raw materials/labour/overheads;
- **Add the relevant proportion of indirect costs to these figures;**
- Assess the resulting total cost of supply;
- Add the required (or target) profit margin;
- Compare this selling figure with the original quotation estimate;
- Judge whether the revised cost plus margin figure is realistic;
- Agree a firm cost quotation for the product/service;
- Await the result.

3.13 If the quotation to the customer is too high, this should not be the time to reduce the tender unless the business has no other work in the foreseeable pipeline and the priority is to keep the workforce in employment on a no-profit basis for the business, with the reasonable assumption that more profitable work is imminent. The list above highlighted the reference to indirect costs. Small businesses tend not to account properly for indirect costs in their tendering and, if they do, they tend to allow for this element in a 'broad brush' percentage increment that is not monitored or changed regularly. It is imperative that businesses account for all indirect costs on a regular basis when setting tender or product prices.

Minimising overheads

3.14 Some general points can be laid down when a trader wishes to minimise the business overheads. The options tend to be either a review of existing suppliers so that the best quotation for services can be obtained, or a review of existing cost budgets and how alternative sourcing or cutbacks may reduce them. The table following sets out some of the more significant areas to view:

3.14 Existing Products and their Costing

Operational area	Cost	Considerations
Sales	Labour	Have the source(s) of sales been fully 'logged'
		If so, have superfluous associated costs been eliminated
Production	Machinery	Would the equipment be more productive if replaced
		What are the relative costs of replacement v. maintenance
		Can the equipment be utilised more
		Financially, can equipment be leased rather than bought
	Labour	Has the workforce been appointed tasks most efficiently
		Can the workers time be more flexibly used
		Is the payment method (eg piecework) minimising their cost
		Can some tasks be sub-contracted
		Can more part-time/casual labour be employed
	Stocks	Can the stock of raw materials held be minimised more
		Is there a need to maintain 'buffer' stocks
		Can long-term supply agreements reduce their costs
		Can finished goods deliveries/invoicing be expedited
	Transport	Is it cheaper to run an own fleet or contract deliveries out
Marketing	Selling	Is a dedicated sales team beneficial relative to cost/results
		Are salespersons best used for telesales or on-the-road selling
		Are target promotions/advertising productive to their cost
		Have the results of marketing been proved by subsequent monitoring
Administration	Office	Are the key operatives flexible in their work roles
		Can some of the jobs be done with part-time staff
		Will further computerisation of tasks save money
		Have competitive tenders for utility etc. supplies been tried

Chapter 4

The Business Assets – Plan for Growth

4.1   It would be unwise to promote an employee into a position of greater responsibility if the person was not capable of making a success of the tasks that went with the new appointment. Likewise, a business should not attempt to attain objectives that are beyond its capabilities. Perhaps the most common failure for a business is to try and expand its operations without having the right form or size of resources to back up the intent.

4.2   The resources of the business in this context will be a mixture of:

- Fixed Assets – tangible buildings, plant, equipment and motor vehicles.

- Living Assets – the management and staff employed.

- Disposable Assets – stocks, debtors less creditors, and cash held.

- Intangible Assets – the goodwill, brand name and reputation of the business.

- Convertible Assets – the capital and creditworthiness of the business.

- Asset Earning Power – self or independently generated.

4.3   Each of these assets should play their part in promoting future growth. Unfortunately, a financial Balance Sheet only shows part of the business resources, and these are on an historic value basis. This shortfall becomes more noticeable when the business reaches a time of change. For example, if retirement is being considered the owner(s) as sellers will be arguing with the buyers what the business is really worth. It will then be too late to 'groom' the business Balance Sheet to obtain the best price.

4.4   When planning for growth two basic scenarios should be examined: whether the business strategy is to expand its capital value (i.e. the net worth of the business to the owner/s) or its earnings. The latter through retaining profits will enhance the former. Equally, the former can be used as a springboard to expand earnings by gearing up investment (through borrowing) or saving resources until it is judged they can be spent on acquiring new business interests. The difference is essentially a matter of timing; growing earnings are received immediately and, if not distributed, will add to the capital value of the business and be available to be spent at some future time.

Characteristics of growth

4.5   If a business is pursuing in the main an earnings or capital value growth strategy it should have regard to the following options that are shown in the table. Some of these points are discussed in greater detail thereafter.

Resources	Earnings	Capital Value
Fixed Assets	Rent/lease	Ownership
Living Assets	Sub-contract labour	Retain core staff long term
Disposable Assets	Minimise Stocks	Positive Net Current Assets
	Minimise Debtors	
	Maximise Creditors	
Intangible Assets	Less important	More important
Convertible Assets	Minimum necessary	Retain critical mass
	Consider gearing up	Important to enhance
Asset Earning Power	Profit margin	Reputation
	Competitiveness	Long term market outlook
	Demand	Fixed rate long-term loans

Fixed Assets

4.6   The business property may be leased or owned. High growth businesses that may rapidly outstrip their initial floor area needs are best advised to rent short-term so that future expansion can be easily accommodated. The preferences of staff should be noted, as a change of address may lead to resignations due to the time and cost of transport. The best location of a retail shop is vital if its success depends on easy car parking access, regular passing trade and minimal competition. If the business is high-tech it may be more appropriate to lease equipment if it is likely to get rapidly out of date. Regular office tasks such as road fleet management can be delegated to specialised rental organisations.

Living Assets

4.7   Employing staff is becoming increasingly expensive, so the greater the opportunity for the business to contract out jobs or to pay for piece-work, the less likelihood there will be of having to pay staff in unproductive periods. For continuity in the longer term, however, some key personnel should always be retained either in a supervisory/training role or to act as trouble-shooters to ensure that quality control and delivery deadlines are met.

Disposable Assets

4.8 Major (valuable) stock items should be controlled at all times in respect of buying orders, delivery, safe custody and issue. There should be laid down minimum quantities of raw materials stocks based on future production requirements. If the stocks are for resale, it should be calculated in advance what value can be purchased out of expected cash flow resources. More credit should endeavour to be obtained from business suppliers than is allowed to customers. In these ways earnings growth may be maximised.

Intangible Assets

4.9 Business reputation is probably more important for a business than being long established and identified with a particular sales brand. This is certainly true for service businesses where the customer objective is to get a reputable firm to do the job acceptably. Retail selling is likely to depend more on accessibility and choice: if brand X is not in stock then a substitute may suffice.

Convertible Assets

4.10 By this term is meant the ease and extent that the business can convert its credit rating into raising finance for investment or working capital, or convert its net worth into liquid funds for reinvestment elsewhere in the business. The credit rating will be determined by the track record of the business (as demonstrated by its financial results) and the quality of its management. The second definition may be described by a Balance Sheet example:

Freehold assets		£150,000
Other fixed assets at written down value		£ 20,000
		£170,000
Current Assets – Debtors	£ 10,000	
Less Creditors	£ 30,000	
Bank overdraft	£ 40,000	£–60,000
Total Net Assets		£110,000
Long-term borrowing		£ 30,000
Proprietors' Capital		£ 80,000
		£110,000

4.11 *The Business Assets – Plan for Growth*

The Net Worth of the business is the Proprietors' Capital of £80,000. The business would like to purchase a new machine for £40,000. Where will the money come from? Debtors are insufficient to factor. The existing borrowings are high relative to the Net Worth of the business. Hire purchase may be a possibility. The net assets are locked up in freehold assets that, presumably, cannot be sold and leased back. If earnings (not shown) are poor, the business has a problem without more equity capital to be invested. Its convertibility factor is very low.

Asset earning power

4.11   To maximise earnings the sales demand for the business products and the resulting profitability must be high and competition must not be critical to affect these factors. The interaction of these influences will be self-generated: sales demand may be beneficially affected by a good marketing scheme and it may be possible to pitch profit margin(s) to what the market can afford. Taking a longer term view will suggest different alternatives dependent on external influences: the overall market may be entering a period of recession; the business may wish to operate on a non-growth tack until the market improves, meanwhile its reputation and standing should be nurtured for the future. If finance is being considered, a standby borrowing facility may be arranged as a precautionary measure and converting an existing loan into a fixed interest rate (if appropriate) to stabilise the annual borrowing cost may be prudent.

The gearing (leverage) factor

4.12   To attain increased earnings quickly, excess capital should not be locked away in long-term assets not directly related to trading, but invested in more labour, machinery and stocks to enable in due course more sales to be made and, thereafter, the cash to be received from customers. This may demand additional funds to be invested through gearing up the profit return by borrowing finance.

£'000	Without gearing	With gearing
Capital employed	100	100
Borrowing	0	40
Overall capital employed	100	140
Return on Capital employed	20%	20%*
Net Profit	20	28
Less borrowing cost, say, 5%	0	2
Revised Net Profit	20	26
Net Profit margin achieved on sales	6%	6%
Sales implied	333	433
Sales and Profit growth		+ 30%

* *Note*: The critical assumption is that the same return can be achieved on higher sales.

4.13 Looked at another way, some types of business are more conducive to achieve a growth in earnings than others. The table below offers some common characteristics of earnings intensive and capital intensive businesses:

Business situation	Use of Earnings growth to	Use of Capital Value growth to
Mature sector	Retain current earning power	Retain for future use
	Improve distributed rewards	Consider new investment
	Consider product diversification	Prepare for a future sale
Start-up/developing	Reinvest to expand	Obtain critical mass
	Develop the markets	Achieve good asset base
Cash generator	Offer competitive margins	Possible diversification
	Accelerate the number of sales outlets	Consider other investments
Labour intensive	Consider more mechanisation	Build an optimum team
Plant intensive	Minimise labour costs	Plan a replacement programme

4.14 Most small and medium-sized businesses opt for **earnings** growth. This is understandable when profits today may change into losses tomorrow. The owner(s) will look to the whole of their annual profits as just reward for their efforts over the past year, with minimal retention of profits in the business. If the business runs short of funds, the owner(s) will have to invest new capital or borrow commercial funds short-term. The potential catch is that if the capital value of the business is not retained at a reasonable level, the latter option may not be possible and if the owners have no funds set aside themselves the business could have a problem to continue trading.

4.15 Sole traders and partnerships are taxed on their full annual profits and if they withdraw their business earnings to invest elsewhere it will be to spread the risk of loss or to gain a better return net of tax. This aspect is often overlooked by small businesses. If their business is earning 10% before tax and fixed interest or equity investments at most are offering 5% before tax, the choice will be: can I earn 10% by retaining the money in the business? This question can be difficult to answer. For instance, if the business borrows at 12% then the retained earnings can repay the borrowing and 'return' the equivalent of 12%. If the business already holds cash throughout the year, just by increasing its cash deposit it may only earn, say, bank interest of 4% and an investment elsewhere would be more appropriate. Finally, if the business buys a new machine out of trading profits it may be able to increase sales at the same profit margin and the annual earnings would best be beneficially invested in the business.

4.16 Family companies, on the other hand, can retain some profit in the business without being immediately taxed. They may also wish to use their corporate strength to set up a self-administered personal pension scheme and this may be based on the (hopefully growing) value of the business freehold properties. In this case, the business strategy will be a **mixture** of sufficient earnings growth to pay for these and all other business commitments and to continue investing longer term for (pension) capital growth.

4.17   In the third scenario, where a business is under-capitalised and has difficulty in not remaining so, the business should adopt the strategy of minimising the distribution of its annual earnings and instead try to build up the **capital value** of the business to obtain what might be described as 'critical mass'. A banker would define this as trading with sufficient capital permanently invested in the business to support its current and future trading aspirations and any commercial borrowings. Where commercial borrowings exceed the proprietors' capital the question arises: for whom is the business trading? The bank will be taking the greater risk for little reward, namely the borrowing margin over its cost of funds. This may be an acceptable banking choice if the trading problem and the borrowing is temporary and the bank has good collateral to fall back on for repayment.

Planning for growth – a check list

4.18

- For a business to grow there must be a suitable infrastructure (i.e. capital base) on which to build a larger unit.

- Remember that to grow will require investment in advance before the reward of sales receipts flows.

- Investment tends to increase in steps; as full capacity is reached for one level of investment so the next step of investment is necessary.

- If the immediate planned growth is not likely to be as profitable as present trading, reconsider why the expansion should be attempted at this time.

- Review the type(s) of product the business is selling and is looking to sell.

- Is it in a niche area that is less expected to suffer from lower demand?

- Does it have a relatively short 'fashionable' life?

- Is it a mature product possibly waiting to be replaced?

- Could it be classified as a high-tech item where competition, new developments and consumer acceptance are significant factors?

- Can the product be in the vanguard of demand?

- Is the product suitable to sell nationally and what will this cost?

- Can the (new) product compete on price/quality/quick service/availability?

- Has the (new) project been planned to be flexible enough to react to changes in demand?

- Have the risks and rewards been calculated and balanced out?

- Have all the limitations of the planned expansion been recognised?

- Have the special characteristics relating to a capital or labour intensive business been allowed for?

- Has the project for growth been objectively planned, proved financially viable and vindicated on a cash flow basis?

Chapter 5

Business Finance – the Options

5.1   Businesses would be better off if they did not borrow money. Is this true or false? Well, not quite true. There are situations when planned borrowing can be financially beneficial to a business. There are also occasions when the establishment of a credit facility can be useful even if not drawn on. Finally, there are businesses that have made themselves reliant on continuous credit and their only option is to try and reduce the finance charges. The characteristics of each of these types are discussed in turn.

Short-term borrowing requirements:

5.2   Short-term borrowing may be suitable:

- When a period of high growth in trading is expected and the benefits would be missed if additional funds were not borrowed to take greater advantage of the opportunity.

- When a temporary cash flow timing difficulty arises and it is the easier and more rapid option to borrow funds rather than cut back on overheads or postpone planned expenditure.

- When certain trading receipts are not due to be received for a short period and the benefit of the money is preferred now.

- When there is a seasonal trading need for additional credit.

- When exports or imports arise and finance is required to effect the overseas settlement.

Longer term borrowing requirements:

5.3   Longer term borrowing may be suitable:

- When the business is undercapitalised but there are firm expectations of earning profits over the period of the borrowing, so that the interest charge and repayment of loan principal can be met.

- When new or replacement fixed assets are deemed to be required to continue the business and the outlay is greater than funds immediately in hand, but the expenditure can be met if the loan cost is spread over a longer period.

- When it is calculated that by borrowing now to take advantage of a particular offer, the purchase will lead to greater earnings than the cost of the related finance. Examples of this may be borrowing to purchase raw material supplies in bulk at less cost per unit, or to incur the expense of relocating the business to take advantage of reduced running costs in the future.

A contingency credit facility

5.4   This type of facility may be suitable when a business wishes to borrow short-term, but in this case the business is able to operate in credit throughout a normal trading year, with the possible exception of periods when certain large payments are known to occur and there is no certainty in advance whether cash flow at these times can meet those obligations. Examples may be payment situations to settle sole trader or partnership taxation assessments; company dividends and corporation tax assessments and, on a more regular basis, VAT and monthly PAYE creditors.

5.5   It is very expensive to incur an unauthorised overdraft and the cost of even occasionally borrowing in this way should be weighed against the small annual fees that would be charged to maintain an overdraft facility up to a modest limit. Larger contingency facilities may be charged a small percentage fee on the daily facility balance that lies undrawn, to encourage the business to borrow more or release unwanted credit that has been set aside by the bank for the business's use. The bank is really saying that the business should plan its finance requirements a little better and only borrow what is necessary and when it is necessary.

Overdraft versus business loan

5.6   The availability of securing an overdraft facility from the commercial banks is steadily decreasing. This is due to several factors:

- The bank's cost of monitoring the account regularly and the generally lower profitability that it offers.

- The freedom that is given to the business to draw funds for whatever purpose and not to have to meet a fixed repayment schedule.

- The fluctuating cost of an overdraft since the rate will be pegged to some form of variable bank base rate.

- The practical difficulty for the bank to obtain immediate repayment.

5.7   Compare these disadvantages with the benefits of a programmed business loan, for example, where the regular payments (say, monthly or quarterly) are of a fixed amount throughout the borrowing period but comprise a changing mixture of the interest being charged and portions of the loan principal being repaid. This type of loan offers:

- A known set cost and repayment schedule for the business.

- A guarantee that the borrowing will remain in place unless the business defaults through missing any repayments.

- Ease of servicing by the business and (computer) monitoring at minimal cost to the bank.

- The benefit to the bank through having some of the loan principal being repaid at all stages of the loan along with interest due.

A derivation of this is where the regular payments are of loan principal only and the interest is calculated monthly on the outstanding balance and is charged separately to the business current account.

5.8   Business development loans may also be tailored more to the individual circumstances of each business. In these cases various drawing options may be included. For instance, the loan may be drawn at a fixed interest rate plus stated bank margin, for a number of fixed periods (1 month; 3 months; 1 year etc.). At any maturity date of the current period drawn the loan may be changed to a variable interest rate basis until further notice by the business, providing the new period chosen is within the overall period of the facility. Repayment of the loan principal may be done annually or at other agreed periods either by set or variable payments off the total facility outstanding.

5.9   A business does not require a sophisticated treasury function to ask its bank to include some of the above tailored options to be incorporated in the borrowing agreement. The branch manager will be able to provide both initial and on-going advice to ensure that the terms of a borrowing facility can be managed effectively. The business should maintain a Treasury Diary if a tailored facility has been negotiated, showing:

- The amounts of each borrowing;

- How much is to be repaid and on what date;

- The date when renewal instructions should be issued and to whom;

- A cumulative total of all borrowings outstanding shown on a day-by-day basis;

- Notes of significant incoming/outgoing cash transactions that are expected in the future;

- Details of facility drawings that are made; on what date and by whom (with any necessary authorisation alongside).

Where currency drawings are made, the same details should be shown in that currency. If foreign exchange transactions are made, a similar record should also be raised, together with a note of the currency exposure (if any).

Loan monitoring

5.10   Different banks will each have their own monitoring conditions for borrowers. This is usually a mixture of passive (historic) reporting of management figures sent by the business regularly to the bank; active (monitoring) visits at least annually between the parties; and daily reconciliations of account transactions that may operate under 'setoff' or 'sweeper' arrangements. Typical management reporting arrangements asked for by the bank will be weekly or monthly totals of:

- Turnover achieved.

- Orders in hand.

- Trade Debtors outstanding.

- Trade Creditors outstanding.

5.11   The bank may also require certain operating ratios and minimum balances to be maintained during the course of the loan facility and certain minimum sizes of net assets and liabilities. Probably the two most common conditions refer to a limitation on the total borrowings of the business compared with its Net Worth as shown by past and future Balance Sheets, and a minimum Net Worth that must be maintained in the business at all times. Net Worth can be defined as the (Share) Capital and undistributed Reserves held, less any intangible assets such as Goodwill.

5.12   The reason why intangible assets are ignored is that by their nature they may represent assets that have no discernible value. Goodwill may disappear if the business becomes unprofitable. Deferred assets may comprise Research and Development costs not yet written off and expenditure on developments not yet completed and therefore having, as yet, a nebulous value.

5.13   Recently, asset values have been put on Brand Names. The conservative recommendation is to ignore such asset values. If a business has shown as having above average growth in earnings due to exploitation of a particular Brand Name, the value of the Brand will already have flowed through in earnings and, if not distributed as dividend, the residue will be held by the business in its Net Worth figure. If the Brand has been purchased, it will show up as a Goodwill figure, represented by the acquisition value paid over its net asset value. If the Brand suffers a marketing disaster, examples mentioned previously being contaminated effervescent drinking water or poorly manufactured vehicle tyres, the value of the Brand Name will, at best, be highly conjectural for some time to come.

5.14   As a preamble, the assumptions to be drawn from the use of any ratio is that they should be viewed with care and their best value is for comparative evaluation purposes rather than the intrinsic value of the ratio itself. The most common of these are:

1. Quick ratio: $\dfrac{\text{(cash \& deposits held + debtors)}}{\text{Current Liabilities}}$

2. Current ratio: $\dfrac{\text{Current Assets}}{\text{Current Liabilities}}$

3. Cash ratio: $\dfrac{\text{(Cash + short-term liabilities)}}{\text{Current Liabilities}}$

5.15   So far the borrowing options have described multi-purpose loans rather than borrowing for specific purposes. Different borrowing purposes may require specific types of loan. Examples of loans tailored for specific purposes include trade finance; leasing and hire purchase; factoring and invoice discounting; and bridging finance.

Trade finance

5.16   There are a number of options available to settle trade finance:

*   Letters of Credit

*   Bills of Exchange

*   Contract financing

*   Stock financing

The first two are covered in Chapter 15, *Trading Overseas*. Contract financing uses the value of the (term) contract (from an undoubted trading company) against which funds are borrowed in advance of the contract payments. The contract terms must be 'watertight' for the lender to accept this security and the parties to the contract must be of good standing. This is because the lender does not wish to be placed in the position of having to complete the contract physically in order to receive its benefits if the borrower reneges on the deal.

5.17   Stock finance in its purest form is also difficult to arrange. Finished products will need selling and to hold the title to finished goods in written form incurs the risk of not being able to sell the goods or having the goods deteriorate and reduce in value. This risk can be assuaged through the lender only advancing a small percentage of the selling value of the goods. Stock finance frequently is offered as a secondary 'top-up' facility alongside a more standard principal line of credit e.g. increasing an 85% factoring facility to 100% with additional stock finance.

Cash Flow finance

5.18   This is not strictly a separate form of finance but rather a different way of judging the size and effecting the repayment of a facility. There may be a project having a forecast cash flow (income less expenditure) with the shortfall being met through borrowing in order to maintain the business in funds. The borrowing is repaid out of the cash flow as it improves in line with the increase in underlying earnings. Close monitoring is essential and there are usually stiff penalties for any shortfall that would lead to a postponement of repayments. This type of facility is used where the income is largely risk-free, e.g. rent payments, and the borrowing can be at a fixed interest rate to eliminate any future adverse interest rate movements.

Asset finance

5.19   Finance supported by fixed assets may be required for speculative, bridging, or investment purposes. Bridging finance is a good lending reason since repayment is expected to be made within a short space of time. Banks are still being caught out by bad loans for 'investment' purposes and this may be a euphemism for property investment and deals of a more speculative nature. It is true that over the last few decades asset values have risen (when speaking of residential housing the annual average growth rate has been around 7% pa). The difficulty arises when prices do not rise but fall for several years and the income necessary to maintain repayments of interest and capital falls away. Borrowers wishing to raise money on the back of freehold or long (over 21 years to mature) leaseholds preferably should be able to show that the servicing of the debt arises from income that is not associated with the asset(s) being financed and this income is itself of a permanence.

5.20   Asset finance is usually synonymous with Hire Purchase, Lease Purchase, Contract Purchase, Contract Hire or Operating and Finance Leases. Their major characteristics are given in the table following. They all offer a cash flow advantage compared with outright purchase and this is their financing benefit to a business. Hire Purchase reduces the immediate need for cash and provides the lessee (the user) with some security of retention once the majority of payments have been paid under the Credit Consumer Acts. Lease Purchase is very similar but offers a degree of additional flexibility in the terms. Contract Purchase enables the asset to be off-Balance Sheet until the contract period ends but VAT cannot be reclaimed. Contract Hire does not offer ownership but the full payments are a deduction from profits. An Operating Lease is usually off-Balance Sheet, unlike a Finance Lease, with other parties taking the risk of the asset's residual value. Because of their different benefits to the lessor the cash flow arising from the monthly or quarterly payments will vary slightly for the business lessee. The business will have to weigh up what benefits it would most like to obtain before making a choice of the options to gain financing.

Agreement aspects	Hire Purchase	Lease Purchase	Contract Purchase	Contract Hire	Operating Lease	Finance Lease
Ownership	Optional at end	Optional at end	Yes, at end	No, asset is replaced	No	No
Tax allowance benefits on deal	Writing down	Writing down	Writing down	Not to lessee	Not to lessee	Writing down
Claimed off profits	Interest	Interest	Interest	Payments	Payments	Payments
End sale proceeds	N/a	N/a	N/a	No	No	Yes
Rentals cover	N/a	N/a	N/a	Cost and interest	Part cost + residual value	Cost and interest
Off Balance Sheet	No	No	Yes	Yes	Optional	No
Maintenance included	No	Yes	Yes	Yes	Optional	Optional
Interest rate	Fixed	Fixed or variable	Fixed	Fixed	Fixed	Fixed or variable
Interest allowed against tax	Yes	Yes	Yes	Yes	Yes	Yes
VAT payable	Yes at outset	Yes at outset	Yes at outset	On each instalment	On each instalment	On each instalment
VAT reclaimable	Yes on asset cost	Yes on asset cost	No	Yes on payments	Yes on payments	Yes on payments
Payments	Fixed	Flexible	Flexible	Fixed	Flexible	Flexible

Other types of finance

5.21   Subsequent chapters cover the raising of commercial finance and investment capital in greater detail. As a general rule, it is easier to raise money for a new project or start-up venture that would not otherwise stand on its own merits if it can make use of the credit standing and cash flow potential of an existing and profitable part of the same business.

Chapter 6

Evaluating New Projects

6.1   Adopting a new project will require the channelling of new investment and personnel effort into the new venture and may take many different forms of which a number of the more important are listed below:

Selling from the current product base:

- investing in a new marketing strategy;
- opening new sales outlet(s);
- extending the geographical coverage of the sales area;
- deciding to open a presence in new markets (e.g. exporting);
- changing the method of selling product(s).

Extending the current product base:

- expanding an existing product line(s);
- adopting ancillary product lines;
- mechanising production more;
- distributing other products already produced;
- franchising some operations;
- accepting new products on an (exclusive) agency basis.

Raising entirely new ventures:

- independently or as a majority partner in a joint venture;
- acquiring a minority interest in a new venture;
- taking a passive investment role;
- taking an active managerial role;
- acquiring long-term strategic investments in existing businesses;
- investing in research and development of new ideas;
- providing start-up venture capital as an investor.

6.2   Each of these interests will have different risks to evaluate and hold the prospect of different rewards. Some idea of the relative merits, or otherwise, of each option may be judged by the examples given in the table following:

Type of project	Potential Risk / Reward		Advantage	Disadvantage
New marketing strategy	Low	Good	Can be modified easily	Costly if ineffective
New sales outlets	High	On-going	Known profit margins	Need time to establish
More geographic cover	Fair	Fair	Spreads product'n costs	Cost of logistics
Open new markets	High	Good	Quick growth	Needs working capital
Change selling method	Fair	Fair	Improve profitability	Could disrupt business
Expand production	Low	Good	Measurable profit	Needs higher demand
Offer ancillary products	Fair	Good	Diversifies trading risk	Needs new knowledge
Mechanising production	Low	High	Lower cost base	Needs working capital
Act as distributor	Low	Fair	No production risk	Possible competition
Franchise out sales	Low	Modest	Spreads market risk	Reduces possible reward
Accept agencies	Low	Good	Exclusivity of trading	High initial investment
Start new venture	High	High	In at the beginning	May fold; expensive
Minority venture partner	Fair	Fair	Buys external know-how	May need more finance
Investing passively	High	Poor	No management time	No control on business
Managing actively	Low	Good	Can influence events	May be joint control
Invest in running business	Fair	Fair	Possible future takeover	May take time to reward
R & D project	High	Good	Profitable if successful	No guarantee of success
Start-up venture capital	High	High	Needs no management	Offers modest influence

Low risks and good rewards

6.3   Scanning the table contents reveals only one indication of a potentially low financial risk being allied to a high reward: through **mechanising production** more. This is because the cost of the equipment and its **production capacity** will be known in advance and can be compared against the present number of workers being employed to produce the same quantity of production. It is assumed that as the business grows the new machine will meet the demand for higher production rather than employing additional workers. If this is so, there is the additional risk of a subsequent fall in sales leading to possible over-capacity. Furthermore, if the aim is to make some workers redundant there will be the one-off costs of settlement pay to include in the calculation. If the capital cost of the equipment is to be raised by a loan or hire purchase, this cost must also be taken into account. The relative benefit template will look as follows:

Aim: *to increase production*	**Acquiring equipment**	**Employing staff**	**Net Benefit**
Purchase cost (say)	£50,000		
Cost of one production worker:			
gross pay + Employer's NI & pension		£12,500	
Number of jobs saved by mechanising		2	
Redundancy packages (say, total)		£7,500	
Annual cost of borrowing purchase price	£12,500		
Maintenance cost (say) annual average	£1,500		
Year One: cost of additional equipment	£14,000		
saving in wages (net)		£17,500	£3,500
Year Two: net saving after 3% wage rise			£14,750

etcetera

Using discounted cash flow techniques

6.4   Where calculations spanning a period of time are required to work out the overall benefit of one option or investment compared with another, the usual method is to use a discounted cash flow model to incorporate the different timings. For example, if the investment at the beginning of the year costs £100,000 and the cash saving from the investment arises at the year end, the use of the £100,000 over the intervening year should be taken into account when calculating the overall benefit. The question arises what is this cost? If it is taken as 10% then a benefit has to arise in excess of £10,000 to make the project worthwhile.

6.5   If the capital employed in the business is generating a profit return (taxation being ignored for simplicity in this instance) of 15%, then it should be shown that the proposed new investment of £100,000, if withdrawn in cash from the business, will provide a benefit of more than £15,000 annually; otherwise the bald financial choice will be not to invest and jeopardise the current profit return. Even this statement is subject to qualification: if the business can raise the £100,000 by, say, extending the period of credit allowed in settling suppliers without injuring the trading relationships, then the working capital of the business will not suffer.

6.6   Returning to the original concept of the cost of raising the investment of £100,000, it will be wise to correlate this always with the cost for the business of raising commercial finance of a similar amount and for a similar period. Discounted cash flow is a valuable mathematical device to provide a level playing field when endeavouring to make financial comparisons over a period of time to aid business judgments.

6.7   The following example assumes that machinery is to cost £100,000 and will have an effective life of ten years; trading is forecast to benefit (either through increased production or lower labour costs) by £30,000 annually as escalated at 3% inflation each year; The business pays tax at 20% and can claim 25% annual tax allowance on the cost of the machinery. It is further assumed that the business has to borrow the money to pay for the equipment. A quotation has been received for a loan (or leasing or hire purchase) over five years with equal annual repayments of £24,138 at an interest cost of 8% p.a. on the outstanding balance. The calculations should be done at monthly intervals if the repayments are monthly, but the difference it makes overall is not significant. The discounted cash flow calculation would be:

Part 1:

Year	Machinery 25% w.d.v.	Tax allowances	A Tax Saved at 20%	B Profit Increase	C Tax Payable at 20%	D Loan Repaid	E Loan Interest	F Tax Saved at 20%	Cash Flow *
0	100,000	0	0	0	0	0	0	0	0
1	75,000	0	0	30,000	0	24,138	8,000	0	5,862
2	56,250	25,000	5,000	30,900	6,000	24,138	6,069	1,600	7,362
3	42,187	18,750	3,750	31,827	6,180	24,138	4,138	1,214	6,087
4	31,640	14,063	2,813	32,782	6,365	24,138	2,207	828	5,920
5	23,730	10,547	2,109	33,765	6,556	24,138	276	441	5,621
6	17,798	7,910	1,582	34,778	6,753	0	0	55	29,662
7	13,348	5,932	1,186	35,822	6,956	0	0	0	30,052
8	10,011	4,450	890	36,896	7,164	0	0	0	30,622
9	7,508	3,337	667	38,003	7,379	0	0	0	31,291
10	5,631	2,503	501	39,143	7,600	0	0	0	32,044
11	etc	1,877	375	etc	7,829	0	0	0	etc

* *Note*: The Cash Flow is calculated as columns **A+B-C-D+F**

Part 2:

Year	Cash Flow *	DCF Factor For 8%	Present Value **	Equipment maintenance (say)	Present Value
0	0	0	0	0	0
1	5,862	0.926	5,428	0	0
2	7,362	0.857	6,309	0	0
3	6,087	0.794	4,833	4,500	3,573
4	5,920	0.735	4,351	0	0
5	5,621	0.681	3,828	15,000	10,215
6	29,662	0.630	18,687	0	0
7	30,052	0.583	17,520	0	0
8	30,622	0.540	16,536	2,600	1,404
9	31,291	0.500	15,645	3,120	1,560
10	32,044	0.463	14,836	5,240	2,426
11	*etc*	*etc*			
Totals	184,523		107,973		19,178

** *Note*: This is calculated as 1/1.08 cumulatively, where the '8' is the discounted cash flow factor (DCF).

In this example, the cost of the equipment was £100,000 and the value of its purchase after its effective life of ten years is (£107,973 less £19,178 =) £88,795. If the assumptions prove correct, the purchase would *not* be acceptable.

6.8 An **active management** in decision-making will always reduce the risk of failure for a new project and potentially retain a relatively good reward factor. This refers to being involved both in the initial viability appraisal and in the on-going trading decisions. Monitoring should always be done through a mixture of assessing regular desk (reports) actual returns against budget together with occasional on-site inspections. The frequency of the latter will depend on the skills and knowledge of supervisory managers given this task.

6.9 New **agency business** has also been graded well for risk and reward in project assessments. There is a caveat in that it is assumed that the agency products being marketed and/or produced are those common, or a natural adjunct to, the existing business; if they are not related the risk of problems in knowledgeable marketing and for after-sales servicing may be significant. Taking on a new agency will incur initial costs of stocking the goods and building an acceptable infrastructure. This latter cost may be shared between the parties involved.

6.10   The business may be well established and might prefer to expand gradually without causing undue strain on or risk for the owner/management. With some situations like this it can be easy to 'forget' the sharp end of the business and not market the services adequately. A new **marketing strategy** could motivate the staff more, enhance the reputation of the firm and improve sales penetration. It could also guard against any future loss of competitiveness or downturn in demand from established customers. A new marketing strategy might entail:

1.   Estimate the likely future trend in market demand;

2.   See how the business is currently geared to meet this demand;

3.   Visualise how the business could improve its sales penetration;

4.   Raise an action plan for implementation.

6.11   The first point may incorporate bringing together trade and public market research and visiting some existing customers in person to discuss their future requirements. This by itself may raise further opportunities for business. Secondly, the business does not want to find out that its future production is being concentrated on one product line that is going out of fashion or has been usurped by the new product of a competitor. Thirdly, if additional marketing expenditure has to be spent, what should it be spent on? Passive advertising? Printing a new brochure? Increasing the numbers of the sales team? Adopting new sales areas? Finally, the funds to be spent should be itemised in a budget showing the timing of the expenditure and a means to monitor the result.

6.12   Other low risk projects would be to act as a **distributor** for a new product(s) or to **franchise** it out to other parties for them to invest money and develop a market at their risk. Acting as a non-exclusive distributor will lead to competition from existing distributors, but there could still be good opportunities to sell to one's own customers and expand the product range. There could arise the additional cost of maintaining a strategic level of stock to offer a rapid sales service. Some businesses have discarded the selling aspect of their service and concentrated on servicing the machines that are bought by customers. For those businesses not having much working capital it may be easier to repair and service through self-employed mechanics rather than stocking goods for resale that require a permanent and expensive sales team.

Fair risks and fair rewards

6.13   There are two types of new project that are suggested as holding a fair risk before success: making internal changes to the **basis of selling** or expanding the coverage on a **geographic basis** or through offering more **product lines;** or making external changes by buying in the expertise of a **minority partner/shareholder** or making an **investment in an existing business** with a view to 'pooling' resources at some future stage.

6.14   Internal changes may disrupt the existing set-up and cause reticence to change from the staff. The advantages and disadvantages for the business and the staff will have to be spelled out and fully understood before any change is commenced. New selling targets will have to be agreed and prove reasonable to attain so that bonus calculations are still seen to be worthwhile to achieve. External changes may be easier to work out on paper but the objectives of each party will have to be completely understood and supported and, in these cases, an exit route should always be available in the event that the parties find it too difficult to work together, no matter how much at arm's length.

High risks and mostly high rewards

6.15   Finally, there is what has been described as accepting higher risks to gain trading success. Opening new **sales outlets** and **new markets** have been so classified because of the commitment that is needed in money, staff and management over an extended period before the full reward of the new base(s) is forthcoming. Similar reasons apply to new **trading ventures** where the entrepreneurs have extensive skills in some operating areas (e.g. technical or marketing abilities) but may not have in others (financial and money raising expertise). Many new ventures fail because there comes at some juncture a shortage of funds. This may apply particularly where the activity is the **research and development** of new ideas and the eventual cost cannot be ascertained. The risks are even greater if the entrepreneur starts out as a short/medium term pure **financial investor** or a longer term **venture capital** investor for tax reasons having only a modest idea of the technical and other risks associated with the venture. In this latter respect the investor will also have to wait several years to gain any reward from the investment and potentially have to accept the risk of not having any direct influence over the management of the investment.

6.16   A useful method of setting out the risks and rewards of a new project is to commence at the conclusion of the assessment and work back to the beginning (see next page):

Project Assessment   Ref *zzz*

Project: .... Name ....

Time span: .... 12 months ....

Commencement date proposed: .... *1 January 2002* ....

Personnel involved: .... *xxxxxxx* ....

Part One – Summary of overall financial commitment:

Working capital available:	From existing resources	£x	
	From future cash flow	£y	**£z**
Less asset requirements costs:	Capital equipment	£a	
	Personnel	£b	
	Bought-in items	£c	**£d**
Surplus/shortfall			**£e**
If shortfall: how to be made up	(description) e.g. borrowing		
Operating Risks:	Higher costs (analyse)	£p	
	Lower income (analyse)	£q	
	Net benefit (annual)		**£r**
Return on investment:	= £r x 100/(£z – £e) %	**w %**	

Part Two – Detailed monthly cash flow for the project:

£	Month 1	Month 2	Month 3	Month 4	Month 5 etc
Income generated:					
(analysis)	I1	I2	I3	I4	I5
Expenditure met:					
Operating costs	C1	C2	C3	C4	C5
Capital equipment	E1	–	–	E4	–
Cost of borrowings (if a shortfall)	B1	B2	B3	B4	B5
Net Cash Flow	N1	N2	N3	N4	N5

Note: There may be attached a DCF calculation to the Net Cash Flow.

At outset the appraiser will see from *Part One* the likely cash shortfall or surplus that must be bridged whether or not the overall return on investing in the project is acceptable. *Part Two* will then show when the cash requirement occurs.

Chapter 7

Forecasting Future Trading

7.1   The occupation of commercial trading does not give an automatic right to make a profit. The aim of the trader is to be profitable, but in order to do so several factors have to interrelate in the correct way and each of them should be considered when forecasting the future. These points will be discussed in turn.

• Sales income has to be of sufficient size to exceed expenditure;

• Expenditure has be controlled sufficiently so as not to exceed sales;

• The business has to function efficiently to enable sales to be achieved;

• Management has to ensure that as many contributory factors to trading have been allowed for when adopting a future business strategy;

• The business overall has to be flexible enough to adjust to future external (and internal) influences on its operations.

Income from Sales

7.2   The type of product(s) and their markets will determine whether forecasting will be easy or difficult. Each business should recognise its limitations in these respects. The size of the overall market may be immaterial to the business. An established market with many competitors will require an effective pricing and marketing policy to enter and succeed. Forecasting, therefore, should concentrate on these areas. A niche player, regardless of the size of the market, will find that pricing is less important than service, quality and supply. Forecasting then will depend more on internal factors of the business to maintain quality supply. A new product will have to create a market and the forecasting emphasis should be placed on performance and in promoting the product and the brand image. Again, in the first instance, pricing is not the most important factor.

7.3   Products may have a relatively large intrinsic value, reliant on a high profit margin rather than bulk sales to achieve income. Forecasting should concentrate on the quantities likely to be sold. Low value goods will be reliant on the size of individual orders and their shipment costs.

Goods with a high labour content will rely on worker relations, incentives and productivity to attain the best returns. Goods having a high materials content will rely more on consistent supply and its costs. The product(s) may have a low shelf or technology life. The former requires replacement forecasting and the latter perhaps research and development costs to maintain competitiveness.

Only after all these variables have been correctly assessed can the trader consider forecasting and projecting sales of his or her own business.

Control of expenditure

7.4   A business with a poor sales team and poor penetration of a potentially lucrative market may well succeed if the underlying operating costs of the business are sufficiently lower than the sales income being generated. Expenditure should be judged by its necessity: premises must be rented if they are not owned. A workforce, raw materials, light and heat will be needed to produce goods for resale but production may be sub-contracted out at less cost. An advertising budget is particularly difficult to judge on cost-effective grounds. Are additional sales being raised now and for the future by passive advertising? Would more active (tele-sales) efforts and direct managerial approaches to potential customers produce more response? Would a simple shop window re-jig and a re-sited interior activate customers for more impulse buying? Is all business expenditure regularly reviewed for possible pruning? Have these aspects been properly accounted for in the forecasting of expenditure?

An efficiently functioning business

7.5   Each principal item of business income and expenditure should be examined as to its efficiency to improve trading returns and whether it can be improved before adopting a forecasting strategy. The marketing team may be judged on the sales they achieve per capita and their returns from different geographic areas. For the larger businesses this may extend to the returns from branches. Production may be judged by the hourly output per worker/machine and the proportion of unproductive hours in each period. The cost of production for the number of units sold will indicate what selling prices may be set for how much profit that can be earned. The costs of transport may be compared with outsourcing this element of service. The investment in, and earnings from, the business will indicate whether the return being achieved is acceptable. The personal drawings from the business will show whether the business is providing a proper income for the owners.

The contribution of management

7.6   The delegatory powers adopted by management may, on the one hand, stifle incentive and innovation and, on the other hand, allow no interaction between different production areas or plants (where one centre may be under-utilised and another fully stretched). Similarly, funds may be invested in business products offering low profitability to the detriment of other, more profitable, product lines. The provision of additional or replacement equipment may or may not have been fully planned ahead and the effect on future trading may not have been calculated insofar as it will affect cash flow and current financial resources.

Flexibility of future operations

7.7   Having a financial strategy for 'a rainy day' were events to run adversely for the business is often considered a luxury for those firms that are constantly operating at the extreme limits of their operational capacity, whether it be on the personnel; productive; managerial or financial fronts. This approach becomes even more prevalent during times of high growth and profitable trading, yet these are the periods when the greatest care should be taken to maintain this growth and profitability.

7.8   Two forecasting scenarios should always be planned in case of need: that more money may have to be spent if trading receipts, temporary or otherwise, drop and, secondly, what action might most easily be taken to reduce overheads with the minimum of disruption to the business were the downfall to prove temporary. The first remedy could be to have cash facilities at hand in case of need or to build up working capital reserves in the business that could either be channelled to cover a shortfall or to underpin the raising of temporary capital from commercial sources.

7.9   The second remedy is a mixture of prevention and rescue: an example of preventive action is not to employ additional permanent staff until it is proven there is a continuing need to increase the workforce. There are many instances of a business raising a rescue plan out of insolvency only to have it abandoned because the money needed to make the required number of staff redundant was not available. There is a strong case for those businesses that can do so to employ permanently the key skilled supervisor personnel and to sub-contract the unskilled labour from sources local to the work sites. Rescuing a business usually requires a knife to cut costs to generate immediate savings and measures to boost sales and thereby create additional working capital. Forecasts of the effects of each of these measures would greatly assist management to be prepared should the worst situations occur.

The forecasting template

7.10   Individual circumstances will determine how each business prefers to set out the detail of its Profit and Loss Account and any Cash Flow statement for management purposes, therefore the example built up hereafter and shown in Appendix B can only be a general guide. Several options to fit specific types of business are discussed in the text.

The calculations are computer-related (specifically Microsoft ExcelTM spreadsheet format) although they can be adapted for other computer formats or even hand-written use. The computer knowledge required is simple: how to add/deduct/divide/multiply/copy and freeze (by using the dollar sign) cells and groups of cells.

7.11   It is suggested that the smaller business shows income and expenditure on a monthly basis for forecasting at least twelve months ahead and possibly for the second year as well; thereafter the calculations may be drawn up quarterly with annual totals. Totals should be added at the end of each accounting year. Thus, a business wishing to compile a forecasting spreadsheet from 1 January but having a year ending of 31 March might show its initial monthly income and expenditure from January to March; then for twelve months from April monthly through to the end of March in the following year with an annual total. It will be easier to insert in the spreadsheet annual totals in a column after first calculating the monthly figures for all the years in question. This is because it will be easier to copy connecting entries across the page without having to allow for intervening columns.

The Profit and Loss Account

7.12   The starting point for spreadsheet entries will be the monthly Trial Balance of the Profit and Loss Account. As each month is entered in the (computerised) ledgers the main income and expenditure heads can be transposed into the spreadsheet. It is assumed that the monthly figures will be taken from postings a week or so after the month end and will include recently received invoices relating to the previous month but will not include adjustments for other accruals (of debtors, creditors and prepayment of expenses) and therefore the Net Profit shown will only approximate to the true (audited) profit for the period were all accruals to have been correctly accounted for.

7.13   The reason for picking a monthly columnar profile is that many costs are paid monthly and the sales/bought ledgers will be ruled off monthly. It will, therefore, be easier to relate the actual monthly trading figures as they arise to the projections made earlier. Monthly usually means calendar months, but the business may account on a four week/thirteen period year if it wishes. It is suggested that before forecasting ahead the historic Profit and Loss Account figures are compiled from previous monthly Trial Balances for each month of the last accounting year as well as for those months so far in the current accounting year. For those microbusinesses that do not compile a monthly Trial Balance, there should be some records denoting what the monthly sales were and amounts for the expenditure heads can be taken from the last set of annual Accounts transposed on to a monthly basis.

An example of the typical income and expenditure headings to be met is given by *Table A*.

Table A

A Business

Income	Month 1	Month 2	Etc
Sales			
Expenditure			
Direct costs:			
Wages			
Materials			
Transport/other			
Sub-total			
Indirect costs:			
Salaries			
Rent & rates			
Light & heat			
Telephones			
Post & stationery			
Insurances			
Motor & travel			
Advertising			
Financial costs			
Sundries			
Sub-total			
Net Profit			

Sales analysis

7.14   Many businesses will incur a seasonal demand for sales. Retailers, in particular, will be looking to see at the earliest opportunity how current sales compare with the same period in the previous year. When forecasting ahead a seasonality benchmark can be built into the projected figures by taking the proportion of sales achieved for each month of the previous year as a percentage of that year's annual total, and then assume that for each month of the following year an identical seasonality of demand will occur. Should any month in the preceding year have been affected by special circumstances, then the ensuing year's forecast should make special allowance to reflect a more 'normal' return. The resulting figures forecast may have to be adjusted should national holidays arise in different months of the year. *Table B* sets out how the benchmarking calculation will look.

Table B

A Business – start of year January 2002

Sales	January	February	March	April	Etc	Year to Dec
Last year:	8,000	13,000	16,000	18,000		150,000
Proportion %	5.3	8.6	10.6	12.0		
This year:						
Projection	9,540	15,480	19,080	21,600		180,000
Actual	8,200	14,000	18,500	23,600		

Note: 5.3% = 8,000/150,000   9,540 = 5.3% × 180,000 etc

7.15   This method is a reasonable guide for those businesses that rely on over-the-counter sales but further modifications will be required for businesses such as building and construction where the incidence of large contracts can significantly affect turnover month by month. In these cases any contract of size should be shown separately so that a better monthly comparison of performance can be made. The sales projections for the ensuing year will be the total of sales expected to be received from each major contract (based on monthly certificates) and an estimate of income arising from other small jobs. *Table C*, on the next page, provides an example:

Table C

<u>A Business</u> – start of year January 2002

Sales	January	February	March	April	Etc	Year to Dec
Last year:						
Contract 1	5,000	5,000	0	1,000		
Contract 2	6,000	0	1,200	0		
Other contracts	4,000	3,000	3,000	3,500		
Total sales	**15,000**	**8,000**	**4,200**	**4,500**		
This year:						
Contract 7	7,000	7,000	3,000	0		
Other contracts	2,000	1,500	3,500	5,900		
Projected sales	**9,000**	**8,500**	**6,500**	**5,900**		
Actual sales	**8,200**	**6,000**	**4,500**	**8,600**		

7.16   Manufacturing businesses can adopt another form of spreadsheet analysis, either as a supplementary sheet or embodied in the final sheet. This can take into account the value of production expected in future months and its conversion into invoiced sales. *Table D*, on the next page, provides an example and shows the monthly production being invoiced in the following month. If required, cumulative totals of orders and sales may also be included.

Table D

A Business – start of year January 2002

Sales	January	February	March	April	Etc	Year to Dec
Last year:						
Orders in hand	*15,000*	*16,000*	*10,000*	*11,000*		
Production value	*3,000*	*4,000*	*2,000*	*500*		
Total sales	**2,500**	**3,000**	**4,000**	**2,000**	**500**	
This year:						
Orders in hand	*19,800*	*16,400*	*17,200*	*15,300*		
Contract 4	*7,000*	*7,000*	*3,000*	*0*		
Other contracts	*2,000*	*1,500*	*3,500*	*5,900*		
Production value	*9,000*	*8,500*	*6,500*	*5,900*		
Projected sales	**6,600**	**9,000**	**8,500**	**6,500**	**5,900**	
Actual sales	**7,200**	**8,500**	**8,700**	**7,100**	**4,800**	

7.17   These variations in accounting spreadsheets have been highlighted to indicate the different situations that arise with different types of businesses. The detail provided might be too extensive to implement in practice where the sole owner or proprietor manages all financial matters in conjunction with his or her other business tasks. A broader brush approach may be necessary but should still facilitate easy updating of the projections to take account of actual sales achieved and any other changes in circumstances. A complete example of what is meant is given in Appendix B.

Expenditure analysis

7.18   When projecting business costs a distinction must be made between costs that are directly dependent on the level of sales (variable costs) and costs that are independent of sales (fixed costs). As the level of sales varies, so will the variable costs associated with producing those sales, either through producing or purchasing more or less goods for resale. The fixed costs will be incurred regardless of the level of sales and its associated costs.

7.19   Forecasting expenditure should take into account the budget laid down for the business. Many items such as rent (varying only at review times) and rates (varying annually as set by the local authority) can be forecast with good accuracy. Other items may be more difficult, such as motor and travel costs, but a reasonable idea will have been gained from the expenditure incurred in the previous year and how many vehicles are being used for what purpose. Most items will accrue each year with increments attached to allow for cost inflation.

The implication of Value Added Tax

7.20   The Profit and Loss Account spreadsheet, of course, will be based on all figures shown net of Input and Output taxes. When it is adjusted into a Cash Flow format this will change to include VAT on both income and expenditure. In most cases the rate to add to the Profit and Loss Account figures will be the standard rate, but fuel will have its own reduced rate and there will be zero rated supplies. Where the zero or exempt rated supplies are significant, separate calculations should be done to ensure that an accurate cash flow income and expenditure is raised. The (monthly or) quarterly VAT net settlement figure to Customs and Excise will be calculated as the result of adding all the VAT due on Inputs and Outputs and this figure should be taken into account as a separate receipt or payment in the month it is settled.

Other expenditure adjustments

7.21   Since the Profit and Loss Account includes a provision for **depreciation** rather than a payment, this item has to be added back to reduce expenditure when calculating the Cash Flow. Equipment or other **fixed assets** acquired for cash during the year will have to be accounted for as expenditure in the cash flow calculation only, but should be shown as a non-operating item after the operating result has been compiled. With self-assessment, estimated calculations of the future **tax** liability on business trading will have been made and these estimates should be included in the Cash Flow spreadsheet. Additional **investment** in the business by the proprietors and **loans** raised by the business (with the repayments as they occur) will also have to be included in the Cash Flow.

Forecasting Cash Flow

7.22   There are a number of ready-made software programmes currently available to convert historic accounting postings into a cash flow basis. It is assumed, however, that the trader wishes to make cash flow projections for the business that can be modified to allow for different operating situations that may arise in the future.

7.23   As has been mentioned earlier, the spreadsheet examples given hereafter show the cash actually received each month from past sales, or that projected to arise from future sales, and will include Value Added Tax on all items if the business is VAT registered. This should not be confused with the Profit and Loss figures compiled from the book-keeping records which will be accounted for net of VAT and will have a year-end debtor or creditor for VAT in the Balance Sheet.

7.24   In many respects a Cash Flow forecast is more important than a Profit and Loss projection because it shows what total net cash is being generated by the business for management to judge whether the inflow of cash and total available resources are remaining healthy or whether reme-dial measures to improve the position should be initiated. Many businesses have reported rising sales and profits but have run out of monetary resources to continue to trade.

7.25   It is also important to read a Cash Flow in conjunction with other operating data of the business gained from the accounting records and sales marketing returns. Consider the hypothetical case of a business with the following trading results:

VAT inclusive	Month 1	Month 2	Month 3	Month 4	Month 5
Orders in hand	20,000	24,000	27,000	30,000	34,000
Sales invoiced	8,000	11,000	12,000	12,500	13,000
Cash received	7,000	8,000	10,000	9,000	8,000

Orders are increasing fairly well month by month but the conversion into confirmed sales is falling. Assuming a two monthly delay for an order to be produced and delivered, in month 3 the order conversion rate into sales was 60%, whereas by month 5 this had dropped to 48%. Management should be looking to see why orders are being cancelled or completion is being delayed. Assuming also that month 1 invoices should be converted into cash by month 3, in the example provided months 4 and 5 indicate a shortfall in cash expectations. This will have an effect on the working capital available to the business and may be a pointer that debtors are not being chased sufficiently.

Scope of the template

7.26   The standard cash flow spreadsheet will commence with the cash brought forward from the earlier period; add the income received; deduct the expenses paid; and then show the cash carried forward to the follow-ing period. The opening and closing cash will be that held in the business bank account and these entries are usually given at the foot of the spread-sheet. As an example, *Table E* (see next page) takes notional trading figures for one month and converts this into a cash flow statement assum-ing that the standard VAT rate is 17.5%.

A more comprehensive example is given at the end of the chapter together with a description on how the spreadsheets were compiled.

Table E

A Business

£'000	**Profit and Loss Account**		*Notes*	**Cash Flow**
	Month	Calculation		
Income				
Sales	4,400	4,400 x 1.175 =	1	5,170
Expenditure				
Direct costs:				
Wages	320		2	320
Materials etc	2,200	2,200 x 1.175 =	1	2,585
Indirect costs:				
Salaries	240		2	240
Rent	300		2	300
Utilities	180	180 x 1.05 =	3	189
Other costs	670		1	787
Depreciation	150		4	0
Net Profit	340			
Operating Cash Flow				749
Irrecoverable VAT		5,170-4,400 – 2,585+,2200 – 189+180 – 787+670 =	4	259
Equipment purchased (say)			4	400
Proprietors' drawings			4	120
Net Cash Flow				– 30
Opening cash				230
Closing cash				200

Note 1: Assumed all items subject to standard rate VAT.
Note 2: Items not subject to VAT.
Note 3: Utilities costs assumed charged at 5% VAT rate.
Note 4: Adjustments for cash flow purposes.

Appendix B: example

7.27

Sheet 2: Actual results of the previous year.

Actual trading results are shown for each month of the year 2000. It has been assumed the quantities of items produced were sold at 1.65 during the first half of the year and a price increase to 1.73 was adopted thereafter when new plant came on stream and produced a slightly modified item selling for 1.50. This enabled a higher production to be achieved by five less workers. Turnover for the year nearly reached £2.5 million and a Profit before tax of £449,176 was earned. Cash held at the beginning of January was £25,000.

When calculating the Cash Flow a one month time lag for invoicing sales at the month end and a further one month credit has been allowed before the cash was received (*Note 1*). VAT at 17.5% has been added to the Profit and Loss Account sales (*Note 2*) and for simplicity it has been assumed that 80% of non-labour costs have also been subject to VAT at the standard rate (*Note 5*). Labour costs have been paid out in the month they have occurred (*Note 3*) but two months' credit has been taken before paying Other Costs, and Materials costs have been assumed ordered in advance and paid in the month of production (*Note 4*). January and February Other Costs are calculated from the spreadsheet since they relate to the last two months of the previous year. The VAT payable is settled quarterly and is the net sum of Outputs and Inputs for the previous three months (*Note 6*).

The new equipment purchased is shown as paid in July (*Note 7*) and the business has had to repay the principal of a bank loan at the fixed rate of £8,000 per month (*Note 8*) with the interest (not shown) included in Other Costs. Taxation paid in September relates to Corporation Tax due on the previous year's profits at the rate of 20% (*Note 9*). A dividend has been declared out of the previous year's profits and paid in March after the audit (*Note 10*). The business shows a healthy position at the end of 2000 with £111,212 held in the bank.

Sheet 3: Forecast results for 2001

With the new equipment installed, the management has decided that production can be increased to 1.8 million units from 1.47 million units achieved in 2000 *(Note 12)*. The quantity of items produced each month in 2001 has been assumed as the same percentage produced in 2000 *(Note 11)* as adjusted up to the higher annual output budgeted for the year. With the new plant output having been established it has been possible to market all production at a standardised selling price of 1.75 per unit *(Note 13)*. The labour costs are shown for either four or five weekly payments per month depending on when the payment days fall in each month *(Note 14)* and the average cost from January onwards is based on the wage bill brought forward and adjusted for a wage increase of 3% p.a. *(Note 16)*. The number of production employees is projected to remain steady at 60 throughout the year *(Note 15)*.

The variable cost of materials has been estimated by multiplying the production output by the cost taken per item *(Note 17)*. Fixed labour costs have also assumed a pay increase of 3% p.a. and been allocated evenly each month over the ensuing year *(Note 18)*. Other Fixed costs have been separately calculated for each item (not shown) and shown for each month when they are expected to occur *(Note 19)*. Depreciation will be calculated on the bases laid down for each asset (ie worked on a straight line or reducing balance) and adjusted as each item of new equipment is purchased. When items are acquired part way through the year, depending on the method adopted for calculating depreciation, either one-twelfth of the annual charge for the new item is added to the depreciation sum, or the depreciation charge for the whole year can be apportioned and charged against the remaining months of the year. The Cash Flow calculation is worked on the same basis as for the year 2000 example *(Note 20)*.

Sheet 4: Actual results for 2001

As each month's trading results are known, the actual figures are substituted for the estimated figures. In the example given, the fall off in sales led, first, to a reduction in selling price from June and, when this did not stem the dropping sales, the number of production (and some fixed cost) employees were made redundant in December. The business also had to suffer an increase in material costs from August. As a result, it was seen that the forecast cash flow of the business could not afford to pay off the loan early and meet the Corporation tax bill due in September. The loan was therefore continued and serviced on its original repayment schedule.

The Balance Sheet

7.28   It is suggested that the forecast Balance Sheet is limited to the principal headings met in the annual Accounts:

- Fixed Assets – showing Land/buildings & Other (less depreciation);

- Current Assets – showing Stocks and Trade Debtors and Cash (if any);

- Current Liabilities – showing Trade Creditors and Other Creditors;

- Borrowings – showing short-term (up to one year) and long-term;

- Capital – of the proprietors.

The first step is to compile an **Opening Position** of these items, taken from the last available set of audited Accounts or possibly from subsequent management accounts if that is preferred. Amendments to the **Fixed Assets** occurring each year can be added (or sales subtracted) and the **Depreciation** figure (calculated either on a straight line basis in equal annual amounts, or on a depreciating balance as a percentage of the previous years total) can be worked out on an annual basis.

The **Net Current Assets** position will arise from the assumptions made for the Cash Flow: if sales and purchases are received and paid respectively two months in arrears and the year end is 31 December, the sales and purchases amounts shown for the previous November and December should be added together (net of VAT) and will comprise the **Trade Debtors** and **Trade Creditors** at the year-end. Similarly, if the assumption in the model has been that Stocks are equivalent to two months' purchases (net of VAT) then this will be the **Stock** figure at the year end. An addition may be made for **Work-in-Progress** (excluding any profit element) if it is substantial. **Cash in Hand or Overdrawn** will be the actual amounts given by the bank statements. **Other Creditors** will be sums outstanding for VAT/PAYE (three months VAT if payable and settled quarterly and one month's deductions for PAYE plus the Employer's percentage portion), and the tax calculated to be due on the profit made in that year. Other items may be added according to the individual circumstances of the business.

Borrowings will comprise commercial bank and leasing/hire purchase/factoring debts and possibly loans outstanding from the proprietors. The lenders should have provided a schedule of the monthly/quarterly repayments due with the balance outstanding after each payment; this balance of the capital and interest combined will be the sum still owing. Net off the totals for Fixed Assets, Net Current Assets and Borrowings to arrive at the **Capital Employed** and retained in the business by the proprietor. A quick approximate check on this figure is to take the opening position of the Capital Account and add the Profit after Tax. Due to several items in the Balance Sheet that have been affected by calculations based on preceding months figures, the two figures of Employment of Capital and Capital Employed will not be exactly similar, and therefore for the Balance Sheet to balance, the **Other Creditors** item should be amended by the required amount. A more sophisticated computation will be needed for an exact balance to be achieved and it is suggested that for broad forecasting purposes this approximate guide should suffice.

Chapter 8

Balance Sheet Management

An overview

8.1   The Balance Sheet is an image of the state of the business at one point in time. Being an historical document based on the book values of assets and liabilities its use as a management tool tends to be overlooked compared with turnover and profit projections and cash flow forecasts. Three examples of a simplified Balance Sheet are illustrated hereafter, each being observed from a different viewpoint after making some necessary valuation assumptions:

The historic book values reflect (intangible) Goodwill and (tangible) Premises and Equipment, all shown net of depreciation that has been charged annually in the Profit and Loss Account and accumulated prior to being deducted from the acquisition value of the assets at the end of each accounting year. These values will differ markedly from their (higher) current replacement values if new assets are soon to be acquired, but the values may understate their current selling value where, for example, the freehold of the site has appreciated from the date it was originally purchased many years ago, or the plant is specialist by nature and has held its value in the second-hand market. In each case, the reader will judge the Balance Sheet values according to the reasons for which they are being examined.

Current assets should hold their values historically and for current replacement values, subject to raw materials' prices changing and possible bad trade debts. On a forced break-up sale, however, their book values are most unlikely to be attained. Conversely, trade creditors will try and obtain the full value of their debts and the bank overdraft will usually be supported by security to obtain full repayment. In the example, the future break-up value of the business for the proprietor given by the Balance Sheet is negative (-25) compared with the historic value of 130.

See next page

8.2 Balance Sheet Management

Balance Sheets (£'000s)	Historic net Book values	Current Replacement values	Future Break-up values
Goodwill	10		
Freehold	100		70
Leasehold	15	20	5
Plant/Vehicles/Fixtures	<u>75</u>	<u>150</u>	<u>25</u>
Fixed Assets	200	170	100
Stocks/Work in progress	60	60	20
Trade Debtors	<u>45</u>	<u>45</u>	<u>30</u>
Current Assets	<u>105</u>	<u>105</u>	<u>50</u>
Trade Creditors	55	55	55
Other Creditors	10	10	10
Bank overdraft	<u>30</u>	<u>30</u>	<u>30</u>
Current liabilities	<u>95</u>	<u>95</u>	<u>95</u>
Net current assets	<u>10</u>	<u>10</u>	–45
	210	180	<u>55</u>
Capital	100	70	–55
Undistributed earnings	30	30	30
Long-term liabilities	<u>80</u>	<u>80</u>	<u>80</u>
	<u>210</u>	180	<u>55</u>

The assessor's view

8.2   The assessor will be looking at certain key features shown by the historic, traditional, Balance Sheet and will not be privy to more detailed management returns. Several years' figures are preferred so that comparative trends can be highlighted, but if only one year is made available the following facets would invoke attention:

1.   Capital employed totals £120k (after deducting Goodwill) and borrowings total £110k, giving a Gearing of (110/120 =) 92%. Most businesses would be starting to become uncomfortable were the gearing to exceed 100%, implying that its lenders are investing the greater share of the business. Ignoring other factors, the business may have difficulty in persuading its bank to increase the credit facilities.

2.   The Net Current Assets position is positive, inferring that the business could stop trading, sell off its stocks, run down its debts and

still have funds in hand before considering a sale of the fixed assets. This is referred to as the Current Ratio; being Current Assets divided by Current Liabilities (= 1.10). It does not mean that a ratio of less than unity shows the business to be insolvent. To be solvent, the business must be able to pay its liabilities as and when they fall due. Re-arranging the Current Assets and Current Liabilities for a solvency test would indicate the following:

Time Period	Solvency Test	Current Assets	Current Liabilities	Net Position A	Net Position B
30–60 days	receive Debtors	45,000			
30–60 days	pay Creditors		55,000	– 10,000	– 10,000
60–90 days	realise Stocks	60,000		+ 50,000	Ignore
90 days +	pay Other Creditors		10,000	+ 40,000	– 20,000
annually	review Overdraft		30,000	+ 10,000	– 50,000

In practice, the Trade Debtors and Creditors would be analysed probably under weekly bands when the receipts were likely to materialise and the bills paid. Other Creditors would be taxes and non-trade debts, again with specific times for payment.

8.3   The *Net Position 'A'* assumes Stocks are realised for cash within a 60 to 90 day period. If management wished to remain within the overdraft exposure shown of £30,000 and a projection of trading for the next three months, for example, gave an exact balance of receipts and payments from future business, the table indicates a requirement of £10,000 working capital to settle all trade creditors and at least a future overdraft of £20,000 on renewal of the facility. In the circumstances the management would, no doubt, defer paying some £10,000 worth of Trade Creditors and ensure that the overdraft renewal was agreed.

8.4   Stocks, however, may consist of worked raw materials or work-in-progress not yet sold and therefore not readily realisable. It would be prudent to ignore this figure in the solvency calculation and this is shown in *Net Position 'B'*. The financing need has doubled in the example to £20,000 before assuming that the overdraft facility will be continued. Again, a projection of future cash flow from forecast trading may indicate that there will be no cash problem to resolve in the months ahead, but do all businesses check this position on a regular basis?

8.5   Many businesses can operate showing a Net Current Liabilities position for part of their trading year. This can be due to a number of factors: the day taken for the year end Balance Sheet may be during a period when the overdraft is close to its peak, whereas during the remainder of the year the cash position is much improved. The stocks held may also not be representative of trading throughout the year. If a Net Current Liability is shown, the shortfall may be made up through drawing additional bank credit where it is available. There are few other alternatives: reducing stocks or accelerating the receipt of debts will improve the cash position but not alter Net Current Liabilities overall. Only an injection of cash will do this, either from increased profits on sales that are paid for, or from additional working capital that is either retained or injected into the business.

Long-term assets shown in the original example have a tangible book value of £190k, which compares favourably with (matching) long-term liabilities of £80k. Sometimes a Debt Ratio is quoted; being Long-term Debt divided by the sum of Long-term Debt and Capital (= 0.40). The important points from this comparison are that, first, long-term debt is classified as capital invested long-term in the business and not short-term working capital. Secondly, it brings into prominence the gearing (or leverage) factor. Adjusting the figures from the original example once more, the effect of gearing would be as follows:

Balance Sheet	With gearing	No gearing with the same capital	No gearing with increased capital	Adding gearing to improve earnings
Fixed Assets	200	120	200	200
Net Current Assets	10	10	10	30
	210	130	210	230
Long-term Debt	80 *(a)*	0	0	100 *(a)*
Capital & Reserves	130	130	210	130
	210	130	210	230
Earnings (say)	40	(48x130/210=) 29.7 *(c)*	(40-8=) 48 *(b)*	(29.7-10+100x22.9%=) 42.6 *(d)*
Return on Capital	*30.7%*	*22.9%*	*22.9%*	*32.8%*

8.6   Column one of the table shows pre-interest earnings assumed of £48k, less interest on debt (*note (a)*) at 10% p.a., leaving £40k to add to the capital invested in the business. The return on equity capital employed is 30.7% p.a. Had there been no long-term debt invested in the business, less money would likely have been spent on fixed assets (machinery) and the production capability would not have supported the same level of sales or profit; hence the lower earnings calculated pro rata of £29.7k shown in column two. The return on equity capital has reduced to 22.9% p.a. and the profit earned has reduced by £10.3k.

8.7   If the owners decide to repay the long-term debt (column three) and have surplus funds available to do so, the business will generate higher earnings through eliminating interest payable on the debt although this will not improve the investment return on equity capital straight off. The management has a decision to make whether present earnings on the surplus funds of £80k that is currently invested elsewhere would be more or less than the £8k interest saved. Taxation has been ignored but will constitute part of the decision assessment.

Finally, the effect of increasing the gearing by £20k is shown in column four. Earnings have risen by £2.6k and the return on equity capital has risen to 32.8%. Debt as a proportion of equity capital has risen from (£80k/£130k =) 62% to (£100k/£130k =) 77%. The earnings cover to meet the interest payable on the debt has reduced from (£48k/£8k =) 6.0 times to (£52.6k/£10k =) 5.3 times.

The management view

8.8 The management should be viewing the Balance Sheet as shown by its current replacement values. The aspects to consider in this case are:

1. To replace the existing assets the business would require additional finance of £30k. The questions to answer are over what period must the replacements be purchased and how will the money be raised for this latent liability.

2. The (short-term) lease is due for renewal and a possible premium might have to be paid, say £5k, if alternative premises have to be found.

3. The freehold owned provides the option for the business to consider a 'sale and lease back' to raise funds. Alternatively, the property may be sold to benefit the owners financially and additional premises leased so that the business can in future be accommodated under one roof at a more advantageous site.

The bank view

8.9 The bank may have monitored the debt to equity capital ratio and for prudence would have noted the possible break-up value of the business. On the figures shown there would be negative equity of £25k and, as part of the continuing relationship between the bank and the business, the bank should be enquiring how the business is trading and what its plans are for replacing plant and continuing the business when the current lease expires.

Three very disparate pictures of the business have been drawn up. In conjunction with profit and cash flow forecasts (not shown) the management should already be aware of the strategic necessity to plan ahead and ensure that future Balance Sheets convey a more acceptable depiction of the state of affairs of the business. Each main asset heading is now examined in greater detail.

Fixed assets

8.10   It is presumed that all businesses wish to trade at a profit and the accrual of fixed assets is a necessary feature of this aim. A business in its most basic form would outsource or contract out any pre-sales work, use agents to sell the product and act purely as administrative manager. Virtually no capital would be required and no fixed assets, apart from a personal computer, would be necessary to operate the business.

8.11   At the other extreme, if an environmentally friendly site and specialised plant and equipment are necessary and the business is capital asset intensive, considerable financial capital will be necessary to trade. Every business should regularly appraise its needs for investing in and maintaining fixed assets. A sample checklist template is given below:

Type of Fixed Asset	*Action check list*
Intangible	Generally amortise under accounting recommendations. What controls are there on Research & Development costs?
Freeholds	Is it necessary to own property? If so, who should be the owner? Consider taxation and owner pension options.
Long-term Leaseholds	Can any part be sub-let for additional income? Is there a premium receivable on relocation? Would the freeholder be willing to sell?
Short-term Leaseholds	Is there a policy laid down for renewal? Would longer lease terms be preferred?
Plant and Machinery	Is there a replacement programme in place? Is maintenance better to be done in-house or by external contract?
Motor Vehicles	Should they be owned or leased? Can the transport fleet be outsourced?
Equipment/Furniture/ Fixtures/Fittings	Have refurbishment costs been budgeted? Can any equipment be leased?
Patents	Are they fully safeguarded? What strategy is planned for when they expire?
Trade Investments	Are they necessary? Would it be preferable to increase the investment?

8.12 A regular Plant and Machinery record should be maintained to indicate the cost of using each piece of equipment, the proportion of time it is in use and when it could most beneficially be replaced. Some of the data will only need to be updated occasionally. Headings to consider for each major item of plant and machinery are:

- Date purchased, the purchase price and age (if second-hand).

- Any attached financing (e.g. hire purchase, with the terms and period of repayments).

- Any contract maintenance with terms (e.g. renewal date and cost).

- Cost of running per hour, including the above indirect costs. (*Note*: the cost of specialist operatives should be included as a direct expense).

- Work sheet details downloaded to give the non-/usage time split.

The last two items will provide the financial information necessary to cost out the machinery when tendering for customer contracts and will show how frequently the machine is used. In this latter respect, the percentage of use to idle time will assist in answering the questions: Is the machine being used efficiently?; When (or not) should it be replaced?

The labour force

8.13 It may appear strange to the small business owner that one type of fixed asset is never shown on the traditional Balance Sheet; that of the valuable labour force that is needed to maintain trading. The closest to a mention, and that in company accounts, is in the Notes to the Accounts describing the pension commitment of the business and the number of staff employed. At any time the business would have a liability to pay staff on compulsory redundancy and this should be a negative addition when evaluating the break-up value of a business. For an on-going business there would be agency and advertising costs associated with appointing new staff. The 'investment' of the business in its staff will be the costs of training and providing for staff amenities and pension commitments. Management should review on a regular basis its labour force incorporating a checklist of:

- Separate lists of 'key' and other personnel and their responsibilities.

- The number of years each has been employed.

- Any training commitment outstanding.

- Current pay/overtime rates, review dates and annual cost + benefits.

- Productive hours worked and the cost per hour for the business.

- Work sheet details downloaded to give non-/productive time split.

- The liability were the employee to be issued with a redundancy notice.

Current Assets

Stocks

8.14 An efficient control of stocks held should be a key feature of all Balance Sheet management. Until sufficient experience has been gained of trading and until adequate finances are on hand to allow for any build-up of stocks, conservative principles should be the order of the day: produce only to firm orders and preferably receive cash on delivery or, if services are offered, accept a partial down payment with regular stage payments thereafter. Many on-going contracts set out specifications and prices but have no firm times or quantities for deliveries, on which the supplier depends for subsequent payment. In this case it may be possible to negotiate that the customer pays and retains ownership of the raw materials until they are used.

8.15 If the sales contract(s) is on-going and dependent on end-user demand, the supplying business or sub-contractor should discuss with the customer (who may be a wholesaler main contractor) what stock is needed as a strategic minimum to satisfy normal demand for the product(s). The cost of raw materials for this element of finished stock and the direct costs of manufacture can be calculated and the customer asked to subsidise or provide credit to the supplier up to this amount.

8.16 If sales contracts are usually one-off and reasonable in size (say, £20,000 upwards) and the customer is an established name, it may be possible for the supplier to finance the contract commercially and therefore obtain finance to obtain raw materials stocks and produce the goods. In this case, stocks can be purchased to fulfil the whole contract rather than jeopardising deliveries through purchasing stocks piecemeal.

8.17 Where the stocks are of standardised finished products and the type of trade demands immediate deliveries, say of perishable goods, it may be possible for similar suppliers, close to one another, to agree to help each other out in supplying raw materials and selling the packaged goods. There would be netting out of balances owing at agreed intervals but no intervening cash payments and receipts.

8.18 The question frequently posed is: How much stock should be held for any given level of sales? Clearly, there is a strategic level of stock that is needed to maintain production or selling capability. This may be adjusted for specific orders or for seasonal demands. Small retailers can usually discern at a glance what goods lines are getting low and previous ordering will show what lines sell quicker and what does not sell well.

Manufacturers need more sophistication with their calculations unless a computerised stock control system is in place. Consider the following example:

Months:

Profit & Loss: (£'000)	*1*	*2*	*3*	*4*	*5*	*6*	*7*	*8*	*9*
Sales invoiced	100	100	100	120	140	160	180	200	200
Materials delivery	20	24	28	32	36	40	40	40	40
Labour cost	40	40	40	48	56	64	72	80	80
Cost of sales	60	64	68	80	92	104	112	120	120
Gross Profit	40	36	32	40	48	56	68	80	80

Cash Flow: (£'000)	*1*	*2*	*3*	*4*	*5*	*6*	*7*	*8*	*9*
Sales receipts	100	100	100	100	120	140	160	180	200
Materials payments	20	20	20	24	28	32	36	40	40
Labour payments	40	40	40	48	56	64	72	80	80
Net Inflow excluding other costs	40	40	40	28	36	44	52	60	80

For simplicity, other months incurring no change, sales progressively increased and doubled over months 4 through to 8. Materials (comprising one-fifth of the value of sales invoiced) for production had to be delivered two months in advance. Customers were given one month's credit and suppliers were paid after two months. Two deductions can be made from the table: first, when and by how much materials should be ordered. Secondly, that cash flow will dip in months 4 and 5 and sufficient cash should be available to meet the direct costs shown, otherwise creditors will have to be deferred for payment until later.

Work-in-Progress

8.19   Management of this aspect of a business that is concerned with sub-contract work largely centres on accurate estimating of tenders; full evaluations of performance risk; prompt accounting for progress payments and regular site monitoring. The costing of job expenditure is only as good as how recent and accurate are the underlying charge-out rates for plant, materials and labour. Performance risk evaluation is only as good as the research into, for example, soil conditions. Cash flow will only be as beneficial as the speed in requesting progress payments. Quality control will be dependent on the efficiency and regularity of site inspections. At outset, an estimate of the labour requirements for each contract should be calculated and, if the present work force is not sufficient, allowance should be made for the time needed to employ additional temporary employees.

8.20 Where work in progress consists of product manufacture, any sizeable sales contract should be broken down into several deliveries with separate billing for each. The management of contracts may require the allocation of plant time and staff depending on the size of the labour force. A rub-off wall chart of available employees' names (after allowing for holiday dates) with their allocation to jobs could greatly assist forward planning. Some customers may ask for prototypes of a new product to be made in advance of placing an order. If the cost of these would be significant and the supplier has to bear the risk of failure, the work should be billed as a separate consultancy or the customer asked to make stage payments, thereby ensuring that as work progresses, the risk of aborting the product lessens.

Trade Debtors

8.21 The collection of trade debts has become almost an industry in its own right. The best way to safeguard against losses from debts becoming irrecoverable is to take added care when agreeing trade credit. The effect on a business of a bad debt may be judged from the following example:

(VAT ignored)		**Sale**	**Loss**
Debtor invoiced		£1,000	£1,000
Cost of sales: Materials, *say*	£150		
Labour, *say*	£450	£600	£600
Indirect costs, *say*		£100	£100
Net Profit on sale		£300	£700
Future sales required to recoup the expenditure			£2,333
Future sales required to recoup the lost profit			£1,000
Future sales required to make up the total loss			**£3,333**

From the example, given that it is easier to achieve sales of £1,000 than £3,333, it would be preferable to invoke caution in allowing trade credit to new customers where there is any doubt over payment or no knowledge of the new account. Equally, it is better and easier to nurture long-standing customers since they are unlikely to call for strong marketing or 'special terms' to gain orders.

8.22 The management of trade debts should include the following characteristics:

- Operate a system of verifying the account risk before allowing credit;

- Monitor the Debtors ledger constantly and keep running records of the ages of each debt;

- Record the date when each debt was chased for payment, by whom, to whom, and the answers given by the debtor when tackled (by telephone);

- Management should review outstanding debts individually at least on a monthly basis;

- Have a formal notice procedure of appointing debt collectors or when it is to be done in-house;

- Decide when a 'without prejudice' approach for partial settlement should be made and by whom it should be authorised. Small debts are usually not worthwhile to pursue above a 50-60% recovery proportion;

- Consider whether quick payment should be encouraged by discounts etc.

Current Liabilities

8.23   There is a clear financial advantage to pay business creditors later than receiving business debts. This must be weighed against the legal right for interest to be added to debts once they have been deemed late for payment (which is either after the agreed credit period has expired or otherwise after a default period of 30 days) and the possible damage to the business' reputation in being brought to Court and a loss of purchasing power through becoming a payment 'laggard'. The interest that can be charged on the oustanding debt is 8% p.a. above the ruling Bank of England Base Rate on the day that settlement should have been made.

8.24   If the business situation gives a choice not an option, then it could not be the best strategy to have one or two large creditors outstanding, since if a voluntary arrangement for settlement is pursued, these creditors may well hold and exercise the power to close the business whereas a more widely spread list of smaller creditors may not be so active. Before this situation is reached, however, it will be found that most creditors will be willing to listen to some form of deferred settlement.

8.25   A business borrower in default to their bank may expect to be treated somewhat differently. First, the bank will show much sympathy for difficult times, especially if it has not been exacerbated through mismanagement by the proprietor(s). The bank will not wish to be seen to have made a poor lending decision. It will be looking to have the debt repaid by some means and the choices are usually two: by letting the business trade profitably out of its adverse situation (if possible) or by recovery of the debt through realising the security held.

8.26   The type of security and its ease of conversion into cash will play a major part in the bank's decision about how to treat the errant account, as will the customer's past account record. A well thought out proposal for repayment should be laid before the bank for their consideration and, preferably sent to the bank before the meeting at which it will be addressed. Even before then, the business management should have fore-warned the bank that trading difficulties were becoming apparent so that remedial action could have been mutually agreed and implemented before the situation became more formidable to resolve.

Long-term liabilities

8.27   Long-term liabilities of a business should not be forgotten when managing the Balance Sheet. They may hold options to convert into less onerous debt, particularly if a loan has commenced at a variable interest rate and there is the option for the borrower to convert into a fixed inter-est rate. If the terms of the borrowing do not allow this choice, a matching deal (for the remainder of the period of the original loan) may be possi-ble to convert the liability from fixed into floating rate, or vice versa, or a similar exercise in currencies. A further alternative that is always avail-able is to replace the debt with a new credit line on more preferential terms. This may demand a change of lender. Before doing so considera-tion should be given to all the ramifications of such a move.

8.28   Comment is made elsewhere about the emotive subject of the bank taking security in the form of a personal guarantee before allowing money to be borrowed. When managing the Balance Sheet it should not be an oversight on the part of the borrower to discuss with the bank whether the (presumed) greater net worth of the business warrants the elimination of this security. If this is unavoidable (and it should be avoided if possible in favour of other forms of security) then it should be remem-bered that the liability can be 'capped' as to the maximum amount and may not have to be 'joint and several' in scope i.e. when the bank can approach one guarantor in preference to another for the whole debt. Of course, a sole trader always holds personal liability, a partnership may do so and a company shareholder does not.

General considerations

8.29   The Balance Sheet provides the viewer with the (historic) state of that business at one point in time. More strict accounting and legal regu-lations over the years have largely eliminated a 'massage' of the entries to show a position that may not be totally relevant to what it was during the best part of the accounting year since the date of the previous Balance Sheet. Banks themselves can still 're-arrange' their maturities quite legally to show a particular position at their year-end if they wish. For the busi-ness and the individual this option is of limited use. Extensive tax regulations prevent a re-arrangement where it is for the purpose of avoid-ing the payment of tax. The usual forms of re-arrangement are to hide the true ownership of a company and to take its domicile abroad.

Chapter 9

Raising Commercial Finance

9.1   For many businesses commercial finance is the only means for them to continue to trade. Any bank (in its widest sense) offering commercial money will be pleased to view any reasonable proposition from a business wishing to borrow funds. The principal aim of the borrower must be to help the banker grant this request. The tenets of a good proposition for a banker lie in what might be termed the proposition's 'Street Cred'(ibility):

S – there is a sound STRATEGY to support the proposition or project.
T – a forecast of future TRADING profit and cash flow is available.
R – RESEARCH has been done into the market for the product.
E – it can be shown that EARNINGS from the project make it viable.
E – the EFFECT of the borrowing is described and shown as understood.
T – there is a satisfactory TRACK RECORD by the management.

C – the borrowing is of a CHARACTER that can be supported.
R – there is a feasible plan as to how the borrowing can be REPAID.
E – the borrowing offers EASE of mind for the lender.
D – there are well DEFINED risks that can be managed by the borrower.

Each of these statements is explained in greater depth in the paragraphs that follow.

S – Strategy

9.2   The lender will expect the borrower to explain why his strategy is sound to ask for credit. For example a wholesaler in the utilities industry was starting a new venture but, with no substantive track record or capital of note, he could not obtain credit by the traditional overdraft route. However, he had sourced his buyers; gained accreditation that the product would perform the way it should; had test marketed and won a small initial order and had lined up an overseas manufacturer. His trading forecast had gained credibility through these actions. The need for short-term finance was to pay in cash for stock to ensure its delivery in this country. The **Strategy** was soundly based for borrowing and, because the principal security lay in the trading stock that was envisaged to be turned over quickly at a high profit margin and with a rapid growth, a factoring facility was easily arranged.

9.3   Many commercial propositions fail to gain credit because the basic strategy behind the borrowing is flawed or, quite simply, no strategy has been planned. A small food retailer would be unlikely to commence trading next door to a supermarket, but a large supermarket might be built adjacent to a small retailer. A more appropriate business example is the situation of a small but well-established manufacturer, just short of his decided retiring age, who was given the opportunity to purchase the freehold of his factory. The best strategy would be not to borrow the purchase cost and tie up funds in the property if he expected to retire and live on the cash already invested in the business. This was not the full story, however, since there was family succession to consider and the property had the opportunity of redevelopment within the next two years. It was strategically important to acquire the site.

9.4   When a business is found to have financial problems and the immediate remedies of recovery have been exhausted (such as collecting outstanding debts; postponing paying amounts owing; reducing overheads) thoughts turn to raising more credit. The plan for the business will be recovery but the strategy behind future trading is not very often queried. It should be the time to go back to basics and ask oneself: What do I want to achieve from the business and what is the best way of doing it? The answers should determine the reason to support the request for finance and the subsequent business plan will spell out the detail of how that is to be accomplished.

T – Trading Profit and Cash Flow

9.5   Cash Flow is important enough to warrant its own chapter. The lending banker will be monitoring the performance of the business day to day based on cash flow of the account. It is prudent, therefore, for the business to monitor its trading in a similar fashion. One cannot do this perfectly for several reasons: there may be credits being received and not known in advance; cheques will take different times to be banked; and the bank will have the singular knowledge of the total of 'uncleared effects' on the account.

9.6   A future profit must be earned and estimated in advance to underpin a request for credit. Its forecast amount will determine whether the borrowing proposition is to be favourably received by the lender. Its historic amount will help determine the future strategy for the business; e.g. the gross trading margin may be shown as inadequate, or it may influence how much can be drawn judiciously out of the business by the owner.

9.7   When forecasting profit and cash flow for the next year or further ahead it is best to work out both projections at the same time and relate the calculations together for accuracy. When doing this it may be helpful to remember that businesses can be categorised into two main forecasting types: those that have a fair idea through orders in hand and work-in-progress what the turnover will be (*Type A*), and those that have little idea how much may be sold from one day to the next (*Type B*). Brief worksheets are given as a guide for each forecast on a monthly basis:

Forecasting *Type A*: (figures include VAT)

Turnover:

- List the value of known and expected orders for each future month.
- Add a sum each month for unexpected orders through past experience.
- Total each month up and start a fresh list of entries.
- Re-write the earlier entries to the months when each order is invoiced.
- Total each month up and start a fresh list of entries.
- Re-write them again to the months when payment is expected.
- Total each month up and it will show the total turnover cash flow.

Direct Expenses:

- Calculate a sum for materials to meet each order.
- Place materials cost in month of delivery needed for production.
- Re-write them again to the month when the cost is expected to be paid.
- Total up each month's payments.
- Add other direct costs, e.g. transport paid in month when shipped.
- Put in labour costs in the month when paid.
- Total all the Direct Expenses paid as shown.

Indirect Expenses:

- Allocate all the expected costs to the month when it is to be paid.
- Calculate the quarterly VAT bill to enter in the month paid (*see note*).
- Total all the Indirect Expenses paid as shown.

Summarise the **net cash flow** (*total turnover less direct & indirect expenses*)

- Add the cash at the beginning of the month.

This leaves the cash to carry forward to the next month.

9.8   The VAT payment calculation requires that for each month for each VAT quarter all the income and expenditure totals subject to VAT must have the tax element (multiply the amount by 0.175 and divide by 1.175 for a 17.5% rate, but note that fuel is currently at a 5% rate and some costs have no VAT). The overall net VAT for each three months is then entered in the month it is paid or to be received. For simplification, partial exemption and the annual VAT adjustment have been ignored.

9.9 For simplification, it is suggested that the gross cost of employing staff without deductions can be entered and the Employer's National Insurance and Pension etc. elements are added. This will show in advance their true payment since the deductions are actually paid monthly in arrears.

Forecasting *Type B*: (figures include VAT)

- Enter monthly the two previous year's actual turnover figures.

- By experience, project the turnover monthly for the ensuing year.

- Adjust this figure for known alterations to occur in the coming year.

- Allow for seasonal variations.

- Total the final turnover figures for each month.

- Calculate the Direct and Indirect Expenses as before, and the summary.

It should not be forgotten that with 12 months in the year, but 52 weeks, some projections will be for a five week period.

With the net cash flow figures already calculated, they can then be adjusted to a **Profit** forecast basis.

- Take the monthly cash flow figures already estimated:
  - – for Turnover it will be the month of invoiced entries.
  - – for Direct Expenses it will be the month of deliveries.
  - – for Indirect Expenses for simplicity it will be the month when paid.

- Each monthly total needs to be divided by 1.175 (for a 17.5% VAT rate, or by 1.05 for a 5% VAT rate) with those items not subject to VAT having no adjustment made to them.

- The VAT payment entries each quarter can be eliminated (*see note*).

- Summarise the **net profit** (*total turnover less direct and indirect expenses*).

Some businesses may have irrecoverable VAT to charge separately against the profit. Where this is significant it should be estimated and, for simplification again, past experience will be a guide as to the amount.

Appendix B shows a typical example of how such calculations can be worked out in practice. Your lender will be pleased with this work.

R – Research

9.10   Too many new projects or start-up ventures ask for finance to support ideas without conducting research on the suitability of the product or its acceptability in the market. Where there is no new product but just expansion of the existing business the same reasoning applies. A number of pertinent questions will have to be satisfactorily answered:

- Will the market absorb additional production and for how long?

- How will the competition react to a potential reduction in their own market share?

- Has the selling price been thoroughly thought out and will it be accepted?

- Will the selling price satisfy the gross margin required for the borrowing to be viable?

- Has the typical customer been researched adequately for repeat business?

9.11   It is surprising how many small businesses reliant on winning orders from regular customers just take this for granted. An example of this was a small engineering concern that had painstakingly dismantled the customer's own product when asked to quote a supply price; had shown the customer where modifications were needed to strengthen or improve certain parts to which the customer had gratefully agreed; had supplied the first order and then discovered that the customer had gone to a competitor who had taken the improved product and quoted a lower price to obtain the future business. The engineering concern had not backed up its product research with adequate marketing to gain alternative orders.

9.12   There was also the case of the retailer who spent little on passive advertising in newspapers, but instead would send a personal card or little gift occasionally to regular customers thanking them for their custom. In this way existing customers were pleased with this personal attention, and retained, and they spoke well of the retailer to their friends who became regular customers also.

9.13   The other form of research to be done on a regular basis is to keep abreast of what products the market is wanting. This means discussing with customers their future plans in broad outline. It will provide an early warning of possible production changes that will be necessary for the business to take advantage of future demand. It may lead to new tooling that cannot be obtained immediately. The retailer is often in a better position to gauge future demand by going to Trade Fairs or hearing from sales representatives what new products will be coming on the market. The lending banker will be pleased to hear that the potential borrower is keeping up to date with future developments in its area of business.

E – Earnings

9.14   Any earnings forecast to support an application for credit must be viable, that is, capable of becoming actual. For business people, especially entrepreneurs of small businesses skilled in production and selling who do not regularly have to estimate in depth what future turnover will be attained and what profit will be earned, there is a real danger that their forecasts will be optimistic. The appraiser of the credit application may be faced with a gradually increasing level of turnover month by month and individual costs shown at the same sum each month with perhaps changes made at the beginning of each year.

9.15   Unfortunately, the real world tends to be different. Large variations can occur month by month to the fortunes of the business, mostly outside the control of the management. Forecasting is an art rather than a science, but there are a few pointers that may go some way to provide more viable earnings projections:

- Although the result may be shown on a monthly basis, first of all work out the income and expenditure on a weekly format and then convert to monthly according to the number of Saturdays in each month. This will best pick up weekly wages where they are paid on a Friday. Apply the same principle to regular costs.

- Monthly returns for past years will help to forecast the same months in the future as it will pick up seasonal trading variations.

- Having made a first estimate, consider what is different for the business now compared with the past. Has production capacity risen? Is there a different sales mix? Are there more staff being employed? Is the gross profit margin on sales likely to have changed?

- For retailing businesses where stock is bought for resale, if the overall gross profit margin on sales is known and up to date, once the sales are forecast this margin can be used to calculate the gross profit, leaving only indirect expenses to be calculated and apportioned month by month.

9.16   The net profit projected for the business has been calculated and the annual cost (interest payments and loan repayments) of the proposed borrowing has been allowed for, but there remains a useful check that can aid discussion with the proposed lender:

- Re-work the turnover (and consequent gross profit) figure on the assumption that sales will only reach at 90% and 80% of the original forecast. If the resulting earnings still make the business and the required borrowing viable, it will be further comfort to the lender.

- Finally, it would be wise to check that the earnings forecasts do not jeopardise other aspects of the business: that salaries and other proprietors' drawings can still be afforded and other necessary expenditure of a capital nature (equipment; loan repayments) can be maintained.

E – Effect of the borrowing

9.17 The lender will want to be satisfied that the borrower understands the commitment that is being entered into and how it will affect the existing business. It will tell the lender the effect (risk) of going into (greater) debt has been recognised by management. This is usually best described by the cash flow profile of the business *Before* and *After* the borrowing has been put in place. Small businesses often offer the bank the latter but rarely include the former projection, yet the bank will be able to judge better what the injection of new finance can do for the business and whether sufficient reward will outweigh the risk.

9.18 Consider the case of a retailer wishing to expand his shop. His past trading profile by quarters was:

The Effect *Before*

£'000	Q1	Q2	Q3	Q4	Year
Turnover	30	50	40	80	200
Variable Costs (40% of turnover)	12	20	16	32	80
Fixed Costs	20	20	20	20	80
Net Profit/(-)Loss before tax	– 2	+10	+4	+28	+40

The cost of expanding is put at £60,000 of which £20,000 can be raised personally. He wishes to borrow £40,000 over two years at an annual cost of 10% p.a. with loan repayments of £5,000 each quarter. What is the risk for the business if turnover fails to increase after borrowing the money?

The Effect *After*

£'000	Q1	Q2	Q3	Q4	Year
Net Profit as shown	– 2.0	+10.0	+4.0	+28.0	+40.0
Borrowing cost: interest	– 1.0	– 0.9	– 0.8	– 0.6	– 3.3
Adjusted Profit/(-) Loss	– 3.0	+9.1	+3.2	+27.4	+36.7
Loan repayments	– 5.0	– 5.0	– 5.0	– 5.0	– 20.0
Effect on the business	– 8.0	+4.1	– 1.8	+22.4	+16.7

9.19   Comparing the two trading results first: break-even point for sales in the first table was £133,300 and in the second table £138,800. The higher break-even point appears to be well within the achievement capabilities of the business. (*Note:* the calculation is for break-even point: Sales = Fixed costs divided by (1 – 0.x) where x after the decimal point is the gross profit margin; in this example being 0.4).

9.20   Now compare the cash flow break-even point (for simplicity the same figures are assumed, i.e. no adjustment for VAT): in the second table; the effect on the business gives a break-even point of sales to be £172,200 to generate sufficient cash to break even. If turnover fails to increase and falls by, say, 10%, the new sales forecast will be £180,000, much closer to the cash break-even point of £172,200. (*Note:* in this example Turnover will need to drop by 13.9% to reach cash break-even point). Note also that during the peak (Christmas) selling season 40% of sales are attained. A poor trading season at Christmas heightens the risk of a possible earnings shortfall.

T – Track record

9.21   The past record of a business and its management says a lot to a lender. In the absence of other information it will be perhaps innocently assumed that what has been done in the past will continue in the future *or* if it does not, the experience and skills of the management will ensure that the business survives and is profitable.

9.22   Compare this view with that of an investor about to risk his funds by investing in the business. The investor will add one particular ingredient to the track record: the type of business being undertaken. Some types of business are volatile by their nature and consequently hold a greater potential risk when projecting future trading returns. Their track record can be less of a guide to lenders than a business operating in a more stable environment. The applicant for credit should emphasise how his past trading record (if good) is an accurate guide to the future (if that is so) or, conversely, the forecasts provided have allowed for any volatility.

9.23   If a track record is being quoted by figure comparatives, significant changes should be highlighted so that the lender can make a better evaluation of what has happened in the past, what is likely to be continuing and what will not recur. These adjustments may arise as follows:

Turnover last year (monthly)	x	x	x	x	x	x	x
Deduct sales of a business sold	y	y	y	–	–	–	–
Add insurance claim re fire	–	–	–	z	–	–	–
Deduct special one-off sale	–	p	–	–	–	–	–
Adjusted Turnover for comparison	*q*	*q*	*q*	*q*	*q*	*q*	*q*

Similar adjustments may have to be made to Expenses before the Net Profit figure for that year is suitable to compare with projections for the year ahead.

9.24 Where a track record has a 'blemish' due to a poor judgment having been made by the proprietor, it may show up in past management returns or audited accounts or, if not otherwise apparent, the facts should not be hidden from the lender. If the error is significant, in most cases the bank manager will have known about it due to its effect on the business bank account. Every blemish offers the sufferer the experience of what occurred so that it may not happen again.

9.25 It is really the management capability that is under review when one speaks of a track record. Evaluating the actions of management, unfortunately, may or may not give a correct picture to the lender and it is up to the potential borrower to emphasise where a good action by management has led to great benefit for the business. Consider two examples of businesses trading overseas and being paid in currency. Management 'A' is active and decides to sell the currency for sterling now in advance of the payment date. In the event, by the time the currency was received, a fortuitous movement in exchange rates would have led to a currency gain had no forward sale been done.

9.26 Management 'B', through inertia, had not even considered the currency risk and therefore gained the windfall on conversion, thus making more profit on the deal. On the face of it, Management 'B' can show the better track record although Management 'A' has demonstrated better business thinking. In fact, it is not the best business thinking: had Management 'A' taken an option to choose whether or not to sell at the earlier currency rate, it could still have chosen the better exchange rate at the expense of paying a small fee.

C – Character

9.27 A person must be of good enough character to be able to obtain credit. The same principle applies to the reasons that are put forward to borrow money for business purposes. For example, standard commercial finance should not be available from banks to be used as risk capital for speculative ventures. There are specialist venture capital divisions or organisations geared up to lend for this purpose.

9.28 Neither is commercial credit provided in the form of an overdraft facility suited to finance a business, open-ended, over a long period of time. The traditional overdraft facility was set up to meet a fluctuating demand for credit by businesses. It is surprising how many businesses not subject to seasonal sales peaks but permanently short of working capital assume that an overdraft facility can be put to use virtually as if it were the same as long-term investment capital. Banks may allow this to occur, however, providing they hold the right to be able to withdraw the overdraft facility on demand were the business to get into difficulties such that grave doubts arise for the recovery of the money lent. You have been warned.

9.29   The character of the request for finance should determine the type of facility to be used. A general guide to the choices that are matched is given below. Short-term may be considered as three to six months; medium-term up to three or five years and long-term ten years or more.

Finance character	Usage	Type of facility
Occasional or seasonal use	Trading purposes	Bank overdraft
Borrowing for:		
Property	Long-term	Secured loan
Plant & equipment	Medium-term	Loan over life of asset
Motor vehicles	Medium-term	Loan or Hire Purchase
Stock in Trade	Short/medium-term	Contract finance
Import/Export	Short-term	Letters of Credit or Bills of Exchange
Debtors/Creditors	Short-term	Factoring or Invoice Discounting
Specific Projects	Variable	Ring-fenced to Project Income
A lack of business capital	On-going	Borrowing against Net Worth or venture capital

Stock in Trade may consist of finished goods ready to satisfy contracted orders. Depending on the 'firmness' of the sales contract, the receipts may be pre-drawn by agreement in cash subject to the credit standing of the parties.

9.30   Many businesses can get in the position of suffering an on-going lack of business capital. Where the business is strong enough to operate permanently with outstanding borrowings (on the basis that as existing loans are repaid they are replaced with new loans), it is a matter of judgment whether the business wishes to gear (leverage) itself up to earn more profit through utilising commercial financing or not. In these circumstances, this borrowing against the value of Net Worth (Proprietor's Capital) employed in the business can range from short to long-term.

The effect of gearing	Example without	Example with
Net Worth employed:		
Proprietor's Capital	500	500
Borrowing (long-term)	0	50
Combined	500	550
Profit return earned on Net Worth	20%	20%
Profit, say	100	110
Borrowing cost (*say*, 10% p.a.)	0	5
Profit after borrowing cost	100	105
Additional profit due to gearing	0	5

In the illustration the description Borrowing could be substituted by Venture Capital investment from Business Angels or other sources.

R – Repayment

9.31   All applications for commercial finance should be accompanied by a firm repayment plan. The lender will want to be satisfied that the money lent can be repaid providing future trading meets the income and expenditure assumptions on which the borrowing has been based. If the application has been properly drawn up it will be the lender's job to evaluate these assumptions and either grant or turn down the application. The method of repayment will be based on the type of borrowing requested. In this respect, the business will have two important disadvantages to overcome:

- Every lending bank will be careful to operate with a 'balanced lending book'; that is, it is not unduly biased towards one particular type of loan (unless it is a specialised institution) and adheres to the particular policy laid down from time to time by Head Office. The snag is that the borrower will not know what type of loan is likely to get more favourable treatment from which bank in advance. It may be a case of try and try (other banks) again if the 'house' bank of the business refuses the lending request.

- The applicant may not be certain how best to structure the borrowing requested. For instance, banks will prefer to see a regular part repayment schedule being met rather than a single ('balloon') full repayment to be made at the end of the loan period.

In respect of the last point, the various instruments of credit will each have their own repayment characteristic:

Type of Borrowing	Repayment Advantages	Repayment Disadvantages
Overdraft	Flexible	No discernible schedule
	Can be the cheapest	Requires constant monitoring
		Mixes in all borrowing needs
		Can be demanded on renewal
Set-off	Automatic when in funds	Assumes credit balance periods
	Reduces net borrowing cost	Still requires repayment profile
	Can reduce tax liability	A matching of terms is required
Rollover	Can be until further notice	Of a short-term nature
	Can have flexible period	Requires good credit record
	No part repayments	Some types may be unavailable
Medium-term	Repayable on default	Usually more expensive
Long-term	Lower regular repayments	May offer repayment 'holiday'

9.32   A set-off arrangement allows the borrower to take advantage of periods when the business is in funds by reducing the cost of medium or long-term borrowing through setting off the interest receivable on the credit balances against the interest cost on the loan, subject to an agreed interest margin being paid to the bank. The tax liability on the full interest receivable is mitigated by that set off against the loan. This profile would suit a business that for certain periods of each year is holding surplus cash, but still requires continuing long-term funding overall.

9.33   Rollover facilities include those for trade credit by way of Bills of Exchange that can be discounted early by a bank for cash and then repaid when the bill matures for payment, usually after three months. Another form of rollover credit is commonly known as an 'evergreen', where the facility, say, is for an initial period of three years but is automatically renewed after every twelve months for a further year. The bank can revoke the right to an annual renewal, but it would still allow the borrower to have a final two-year credit period before repayment must occur.

9.34   The Clearing (High Street) banks each have their own lending agreements and forms of charging and repayment. For example, repayment may be structured so that an identical sum is charged every month which itself comprises an element of loan interest and an element of loan capital (principal). Another method is to charge interest and repayments of capital separately, the interest varying according to rates in force and the outstanding amount of the loan, and the capital part comprising the same fixed sum at each repayment date. Other methods require quarterly or annual repayments of loan capital. The potential borrower should decide according to the future projected cash flow of the business which method is most suitable in the circumstances.

9.35   A very important point about loan repayments is that one should always realise that making a business (paper) profit does not necessarily translate into receiving the same amount of cash by which to pay off borrowings, and it will be cash that is required for repayment.

E – Ease of mind

9.36   It is the potential borrower's task to provide the lender with a certain ease of mind before the loan application is granted. At some stage in the negotiations the banker's thoughts will turn to security. Apart from an outright loan refusal there seems to be no other topic to create so much disharmony between lender and borrower. This relates to existing borrowings as well as new facilities. It may be epitomised as follows:

The Net Worth of the company, according to the Balance Sheet, is £100,000.
The banker is being asked to finance expansion to the extent of £100,000.
All financial and other appraisal checks have been to the satisfaction of the banker.
The business earnings are currently £30,000 but are forecast to expand to £60,000.
The loan is over 5 years costing £10,000 interest and £20,000 repayments annually.
The owner of the company is asked for a personal guarantee of £100,000 by the bank.
The owner says that the business is worth £100,000 now and is increasing its profits.
Why should the owner, a long-standing customer, have to give a personal guarantee?

9.37   This is not an examination question to answer, but certain facts should be understood by the owner:

- There is a risk to the bank in advancing £100,000;

- The bank will view its advance (per the example) as doubling the

Net Worth of the business, only half of which can be attributable to the owner;

- For its apparent generosity the bank is gaining a gross return of 10%, out of which it will have to set aside some of its own capital at market cost;

- The return to the bank's shareholders, on this particular deal, may not attain the reward they would normally wish;

- Meanwhile, the owner(s) of the business will reap the benefit of an additional £30,000 earnings forecast annually, less the interest cost of financing the £100,000 loan.

9.38   The bank must be satisfied that the business can generate sufficient additional earnings to enable it to pay both the annual interest charges on the loan and the capital repayments that become due. It is the bank's decision and the loan proposition is likely to stand or fall according to the safety margin the bank deems the business can offer in this respect. In the example, during the first year the expected additional business earnings (£30,000) correspond to the total cash to be paid to the bank. There is no margin for any shortfall should projected earnings fall below budget, other than to meet any shortfall by using some of the existing trading profits that may, or may not, be available. The bank is well advised, for its ease of mind, to ask for (additional) security from the prospective borrower.

9.39   Frequently the borrower has limited assets to pledge to the bank to support additional borrowing. He, or she, will probably have title to the family residence, in itself an asset to which other family members may have legal recourse, and perhaps some stocks and shares, but little else of worth that can be readily realisable. The bank will usually accept tangible assets, such as property (unless it is a short leasehold), at market value less a margin for valuation error and any realisation costs. Commonly, this may accord to 60-80% of the security valuation, depending on the location and type of property.

9.40   There is also the intangible asset of the management expertise of the business owner. Again, for its ease of mind, the bank will be pleased to hold the personal guarantee of the owner(s) where the business is structured as a company and in this way will be secure in the knowledge that the owner(s) will not easily be able to 'walk away' from their business obligations if trading subsequently founders. The bank will not wish to stand in the shoes of the owner(s) and have to manage the business physically.

9.41   Jumping forward in our example, say, to year three, the financial position has changed: the (additional) bank debt, after two years' repayments, now stands at £60,000. At the same time the extra earnings of the business, thanks to the loan money, have boosted the owner(s) value in the business to £160,000. The bank debt, rather than having a Balance Sheet asset cover at Day One of the loan of 100:100 now stands at an enhanced 160:60, the loan being covered 2.67 times. Assuming the business trading and outlook is still satisfactory, it would be pertinent for the borrower to ask the bank to release some (or all) of its security. The bank may be judged to be holding security in excess of what may be considered prudent and, for the borrower's ease of mind, a revised security arrangement should be negotiated.

D – Defining the risks

9.42 The potential borrower should be aware of two basic types of risk and be prepared to refute that they will have an effect on the proposition. The first is influences affecting the specific project (or start-up) for which the finance is required and the second is influences inherent in the business itself. The former may have an adverse or beneficial effect, although the banker will probably only query the adverse element. If the lending banker asks 'what can go wrong?' it would not be appropriate to have difficulty in answering the question. Different businesses will have their own risk table. An example of two of the more common risks met in business are:

Specific Risks met	*Likely action the business will take*
Reduced sales	Lower selling prices and/or
	Increase special marketing plan and/or
	Curb operating costs and/or
	Downsize operatives and/or
	Freeze capital expenditure and/or
	Halt expansion plans
Cannot keep up with demand	Raise selling prices and/or
	Freeze lower demand product lines and/or
	Increase the production in demand and/or
	Outsource some production and/or
	Employ more operatives

9.43 The more general risks and their effect on the business should be shown to be understood so that remedial action can be planned in advance and/or already set in motion. The table following sets out some of the more obvious general risks met with actions that may be taken. One risk difficult to offset is where the business is operating in a cyclical industry that has long periods of boom and slump associated with the national economy or changes in world production capacity or sales demand. In the former case an export business can be built up in several countries. In the latter case long-term fixed price/delivery contracts may be possible to be negotiated. Alternatively, the business should be prepared for these changes in demand and act swiftly to reduce production, lay off unwanted labour; prune unnecessary overheads and conserve finances.

General risks met	Expected action the business will take
One customer accounts for the majority of sales	Constant effort to gain more customers and/or Diversify the product range and/or Endeavour to obtain long-term contract(s).
Majority of turnover consists of one-off contracts	Diversify into repeat contract business and/or Market more and increase size of order book.
Selling prices are 'controlled' by competition or the customer	Outsource production to retain profitability and/or Negotiate longer-term set margin contracts and/or Market for additional business outlets.
Turnover is very seasonal	Use off-peak periods to build for stock and/or Diversify into products sold in off-peak periods.
Business is heavily dependent on occasional/part-time labour	Make use of self-employed workers and/or Maintain key workers and outsource the rest.
Business is heavily dependent on sub-contractors	Use several sources of supply and/or Manage contracts rather than do the work.
Known external influences can affect sales demand	Get customers to buy more in advance and/or Maintain strategic stock of raw materials and/or Build up finished product stocks of regular lines.
Known external influences can affect purchases procurement	Buy supplies in advance of need and/or Order in advance and control deliveries.
Financing costs are subject to external influences	Agree funding at fixed interest rates and/or Agree credit lines with fixed/variable rate options.

9.44   There are two mnemonics that bankers have used for many years which cover similar ground but offer less guidance on all trading aspects that the borrower will encounter to be fully prepared when requesting finance.

CAMPARI – Reminding the banker to check the **C**ommitment by the borrower; his **A**bility to manage the business; the quality of key **M**anagement; the **P**urpose of the borrowing; the **A**mount of finance the borrower is committing to the business; the ease of **R**epaying the debt; and the **I**nsurance provided through any security taken.

PARSAR – The track record of the **P**erson asking for credit; the **A**mount of finance requested; whether the **R**epayment terms are realistic; the viability of the **S**ecurity that may be available; the **A**ssumptions laid down in the business plan; and the **R**eward to the bank in the lending proposition.

9.45   It is a good principle of lending to established businesses when judging whether or not to accept a credit risk, that reliance should not be placed on security either provided by the borrower or requested by the lender and it should not affect the decision to lend. After turning down a credit proposition probably the next most aggravating decision for the businessman or entrepreneur is to get what one might describe as a 'qualified' approval. That is, the banker is willing to accept the risk and offer the loan, but on condition that the borrower provides additional security of a personal nature such as a guarantee or a charge on personal assets. The reasons for this have already been discussed in paragraphs 9.37 et seq under 'Ease of mind'.

9.46   The borrower should also be aware that security taken in the form of a charge on the business assets will not affect trading and is legally necessary to ensure that the assets do not 'walk out of the door' or are pledged to others. Where the business Balance Sheet has no realisable assets to speak of and/or is a start-up venture with a relatively high risk of failure there will be no effective security to take. In the first case the question should be asked 'Why is there no value in the Balance Sheet?' The answer may well provide the reason for a negative lending decision. In the latter case the Balance Sheet may well show liquid assets, but these will be used up as the business gains its feet. Witness the dot com companies with millions of pounds of cash that will be used during the next year or two in marketing their services to try and gain a regular income stream.

9.47   As has been stated, both lender and borrower should always be aware that the established business could grow out of the need for supplementary security from the company directors to support company borrowing. This will require regular monitoring and discussion between both parties. Sole traders do not have a choice since their personal assets are already at risk should the business fold.

Chapter 10

Raising Investment Capital

10.1 An entrepreneur wishing to develop a new product, idea or service will usually commence with great enthusiasm and a little money, some business contacts and much time. He or she will concentrate on developing the product alone or with family assistance at first. At some stage the funds available are likely to run out and progress will falter. It is at this point that thoughts on raising external funds become more prominent. Local banks will be approached and may be receptive only if suitable and sufficient security is made available. Few entrepreneurs will accept this, although they may expect other individuals to put up finance at the same risk. Government agencies will also be tapped for advice and eligibility for regional or technical grant aid may be possible.

10.2 If the entrepreneur already has a successful business operation, it will be easier to piggyback on to these facilities, including drawing on funds under existing commercial borrowing arrangements, to develop the new product. This will be by far the easier choice but it will require adoption of the same financial viability tests as with any new business venture to ensure that the existing business will not be jeopardised through the drain on cash resources when developing the new product.

10.3 Entrepreneurs who have good business connections will have two alternative choices to raise funds for the new product: they may ask their acquaintances whether they wish to subscribe risk capital, or they may wish to have some joint venture arrangement with another business whom they know well. This may take the form of setting up a new company with agreed shareholdings, each shareholder putting in know-how and/or assets/cash and/or management time.

10.4 If the new product is 'proven' up to a point, so that a fair idea of the risks and rewards of participation can be ascertained, and the finance required is of sufficient size to warrant a number of investors, the entrepreneur may wish to try at outset to raise money through a private issue of shares. This will necessitate a formal Offer of Shares by Subscription and the services of an established promoter and other professional advisers. The promoting firm will underwrite the Offer sufficiently to ensure success or will state a minimum subscription level below which any funds subscribed will be returned and the Offer will not proceed. Typical Offers may aim for a total subscription receipt of between £1-5 million. Below £1 million the costs to be borne will tend to make this form of raising finance unattractive.

10.5   There are no strict demarcations when one type of raising investment capital becomes preferable to another. A broad guide is shown below:

Funding size	Type of venture	Suggested sources	Comments
Up to £50,000	Any. No prior start.	Family & friends.	A modest bank loan may be possible.
£50,000 up to £200,000	Any. Probably some prior start.	Approach private individuals or local or national agencies.	A more formal Business Plan will be needed.
£200,000 up to £500,000	Selective by the funders.	Commercial venture capitalists.	E.g. High Street & other specialised banks.
£500,000 up to £1 million	Selective by the funders.	Limited number of specialist venture capital investment companies.	Many funders require the business to be already operating.
More than £1 million	Selective but a greater choice.	Larger venture capitalist investment companies and investment banks.	Choice of private investors or through a private offer or placing.

Funding up to £50,000 investment

10.6   For the smallest sums of finance and especially if the project is only at the drawing board stage, the more control the entrepreneur can exercise then the better. Even if family and close friends are involved, a written agreement should be raised and signed by all parties to ensure that any differences of opinion that may arise later can be easily resolved. A simple check list would include:

- Ownership of product rights;

- Development strategy (including adoption of expansion plans and possible raising of additional finance in the future);

- Operating responsibilities of the investors;

10.7 *Raising Investment Capital*

- Sharing of assets and liabilities;

- Sharing of profits and losses;

- Method of decision making;

- Calling of management meetings and voting rights;

- Powers of veto (if any);

- Transfer and valuation of investment share (offering the share to the other shareholders first);

- Disposal of the business.

10.7   At this stage the Business Plan might comprise a financial summary of cash flow along the lines of:

Development costs (estimated)	Pre-production	Production pre-sales	Operating
Materials	Yes	Yes	Yes
Labour	Possibly	Yes	Yes
Consultancy	Possibly	Unlikely	Unlikely
Outsourcing	Unlikely	Possibly	Possibly
Fees	Yes	Possibly	Possibly
Establishment/Travel	Yes	Yes	Yes
Sundries	Yes	Yes	Yes
Drawings	No	No	Possibly

At the pre-production stage materials costs will have to be met and also some labour if prototype model(s) and testing is necessary. Consultancy advice may have to be bought in. Fees relating to professional advice and perhaps patent applications may arise. The management will incur office/laboratory/workshop expenditure and travel/telephone overheads. Drawings should not be budgeted until the business starts earning.

10.8   Once production commences other costs will be incurred until receipts from sales appear. Production itself may be in-house or out-sourced. At the operating stage the business will be income producing and monthly estimates of cash flow can be projected. The first two stages and possibly the initial months of the third stage will need to be financed with start-up investment money.

10.9   It should be noted that the time period for financing can be short, particularly if the investors have already been sourced and approached. There is a real risk, however, that expenditure may not be regularly monitored and should further funds be required this may not be tackled until far too late, thereby causing at best a delay in completing the project and at worst its abandonment.

Funding up to £200,000 investment

10.10   Approaches to private individuals, otherwise known as professional Business Angels, who are willing to invest funds in projects that are attractive to their own investment criteria may take time to set up. A period of two to four months is not uncommon before the funds are invested. In most cases the Angel will be a higher rate taxpayer who will wish to invest for a sufficient length of time to gain the most advantage under the Government's Enterprise Investment scheme. The entrepreneur will have to ensure that the investment terms fit these criteria. The main options may be summarised as:

	Characteristics	*Cost*	*Advantages*	*Disadvantages*
Active Angels	Wish to take an active role in some part of the operation.	Negotiable between the parties.	Once on board the Angel will expect to share in management	Some loss of direct control.
Passive Angels	Happy only to be informed of progress at regular intervals.	Negotiable between the parties.	Involvement cost based on investment return.	May have specialised tastes in investment.
Agency services and listings	Information circulated via database of 'interested parties'.	May be free or a single payment.	Some agencies may have a list of local Angels.	A hit-or-miss method. No guarantee of success.
Specialised fund-raising businesses	May act as an introducer or take a part of the action.	Down payment with a success payment.	Professional guidance, including provision of a Business Plan.	No guarantee of success. May have a limited database of Angels.

10.11   Active Angels expect to bring to the venture their particular expertise in certain skills or knowledge. This may, for example, be in production, selling or financial control. If the entrepreneur has a weak spot in the area that the Angel is skilled in, and both parties believe they can co-exist operationally, then the chances of success are high. Passive Angels usually require more convincing before they will part with their money. This is understandable, since there may be no rapport between the Angel and the type of business requiring the investment. The passive Angel will be relying on the reward carrot and may ask for a larger equity share of the business to ensure this is so.

10.12   Agency services offer the entrepreneur a basic 'advertisement' (for which guidance is offered in its compilation) to sell their investment opportunity through a published listing sent to all investors subscribing to that particular database. Some locally based agencies will also offer a meeting place where investors can shop around and talk to entrepreneurs to see if there is an investment opportunity of interest. If necessary, the respective parties can continue the dialogue privately at a future date. The agency will be on hand to assist everyone to attain a satisfactory conclusion. A recommended start is for those interested in meeting others on this basis to make contact at their local Business Link/Small Business Service.

10.13   There are also the specialised fund-raising businesses, frequently franchised out regionally to consultants having proven financial skills, who usually charge in two parts: for some initial work and then a success fee calculated as a fixed sum or a percentage of the finance raised. The consultant will have the backing of a central organisation with a database of potential investors. Before any investor is shown to the entrepreneur, the consultant will ensure that a Business Plan is evident that is viable and can be shown to potential investors. If an existing Business Plan is to hand, this may have to be 'moulded' to improve the chances of success.

Funding up to £500,000

10.14   In practice, compared with lesser and larger amounts, there are reduced financing opportunities in the range £200,000 to £500,000. It is a size that is rather large for all but the wealthiest investors if they wish to spread their risks through taking on a number of separate investments. Alternatively, several investors can join together to raise the required sum, but the more players there are, the greater the difficulty in gaining compatibility of terms and the longer it may take to raise the necessary number of investors. Some banks will offer finance through their own venture capital offshoots, or take on the whole investment and then privately re-distribute shares to their clients.

10.15   There are not many venture capital organisations willing to invest £500,000 due to the relatively small size of investment for them compared with the cost of their services and the need for regular monitoring. The attraction to them of start-up businesses is less than for an established concern where the additional finance can more easily be shown to improve returns. Furthermore, investment in 'high tech' businesses tends to offer potentially a higher reward than from a staple engineering or manufacturing industry that has already been well developed in the market.

10.16   Venture capital organisations, as a guide, will expect to receive a cumulative return of 25-35% p.a. from the time of the investment to the time it is repaid. Repayment will usually be retrograde and not commence until the second or third year of the project's development. This is to allow the business to get on its feet operationally and begin to expand.

There may be an annual 'sweetener' requested by way of a small preferential dividend or loan interest, but mostly the organisation will look for repayment to the generation of earnings or a flotation or sale of the business after three or five years. A small residual equity interest is then continued in the business unless the requirement is for a full sale.

Funding up to £1 million

10.17 For a larger venture capital organisation to consider this size of investment the project has to offer high growth potential and preferably show some operating assets for the cash injected. Start-up projects, therefore, are rarely financed unless the reward can be quickly realised. Smaller venture capital organisations will be looking to spread their investment and to invest in a project of this size may not suit their investment book. The potential choice is further diminished in that many venture capital organisations specialise in particular segments of industry to match their executive skills and investment objectives of their backers.

10.18 Most banks will be interested in examining the possibility of financing a project requiring £1 million, even if it means offering a mixture of a commercial loan and a small equity stake in the business. This is unlikely to be offered to a start-up venture, because the loan element will have no means of support for servicing the interest charged and neither will there be a firm base to repay the principal. A further potential problem for the entrepreneur will be the bank's expectation of the sum(s) to be invested by other parties if the bank is to advance a proportion of the overall finance. Each case will be individually judged, but the bank may agree to advance £300,000 by way of loan and £50,000 equity providing that the entrepreneur finds the initial £650,000. This may not be an easy task.

Funding over £1 million

10.19 There is some merit in the statement that the greater the finance to be raised the easier it can become. Of course, there are many factors that go into the decision to invest in a project and every viable project has a finite investment limit at some point, but sizeable projects by implication will already offer substance of some measure, be it net worth, earning power or opportunities. A careful survey of possible funders should be done before any approach is made, if necessary by an independent party.

10.20 A professional presentation should then be raised and the initial introduction made through that independent party. Banks and venture capital organisations prefer to have 'weak' projects weeded out before they are approached. The likelihood of success increases in proportion to the pertinence of the presentation and how it can answer the questions the funders will wish to know before they raise it themselves. Once the initial presentation has been made the funder will have its own method of advancing the project and it is they who should then take the initiative.

General points

10.21 With all propositions to funders (be they venture capital institutions, banks or wealthy individuals) certain cardinal sins should be avoided. An approach to them should be planned in advance and cover

- What is to be said;
- Who is to say it;
- How long the presentation should run;
- Why specifically the finance is required; and
- When the money is needed.

What is to be said	Bullet points only, in plain language.
Who says it	The best speaker on the team.
For how long	Probably 20 to 30 minutes maximum.
Why finance	Specifics not generalities.
When to provide	To show to what depth the project has been tested.

10.22 The trap to avoid is to concentrate on a sales talk and end up with a jumble of disjointed positive reasons for investing in the project. The listeners will ask for more detailed explanations if they require it. The most friendly approach is to allow questions as the presentation progresses, but to give succinct answers and to return to the same point in the presentation before the question arose once it has been discerned that the answer is accepted.

10.23 The person presenting the project must have two attributes: a sufficiently detailed knowledge of the project to be able at least to start to answer any question, however technical, and to be confident in speaking well. If no questions are put during the presentation, twenty minutes is long enough to retain attention and to put forward the salient points of the project for further general discussion to proceed thereafter.

10.24 It will be beneficial to let the audience know why money is being requested. A bland answer that there are insufficient funds to hand and previous attempts to raise money has fallen on deaf ears will not indicate enough reasoning for the specific funding request now put on the table. It should be spelled out, for example, that other avenues were not conducive to an investment (reasons being ...?) and the structure of the package proposed will enable the project to proceed to the best advantage to all concerned. It can then be said that the investment will be phased in accordance with the projected cash flow requirements and this has raised the particular model now tabled to the prospective funders for their examination.

10.25 The approach should be singular, in that one funder should be given first choice of accepting or rejecting the proposed deal. There is nothing quicker to deaden a deal if it has been touted around the financial market. Any approach to friends or persons with City connections may backfire in this respect. Think of the project as being confidential both to competitors and all possible interested parties. Once there is partial acceptance to take the project to an appraisal stage a Confidentiality Agreement binding all parties should be issued. If the original funder rejects the project in spite of the careful research done, an approach to another source can be made, but not before it has been ascertained why the project was rejected. The second presentation can then be modified accordingly.

10.26 There is a practical difficulty when writing the Business Plan for the project when it comes to showing the projected return for the investors. They will want to know

- How much finance is required of them;

- When it is to be paid over;

- What reward is offered in return;

- How is it to arise; and

- What are the risks involved.

How much finance	There needs to be a cash flow projection of expected future trading, giving the monthly shortfall in cash until such time as it can be seen that the net revenue is cumulatively increasing.
When is it to be paid	The cash flow will show the months when more finance is required.
What reward is offered	This will be determined by the positive cash flow generated through trading and when distributions of profits can be made.
How is it to arise	The return on the investment may be annual, periodic or at the end of the investment period; or it may be apportioned as to some dividend/interest annually and the major share later.
What are the risks	Since the project may be technical, the trading risks should be seen to have been acknowledged by the project promoters.

10.27 The cash flow projection will have to make assumptions concerning the structure of the investment funds requested. This may be far from the actual model eventually adopted, but it will be the job of the funder to decide on the final structure. They will be fitting the needs shown by the Business Plan to their own financing objectives and adopting the best taxation planning. In the absence of any prior guidance a basic form of financing cash flow deficits should be adopted as follows:

Monthly periods	1	2	3	4	5	6	7	8	9	10	11	12
Cash flow (£'000)	−60	−45	−22	−1	6	15	26	−58	51	67	84	96
Financing part 1	130											
Financing part 2							20					
Investors' repayment										100		100
Revised cash flow	70	25	3	2	8	23	69	11	62	29	113	109

10.28   The notional example shows an initial expenditure in the first four periods amounting to £128k. Forward funding of £130k has covered this. In practice, a margin for contingencies would be allowed and the funds raised would be slightly more than £130k, say, £150k. As trading improves so does the cash flow, except that in period *8* there is a need for the purchase of capital equipment. In advance of this there is shown a further drawing of investment funds of £20k. The timing of the required financing is now shown to be in periods *1* and *7*. By period *10* the improved cash flow position means that some repayment of the original investment can be contemplated of £100k. A continuing improvement in trading enables a further repayment and dividend of £100k to be made in period *12*, leaving sufficient working capital to finance further expansion.

10.29   The example also shows the reward expectation for the funders: two thirds of their original investment will be returned by period *10* and the balance with a bonus in period *12*. It will not be necessary to convert these repayments into investment yields or discounted returns. The funders will look to these projections and decide how the finance is to be made. This may take the form of loans, ordinary and/or preference share capital and/or capital divided into part/fully paid up shares and/or with shares having £1 or 1p nominal values and/or with issues of shares at par or at a premium. Mezzanine finance may also be proposed.

10.30   The risks to be shown will usually concern external influences to future trading, i.e. acceptability of the product to be sold, but may include internal factors such as the test results of the product not being acceptable. Emphasis should be placed on risks inherent in the nature of the product, since all funders will be aware of what a trade recession or significant interest rate increase may do to sales projections.

10.31   Some investors will be wishing to discover the Internal Rate of Return (IRR) for the project. This shows over the period from commencement of funding to the repayment of borrowing and reward of investment, on a discounted cash flow basis, what is the yield on their participation.

This return does not have to be achieved on an annual basis by the nature of the investment, but it is quoted as an annual figure. On the basis that best investment public companies and fixed interest Government securities will yield somewhere up to 10% p.a. and second line companies will yield perhaps 10% to 20% p.a., it may be understandable that venture capital investors will be looking to receive 20% to 35% p.a., depending on their perception of the relative risks and rewards.

10.32   As a consequence, for greatest success in raising venture capital, the project must offer a potentially high reward in as short a period as possible. This will outweigh the high risk of failure if there is an attraction to the type of business being put forward for investment. Hence there is the apparent attraction for investment in the high-tech and medical sciences fields rather than for more mundane capital-intensive utilities with the liability of public regulation.

Equity or Debt

Equity investment

10.33   If the new business is high risk with a potential return that is speculative and not amenable to easy evaluation, but the reward for success is significant, these are prima facie grounds for raising equity (risk share capital). The capital may arise from institutions or individuals and, in the latter case, the immediate tax benefits to accrue through investing for a period of years under a Government-sponsored scheme is attractive notwithstanding the regulations that are involved and the steps that the business has to satisfy to be accepted for the required investment status.

10.34   The present **Enterprise Investment Scheme** allows individuals wherever resident and not connected (i.e. controlling more than 30% of the voting power or owning any loan capital or is a paid director or an employee) with the company for two years prior or three years subsequent to issue of the shares, to reduce their liability to income tax for the year of assessment when the shares were purchased by the amount invested calculated at their lower rate of tax. If not fully used, the relief may be taken back to the previous year. There are conditions to be met as to the business being a qualifying company (during the initial three years of the investment and unquoted) carrying on a qualifying trade (with a view to making a profit and not being a financial services company) wholly or mainly in the UK.

10.35   The present **Corporate Venturing Scheme** allows companies to invest up to 30% in an unquoted trading company and obtain a reduction in corporation tax of 20% if the shares are retained for three years. Thereafter, any gain on disposal can be rolled into a further investment or, if a loss net of the original investment relief, can be allowable against capital gains subject to corporation tax.

Debt

10.36   If the new business project holds a discernible risk and the period of investment required is medium-term (preferably from three to seven years duration) with a forecast cash flow that becomes strong enough to repay all borrowings within that time, it will be more beneficial for the business to raise Debt without having to give up a high percentage equity share of the business. Debt itself may consist of having a number of rights or options and some of these are listed below:

- Subject to a fixed interest rate;

- Subject to a variable interest rate;

- Participating in profits;

- Receiving a turnover commission or royalty;

- With cumulative or non-cumulative dividends;

- Preferred or subordinated for security;

- Having a (large, final) balloon repayment sum;

- Having a (small) portion convertible into equity.

10.37   Depending on the start point, it would be an advantage to accept fixed interest debt in the knowledge that as the business grows the increase in earnings will not be eaten up by interest costs, particularly if the future trend of interest rates is upward. Those options that offer add-ons to the lenders, e.g. participating in profits or offering some preferred security for lending, will enable negotiation for a lower interest rate than would otherwise be the case.

10.38   Looking at the Debt from the borrower's point of view, it will be advantageous to be granted the occasional repayment holiday should trading for a temporary period not meet forecasts. The borrower will also prefer to have an early repayment option if success is greater than that expected. In the latter respect, this option must be balanced with the take up of fixed interest Debt over a set period; in this case the borrower is 'locked-in' until the fixed repayment period ends. It is possible to 'unlock' a previously drawn period but the penalties may be great if interest rates meanwhile move in the wrong direction, i.e. fall relative to the cost of the original borrowing.

Chapter 11

Joint Ventures

11.1   Whereas a Partnership presupposes a close, continuing and complete relationship between the partners, each binding the others to the actions of any partner, a Joint Venture has more of the nature of a specific cause joining the parties, each associated with their allotted task(s) and creating by a combined effort, so that the actions of each brings about a trading result that neither could achieve as well without the other's involvement. The joint venture may be initiated at the outset of the mutual business relationship or raised at a later stage of the business's development.

A joint venture from the outset

11.2   Most business start-ups do not commence as joint ventures because the entrepreneur(s) will be looking to develop the product(s) or service(s) their own way and will wish to safeguard any technical know-how in the process. There have been numerous instances in the past of good ideas being punted round established companies for development assistance to no avail, only to find at a later date that the basic idea has been copied and developed by the larger firm for its own benefit. Where financiers have been involved, they have asked for a majority or large minority share as reward for developing ideas successfully and have often required the patent rights to be lodged with another entity and out of the direct control of the entrepreneur.

11.3   Businesses that are already established may have insufficient funds; production space; labour or management capability to undertake the development and marketing of an ancillary product, service or to run a completely separate business. Any of these shortfalls can be made up by bringing in another party of like mind through the relationship of a joint venture. The relationship may be receptive or animated. With the former, one party assists the other only when called on, say, to assemble the finished product from the completed parts, or to fulfil orders already received. An animated relationship would occur when one party has the responsibility of building a prototype that works and then the other party markets the product to obtain business.

A receptive relationship

11.4   The driving force and control of the joint venture will remain with the animated party. There will be a trading agreement stating what the receptive party will do under the instructions provided by the other party. Commission or a profit-sharing arrangement or royalty payments may be chosen to reward the receptive party. This relationship is more at arm's-length between the parties and the receptive party has a trading risk little more than with a customer: the orders for the services provided may cease and/or the money due for the service may not be paid over. No separate investment is necessarily made in the joint venture.

An animated relationship

11.5   With this type of joint venture the relationship is more formal and should be accompanied by a contract of services. Each party relies on the other to make a success of the project and at some stage each party becomes the animated party, or the driving force to see that strategic decisions are made to enable the project to come alive and prosper. The risk for the receptive party at each stage is greater because little day-to-day control is exercised over the project and therefore regular monitoring of progress and cash flow is essential. This type of relationship is frequently met where special technical know-how is required to develop a service or product and only one party can provide it.

A joint venture by an established business

11.6   The established business will be looking for another party to provide added-value, perhaps through a patented application that could enhance the established business's product. If this application is not for sale or would be too expensive to purchase, the result may be obtained by acquiring exclusivity for its use in return for a fee or share of the profits. The agreement should extend over a number of years to enable the established business to recoup any setting up and marketing costs. The risk to guard against is that should the application prove faulty it may harm what was otherwise a successful product.

11.7   So how is the small business to develop successfully under a joint venture relationship? The key is to compartmentalise the stages of bringing the (joint) product to market and only adopt the joint venture approach when it becomes necessary either for technical or financial or marketing reasons. The steps may be:

- Decide whether your own business can develop the project to completion;

- Identify the weak links in this chain;

- List the options that are available to obtain good performance;

- Consider the advantages and disadvantages of each option;

- Evaluate the options in financial/non-financial costs and benefit terms;

- Choose which option (type of joint venture) should be pursued;

- Address the other potential party(ies) to the project;

- Negotiate the optimum joint venture trading relationship;

- Draw up a suitable agreement;

- Commence the joint venture and monitor progress.

11.8   The terms of the agreement should encompass:

- Which party has the prime responsibility for what part of the project;

- List what each party will bring to the deal;

- If the entry is know-how, ensure that it can be legally shared;

- This sharing may have to be through a separate project company raised for the purpose that would 'own' the know-how;

- Indicate the managerial working responsibilities of each party;

- Set out how the rewards of the project are to be shared and when;

- Set out how any losses incurred may be recovered from whom and how;

- Set out how the joint venture may be rescinded if disagreement arises;

- Arbitration procedures should be laid down in case the venture runs into temporary difficulties;

- Provide the machinery for amendments to the terms of the joint venture that may be necessary due to internal/external events;

- Indicate how additional capital may be provided for the venture to continue if the existing capital becomes exhausted;

- Provide a framework should another party wish to join the project or a founder party wish to relinquish its responsibilities to a new entrant (in such a case it is usual to allow the remaining founder to have first offer to take over the complete project).

A summary of the characteristics of the more common types of joint venture are provided in the table following:

11.8   *Joint Ventures*

Type of joint venture	Characteristic	Advantages	Disadvantages
Horizontal	Each party provides part of the infrastructure	Both parties can control their own activity	The product relies on each party's coincident performance
Vertical	One party adds to the product prior to the other party	Both parties can control their own activity	The latter party relies on the former party for performance
Receptive	Dominant party calls for performance from the other party	Control is exercised by the dominant party	Receptive party is dependent on the other party to the joint venture
Animated	Each party is relied on in turn to make the product/service a success	Each party can offer their own expertise to the other party	Non-performance by one animated party will cause failure of the venture

Chapter 12

Starting Up a New Business or Project

Start-ups

12.1   Most entrepreneurs start their business to develop an idea or vision with inadequate backing; either of detailed technical knowledge, market research, strategic planning or finance. By their nature they have a resistance to financial detail and will look to expanding sales as the key to business success. Very often the idea will be good and when their own money has nearly run dry they will expect, first, their bank contacts to provide sufficient finance and, when this is not so, they will turn to prospective partners to bring in venture capital, the so-called 'Business Angels' network, on a future reward basis.

12.2   The entrepreneur will want to maintain majority control of the venture and will show great industriousness in marketing the product or idea. He or she will expect new partners to accept past expenditure as the entrepreneur's equity and the 'business plan' offered will be many pages long, strong in advertising the product, and short on financial detail. The few figures that are provided will show a cumulatively increasing trend of turnover and profit (but no cash flow projections).

12.3   Is this familiar? It is met all too often in practice. By this time money will be running short and the entrepreneur will ask financial professionals to work with him for no reward except a share of the future profits and possibly a Board appointment. At the same time many other avenues for finance are tapped on a no-cost basis (personal friends, Grant agencies, the Small Business Service (Business Links); venture capital companies and databases). The time spent on these avenues is long and the success rate questionable.

12.4   All entrepreneurs should be encouraged and the reward of success can be huge, but a small amount of guidance in the early stages of the project development will greatly improve the success rate and the time taken. There are three steps to pass through: the Formative stage; the Development stage; and the Operational stage. Each of these is examined in turn.

The Formative Stage

12.5   The entrepreneur should critically examine the idea or project for weaknesses and be prepared to answer the following questions:

- Will the market accept the product?
- Is it a new idea requiring high marketing costs?
- How will any competition react?
- Is there competition?
- How will the product come to the market?
- How will the product be produced?
- Should it be self-manufactured, outsourced, franchised out or promoted through a joint venture?
- What are the financial objectives? Are they realistic?
- What additional money will be needed to float the venture?
- Does this money requirement include future working capital?
- What are the financial rewards if the product is a success?
- Has the general business strategy been agreed on?
- Should test marketing be done and, if so, how?
- Is the idea to be patented?
- What can adversely affect the business once it is started?
- Does a prototype need to be built? How much will it cost?
- What regulatory approvals are necessary?
- Is it a real business prospect or more a 'hobby' interest?
- Has a Business Plan been put together?

It is deliberate that the formation of a Business Plan is put last, although the timing of many other observations can be coincidental. Some stages are important to settle early on and among these are:

Patent applications

12.6   If an idea can be patented (i.e. that it is technically a new solution on merit) it must be lodged before any publicity is given or the idea is made available generally in the public domain. Such acts can make the application invalid. Advice from professional Patent Agents should be obtained.

Does the market want the product?

12.7   It is a fact that success in promoting a product already having an established market will be far easier than offering a new product and having to get the market to accept it. For example, there are many commercial vehicles constantly on the road network. The idea to use their external bodywork for advertising other products requires no public acceptance and can be a source of revenue for the promoter and the vehicle owner.

Business strategy

12.8   Will the business wish to pay the costs of own production and marketing or act as a distributor and take a smaller share of the sales income? Going further on this theme, will the entrepreneur be willing to give up a sizeable share of his business for the backing it will bring and potentially the greater reward of having a smaller share of a much larger business operation?

Test marketing

12.9   It will be important before trying to raise backing for the venture to assess the likelihood of success through judging the demand for the product. This may have to be done by specialist organisations through research and possibly canvassing.

The Business Plan

12.10   There is considerable advantage for all businesses to have and to regularly update an effective Business Plan. The owners of small businesses tend to carry their plan in their head. If it is written it is usually in the form of showing general aspirations for the future and as a means to gain finance, following which it is quietly discarded as having done its job. The plan should be the living representation and icon of the business and as such it should provide the detailed means at all times as to how the business is to achieve its strategic aims.

12.11   There are a number of topics that should be covered in a typical business plan and these can be tailored for specific purposes e.g. to raise commercial or Business Angel finance, or to set out how a new project or business can be assimilated into existing operations. It is also a reminder for the business owner how the business should develop and it acts as a blueprint on which to base subsequent changes. To this extent it states what the owner already knows but what other readers may not know. The contents should not get cluttered up with too much detail so that the overall message gets lost. Use should be made of appendices, particularly for items such as spreadsheets showing profit and cash flow projections, sales leaflets of the principal product(s), a profile of management, or a SWOT analysis, and it is useful to include a copy of the last audited accounts.

12.11   *Starting Up a New Business or Project*

A typical Business Plan

Chapter	*Content*
• Executive Summary	Stating the main conclusions on one page.
• Contents	Include page numbering.
• Introduction	An overview of what the business does; its strengths and/or niche areas.
• Track record	Comments on recent years' trading and reasons why they occurred (good and bad).
• The product(s)	Non-technical overview; their market share; their attributes.
• The market(s)	A description; how the product(s) fit in; what changes have occurred and why.
• The business set-up	How the business operates; its structure and ownership.
• The business resources	Human: the organisation & their responsibilities Asset: description of Premises/Plant & replacement.
• Production	A description; how it is produced.
• Marketing	A description; how it is effected & monitored.
• Strategy	Future trading aims and targets; how they are expected to be achieved.
• Financial	How the existing business is financed; the terms/security laid down by lender(s).
• The trading outlook	Sales and profit and cash flow forecasts; reasons for the basis of the forecasts, including general market projections.
• The new project (if any)	A description; with reasons for the project; how it will affect the existing business.
• Raising new finance (if any)	What for; how much; what type; how will it be repaid; is security offered?

Appendices:

Cash Flow forecasts. *
Profit and Loss forecasts. *
Balance Sheet forecasts. *
SWOT (1) analysis & Sensitivity (2) analysis.
Contingency Plan & diversification policy
Copy of last audited Accounts and any subsequent management returns.
Profile of management and organisation chart with key person career profiles.
Lists of key customers and suppliers.
Sales leaflets of principal products sold.
Trade data about markets/products/trends.
Correspondence support (if new venture).
Diary of description/date of revisions.

* The above adjusted to include the new project and/or the new finance to be raised and repaid.

1. SWOT analysis: Listing Strengths; Weaknesses; Opportunities; Threats. The first two reflect the business's own trading position; the latter two are market based reflecting external influences.

2.   Sensitivity analysis: summarising the Profit and Loss and Cash Flow forecasts re-worked with more optimistic/pessimistic assumptions. The usual re-workings are the main headings (sales; gross profit; net profit) based on different trading assumptions (e.g. sales higher or lower by 10% and 20%; debtors taking longer to pay or selling prices changed) and also showing the break-even sales target.

12.12   A practical example of a Business Plan is given in Appendix A. The contents listing above has been formulated in this order for several reasons: it tells the reader first what the business does; then how past trading has fared; selling what products and in what markets. A flavour of the business should have been gained by now and the plan moves on to consider the organisation's structure and what resources are being utilised.

12.13   The Business Plan then turns to a more detailed description of how the product(s) are produced and sold, followed by the strategic aims of the business. The reader can compare how the present marketing will dovetail with this strategy. All this data is then brought down into a possible financial returns forecast followed by the trading outlook. A comparison can be made of the financial projections with the general trading outlook. Finally, where a new project is to be assessed or finance to be raised, specific chapters can be added as required.

12.14   The appendices ideally should cover, on a monthly basis, historic trading figures for at least the past twelve months and forecasts for the next two years. If a new project or venture capital funding is involved, further years should be projected until the payback period has been covered. Forecast Balance Sheets should be compiled at the end of each year, preferably coinciding with the business's existing accounting year-end. Once the forecasts have been worked out for the existing business, adjustments may then be made to allow for development and trading and financing of the new project.

12.15   The Contingency Plan outlines what the management specifically will do (or has already set up) should there be a future trading crisis due to a cash shortfall; downturn in sales; uncompetitive pricing; problems with materials/sales deliveries; a significant loss of trading market(s) or in market share.

12.16   The lists of key customers and suppliers can show the proportion of business traded with each over a given period and any (confidential) significant tender or supply price data. If the Business Plan is being issued externally, depending on the recipient, the confidential data should be withdrawn. Instead, a list of names of the more important customers and suppliers could be retained together with a summary of the value of sales orders outstanding.

The Development Stage

12.17   At this point the entrepreneur has commenced the project and, hopefully, provided the groundwork through a viable Business Plan to ensure that the venture is able to proceed as forecast. Each venture will have its own gestation period before it can be brought to market. This period must be as carefully planned as any other. The critical assumption will be the length of time it will take: too long a time and financial partners may disappear and competitive products may edge out the sales impact; too short a time and marketing arrangements may disappear and quality control may suffer.

12.18   A Critical Flow analysis should be raised to plot in a logical sequence each development step as it arises to match future requirements. An example of a poorly executed project that excludes the procurement of labour and production plant was as follows:

Topics Periods	1	2	3	4	5	6	7	8	9	10	11	12	13	14	15
Business Plan agreed	x														
Prototype built		x	x	x											
Prototype tested					x	x									
Trials of prototype							x	x	x						
Type approval given								x	x	x	x				
Grant application		x	x	x	x	x	x	x	x	x	x	x			
Commercial funding	x	x	x										x		
Test marketing										x	x	x			
Venture capital seek													x	x	x
Ready for production															??

12.19   Type approval had been applied for while the prototype was still on trial, rather risky but possible. Foresight had been shown to apply for a Government Grant and allowance made for the time needed to obtain a response. Commercial funding was lodged as soon as the Business Plan was ready to give to the bank. A formal decision was deferred until the result of the Grant application was known. Test marketing was commenced as soon as the prototype was ready to be shown to prospective customers. In the event, the Grant was refused and this prevented the bank from sanctioning an advance. Resort was then given to searching for venture capital finance. The time extension necessary left the development short of any idea when production might commence.

12.20   What could have been done to prevent this loss of momentum? Clearly, the venture capitalists should have been approached at the same time as the bank. When results of the test marketing were being received, the entrepreneur could have revised future strategy to consider a joint venture with a customer (or supplier) who might have been prepared to part finance the venture for an equity stake in the business, a sales royalty agreement, or both. During this development stage the product should also be protected by trademark and patent applications, as appropriate. The analysis does not show any time taken for the purchase of know-how, either through consultancy work or self-employed specialists.

12.21 Depending on the financial position of the venture there may be a need to commence some trading in advance of completion of the development stage, perhaps when test marketing, to raise early financial support. This may be done by outsourcing a limited production of the finished product on credit and selling these for cash to targeted customers.

12.22 Consideration should be given to the warranty position of the sold products and public liability insurance. There was the case of a transport company that tried to market nationally its own IT software that had been most successfully installed to run its own business. Unfortunately, when similar firms tried to adapt the software to their individual specifications it was found not practical to do so and resulted in replacement software having to be individually designed under warranty at a significant cost to the transport company.

The Operational Stage

12.23 It is assumed that the entrepreneur will have already covered the general necessities of commencing business. These will include:

- Deciding on the business structure of either a sole trader; partnership or limited company (refer to later text).

- Completing legal matters, that may include raising a partnership agreement; ensuring that local planning regulations are adhered to; raising staff contracts of employment; notifying the Customs and Excise (VAT) and Inland Revenue (NI/PAYE) of commencing business; incorporating a limited company at the Companies Registration Office and registering the business name; contacting local Trade Associations for guidance on working environment regulations; raising a bank account; and perhaps registering on the Internet.

- Making contact with the local Chamber of Trade, Federation of Small Businesses, Enterprise Agency and Business Link (Small Business Service) to gather advice on starting up the business and exploring whether any Government Grant programme is available to help the venture. Most EC programmes deal with larger applications for assistance, but it may be possible to 'piggy back' onto an existing scheme.

- Researching Trade Associations and journals to gain a better idea of the market and possible trade contacts.

• Where the business is already established and not a start-up, market intelligence relating to the new project/product should have been tapped. If the business owner wishes other parties to be unaware that there is another interest in a process or product, third parties should be asked to deal with the research. It may be done through specialised departments of financial publications offering this service or research departments of investment banks and stockbrokers.

12.24 A small or medium-sized business has the choice at all times whether to operate as a sole trader or limited company and, where there is more than one owner, whether to operate the partnership with the partners having limited and/or unlimited liability. The preferences are best chosen with the following aspects in mind (see next page):

Choice	Reasoning
Personal risk	A Sole Trader is personally liable for debts.
	A Partner is liable for the actions of others.
	A Limited Partner may 'cap' his liability.
	A Company shareholder only has the investment at risk.
	A Company Director has legal liabilities of office.
Management	There is minimum formality for a Sole Trader.
	The Partnership should have a formal agreement. Disputes and Cessation terms should be covered. Formal Incorporation and annual Reporting is required.
Setting up costs	A Sole Trader has minimal set up costs.
	A Partnership will incur costs when partners change.
	Companies incur annual compliance costs.
Taxation/NI	Sole Traders & Partnerships are generally best where the profit is expected to be mostly withdrawn.
	Profit may be drawn from Companies by fees or by dividend regularly/annually; use tax planning advice.
Financing	Sole Traders & Partnerships must show trading viability as judged through the annual accounts.
	Companies may require additional security from the Directors if the retained profit is insufficient to support borrowing.
	Business Angels prefer a company setup.
Business sale	If this is likely in the immediate future, decide first what assets the business is to own and whether the sale will be piecemeal or not (e.g. venture capital ratchet purchase).
	Plan for retirement on a tax efficient basis.

Expanding the last point slightly, there is a choice as to who owns the freehold premises out of which the business trades; whether the business or the owner/director retains title, or whether the property is lodged under a self-administered pension scheme for the owner/director's benefit.

12.25   When the Development Stage has been completed the Operational Stage should commence with a number of decisions having been made:

12.26   In practice, unless the project is dependent on permissions or approvals or contracts, trading will commence as soon as the first orders are received and the product can be sent to the customer. The entrepreneur must plan his valuable time efficiently and delegate tasks as much as possible. If production is outsourced and other companies are to sell the product on a commission basis, the task for the entrepreneur will be largely one of monitoring and marketing.

See next page

Status	Comment
Does it work?	This means is the product commercially viable
What will it cost to manufacture?	Include indirect costs in this calculation.
How is it to be produced?	Own production or outsourced; it is safer to outsource at first until demand is established.
Who provides the raw materials?	Will the business have an input on ordering, the purchasing prices and stock control?
Is product assembly required?	Who will do this and ensure quality control?
How will it be marketed?	By franchise, through 'wholesalers', or direct selling. (the latter is more risky at first).
Who will promote the product?	An experienced firm with an established network is best, especially if the product can be added to existing product lines.
What is the marketing budget?	How much can be afforded and spent on what?
What pricing policy is there?	Are sales by bulk contract or set individually. At what price will demand be created? Is the projected gross profit margin adequate? What is the break-even point for sales?
How will sales be delivered?	By contractor or own fleet. The former is best until a firm idea of requirements is understood.
Will 'sale or return' be allowed?	Preferably not at first.
Have terms of trading been agreed?	How much credit is to be given/received? Have sales contracts been legally drafted? How will overseas sales be handled?
Have employees been recruited?	Self-employed or as permanent employees? Are key staff to defer part of their pay in return for a share of the business?
Have all regulations been heeded?	Health & Safety; Employment; Taxes; Planning.
Has the BUDGET been agreed?	What funds are required to commence trading?
Is the necessary finance in place?	For trading to continue until a positive cash flow is reached? If not, it is rather late to start searching now.
Is the CASH FLOW worked out?	And monitoring procedures put in place. Has a contingency plan been mapped out?
When to 'pull the plug'?	If events transpire adversely, at what point is the project to be reviewed and/or aborted?

Chapter 13

Why Businesses Do Not Survive

13.1   The immediate reason behind a lack of survival is running out of money to continue to trade. Up to this time the trading may or may not have been profitable and the owner-manager may or may not be to blame for the cause. The management of the business, however, has been at fault for letting the situation get to this fatal position. In general, there may have been a lack of foresight to account for changing trading patterns; the business may have overstretched its financial resources or, simply, the working directors may have retained insufficient working capital for the business to survive. In each case, warning signs have usually been evident, but management has not acted to improve the position. The assumptions quite often are that the business could trade out of its predicament and therefore there is no immediate need to cut expenditure, or that its banker would come to the rescue with more finance.

13.2   Delving deeper into the reasons for failure one may be able to discover situations less immediately obvious: product failure and warranty liabilities; technological advancements; a failure to market products; too rapid expansion (over-trading); excessive marketing expenditure; not establishing a viable market presence; a lack of price competitiveness; inadequate selling prices; extending too much credit; bad debts; a lack of liquidity due to asset investment; too high operating costs; over-staffing; over-stocking; a failure to promote the strengths of the business; the list could go on. Each problem will have its own danger signals enabling early remedial measures to be implemented by management. The table following indicates in broad terms the warning signs met and some of the preventive measures to take to counteract the problems. Their causes and their solutions can be inter-related (see next page).

117

The failure	Warning signs	Preventive measures
1. Money		
Lack of starting capital	Difficulty to raise money	Raise a viability appraisal
Lack of growth capital	Reducing cash, higher sales	Forecast future cash needs
Lack of contingency capital	Lower cash, higher creditors	Agree standby credit line
Excessive capital drawings	Reducing net asset base	Plan management strategy
2. Products		
Lack of competitiveness	Falling sales	Check market sales price
		Review competition
		Review product range
		Conduct customer survey
3. Trading operations		
Loss of profit	Reduced cash resources	Check profit margins

A lack of starting capital

13.3   Before any business start-up commences or an existing business embarks on a new venture, a realistic assessment of the turnover that is expected and the cash requirement needed to generate these sales, at least on a monthly basis over the ensuing one to two years, should be completed. The cash required, of course, will incorporate the acquisition of assets, both in staff and equipment terms, and the on-going cash need to trade before sales receipts flow into the business. Frequently start-up businesses forget the on-going cash needs and this, allied to over-optimistic sales forecasts, immediately indicate financial difficulties ahead. With an established business, what can be forgotten is how the existing trading set-up can help finance a new venture, either directly through providing money from existing cash flow until the new project is fully established or by providing collateral for additional commercial borrowings to support the new venture.

A lack of capital for growth

13.4   The business may already have adopted an expansionary theme, bought additional equipment, stocks of raw materials and appointed additional staff. If the cost of this is not properly reflected in the business's present cash flow forecast or is not fully recovered through a realistic gross profit margin, then the growth forecast may already be fatally based on incorrect financial assumptions and the profit expectation never achieved in spite of intensive marketing initially boosting sales. The qualification 'initial' is important because as cash resources reduce, it will become apparent that there is inadequate working capital to maintain the early rate of growth in turnover.

A lack of contingency capital

13.5 Few small businesses build into their financial plans a deliberate contingency policy in the event that cash resources, for whatever reason, unexpectedly drop in future. This policy may be either 'active' or 'passive', or perhaps both. An active policy will plan for a cash surplus each year and set aside, after all expenditure and proprietors' drawings have been met, a portion of this to be held in reserve in the business. This 'reserve' may be held in the form of cash or in kind; examples of the latter being raw materials acquired in excess of immediate requirements acquired at a cheaper cost through bulk buying; by paying creditors early to gain discounts; or by spending some of tomorrow's costs in advance through an acceleration of the equipment replacement programme.

13.6 It will invariably be better financially to repay borrowings with short-term surplus funds rather than to leave the money on deposit earning interest (unless the borrowing is at a low fixed interest rate and deposit rates generally rise thereafter higher than this cost). It could be beneficial to purchase stocks or equipment before expected price rises, rather than putting the funds on deposit. A cash surplus each trading year, after allowing for the business's capital equipment replacement programme, should always be the first aim. This is easier for companies to achieve on a tax efficient basis than sole traders or partnerships since the latter are taxed on all rather than part of the profit they distribute each year.

13.7 A passive contingency policy will adopt in advance the setting up of a commercial lending facility to be available for the business to draw on in case of need, should day-to-day cash flow fall unexpectedly. One method of doing this is to set up an 'evergreen' facility, where the bank automatically allows annual extensions to the existing (medium-term) credit limit that will enable the business to tide itself over any temporary trading downturn.

Excessive capital drawings

13.8 Many start-up businesses go through three phases of capitalisation. The first is where the entrepreneur decides to make a business of his or her invention, idea, hobby interest, training skill and specialist knowledge. Money is invested to bring the idea into play. The second stage comes when the initial pot of funds starts to run dry and the entrepreneur realises that external capital needs to be raised. Usually all the local and national Grant schemes are tapped, incorporating the agencies who offer advice and bring in advisory services.

13.9   The third stage arises when money has to be given to organisations and/or individuals on a fee basis to raise private venture capital. By this time the entrepreneur can offer a working model of the original idea and much heartache but little else. There is usually no market assessment of the idea and no realistic financial assessment as to its viability. Meantime living needs have reduced further the capital in hand and what financial plan there is indicates that a proportionately high percentage of any new capital injection will go to provide a monthly salary for the entrepreneur.

13.10   The established business, conversely, may be earning a regular but rather static income for the proprietor. There appears no need to change this status quo, with the result that profits may fluctuate a little each year but the proprietor's drawings will remain at the maximum possible, consisting of a monthly sum, possibly a personal pension arrangement and the annual tax bill. The danger is that the business Balance Sheet will not be sufficiently strong to withstand a downturn in trading and/or a re-equipment programme. Either some money must be returned to the business or the bank will be asked to re-finance the business. The bank will look at the capital remaining invested by the proprietor and make a judgement accordingly. An alternative scenario could be where the proprietor is looking in the near future to sell the business and retire. The value of the Balance Sheet, after several years excessive capital drawings, is not conducive to getting a proper value for the business.

13.11   In each of the situations stated above an effective management strategy has not been planned in advance and implemented. If a sale is likely, the assets employed in the business should be shown to have been regularly renewed and maximum profits earned in the three years prior to a sale so that the best sales price can be obtained. If a retirement is forthcoming but no sale at arm's length is contemplated, perhaps because the business will be passed on to younger members of the family, the business profit should endeavour to be sustained to ensure that any pension payable by the business continues and is safeguarded.

A lack of product competitiveness

13.12   Falling sales may be due to seasonal trading variations, changing fashions or an external general market malaise. If it is internally generated then it may be due to too high selling prices; a product(s) that are not popular; inadequate quality control; poor delivery times; product(s) that have been outmoded due to technological advances; what may be termed market unattractiveness; or just a lack of concentrated marketing effort.

13.13   In each of these cases the priority must be to find out the external cause for the deterioration in sales. Better still, a regular review should be conducted of the business's own market penetration and customers' needs; the effect on sales of competitive products; and how the market might be changing. Internally speaking, the proprietor should check whether there is scope to launch a special marketing campaign; or reduce margins on some products (or tender for contracts on more fine terms) without damaging regular future business or profitability.

A loss of profit from trading operations

13.14   Hidden within the annual turnover and profit figures can be a loss on one or two contracts; or bad debts; or a change in mix of product sales; or a gradual deterioration in operating margins through costs having increased without this additional expense being mirrored in tender prices; or a deterioration in the business's terms of trade (e.g. allowing more credit to customers). A regular monitoring of several key financial ratios should be maintained to warn of any pending difficulties or inefficiencies:

Monitoring area	Warning signs	Action to take
1. Turnover	Reduced Gross Profit %	Check sales mix
		Check contract profits
		Check sales margins
2. Direct costs		
Materials	Higher stocks	Check ordering system
	Slow moving stocks	Confirm future use
Wages	Loss of chargeable time	Monitor work sheets
	Increased ratio to sales	Consider subcontracting
3. Indirect costs	Higher expenditure	Consider outsourcing

13.15   Little or no change in the Gross Profit percentage on Sales can hide large compensating changes in trading. For example, the sales margins on some lines may have been eroded by higher direct costs but compensated by higher sales of larger margin products. If a check is maintained on the broad mix of sales and an adjustment made to the expected overall gross profit margin, a better forecast of future profit will be possible and a more permanent expectation of the future gross profit margin on sales will be forthcoming. Retailers can take the main sales splits of their turnover, allocate the gross profit margin for each and take an average margin in total on the many small product lines. The importance in this respect of operating a cash register with a sales analysis capacity is obvious.

13.16   The table above mentions higher (raw material) stocks and slow moving (finished product) stocks. If the former is reduced it will free cash for more efficient use in the business. If the latter is recognised early enough it may be possible to sell the products at reduced prices and recover at least some part of production costs. It will also show what products are susceptible to lower demand and should not be produced or bought for resale in such quantities in future.

13.17   The very small business will be able to see at a glance whether the production operatives are working to full capacity or not. In other cases, particularly site workers, this may not be easy and visits will be time consuming for the manager if he is not on site as well. In this case a monitoring of the weekly time sheets and comparison on a job basis with the original tender calculations will throw up efficiency discrepancies reasonably rapidly for remedial measures to be taken.

13.18   Indirect costs may not appear to have much scope for improving profits but there could be areas for significant benefits to arise. There is now more opportunity to choose the best competitive supplier of energy, telecommunications, cleaning and deliveries. Vehicle fleet management is a more obvious candidate for consideration. The leasing and maintenance of vehicles will be a fixed cost over the lease period and will enable the full cost to be offset against taxable profits. It will also release cash that would otherwise be needed to spend or to borrow to purchase the vehicles. The disadvantage is that the lease cost will have to be borne for the length of the lease period, otherwise penalties for early cessation will be imposed.

A lack of management implementation

13.19   Of course, behind all business failures is a shortcoming in management skills. The list can be extensive and this is by no means exhaustive:

- A lack of trading foresight leading to having the products marketed at the wrong time in the wrong areas to the wrong customers;

- A failure to foresee how the market will respond in future;

- Inadequate pricing policy on sales products;

- Underestimating the effects of competition;

- A failure to monitor the business properly on a day-to-day basis;

- Inefficient staffing levels;

- Inefficient production methods and under-utilisation of plant;

- Slowness in putting remedial measures into effect when problems occur;

- Over-expansion without the necessary resources in place;

- Too high gearing with borrowings and the attendant servicing costs;

- Simply not acting when the business goes into recession.

Chapter 14

Valuation of a Business

14.1   There are some broad categories to consider when valuing an unquoted business and each of these will be examined:

- Valuing a (company) share, and its entitlement when considering the business as a whole;

- Valuing an embryo business not yet trading;

- Valuing a (continuing) business as a whole;

- Valuing a share of a (continuing) business;

- Valuing a business that is not continuing;

- Valuing a future transfer of a business.

A company share

14.2   A part share in a company describes the extent of the owner's interest in that entity. The interest may be in the form of individual shares or stock of a specified amount. The shares or stock will have designated rights, such as preferential voting rights; dividend rights and winding up rights. In the absence of any designated rights there are general rights attaching to the ownership of company shares that should be taken into account when valuing a holding. These may be split into six broad categories:

Less than 20% holding

14.3   Ignoring special cases where a holding of this size will exercise greater control or influence of the company than its simple proportionate share would otherwise suggest, this will usually be the point when the share of earnings as represented by the shareholding can be consolidated rather than just the dividend income that accrues. The value of the holding will be enhanced accordingly rather than just as a minority investment.

At least 25% holding

14.4   This size (or greater) of investment in a company ruled under the Companies Act 1948 (but not earlier Acts) offers the holder the security of being able to block any changes that have to be adopted through an Extraordinary or Special Resolution. Examples of this would be a proposed dilution or removal of rights pertaining to the shares in issue and how the company may be governed in accordance with the Articles of Association.

Majority holding

14.5   Particularly in respect of private limited companies, the value of an unquoted shareholding is much enhanced if it brings majority control, for the majority shareholder can distribute profits and remuneration and appoint directors at will. The rights of a minority shareholder, in the most extreme circumstances, may only reside in claiming oppression as a minority interest.

At least 75% holding

14.6   The converse of holding at least a 25% shareholding as stated earlier.

At least 90% holding

14.7   The point at which all shares not owned can be compulsorily acquired under section 209 of the Companies Act 1948.

Other aspects

14.8   The Memorandum and Articles of Association will convey the governance and rights of the company's existence and the parties attaching thereto. There may be restrictive covenants over the sale price of shares and their marketability; over borrowing; over the type of business to conduct; over security; over the disposal of assets; and over the cessation and continuation of management (directors). Special covenants can always be attached. Any of these facts may affect the value of the shares in the company.

Valuing the business as a whole

14.9   In its simplest form a valuation may consist of the average profits earned by the business over a number of past years (frequently three years), added to which there may then be a multiple to allow for 'goodwill' of the business and the average may be weighted in favour of the more recent years' returns. This form of valuation is inaccurate and should not be adopted.

14.10   A further method is to take the dividend policy and dividend yield offered by quoted companies in the same industry as the unquoted company, average them and attribute this to the unquoted company after making some allowance for the lack of marketability of its shares. The flaws with this type of valuation lie in the dividend policies of the two types of company, determined as they are by tax considerations and future investment needs to be met by retained profits, and the assessment of lack of marketability.

14.11 A third way is to value the unquoted company on an earnings basis of the number of years' earnings to be acquired by the purchase price. The principle is that if a company shows strong growth in earnings its value to a shareholder is higher because the earnings arise quicker (and presumably the shareholder will benefit from a greater dividend growth and a rising share price). For example, if the company's earnings were £40,000 annually and it was decided that a full payback price would be equivalent to six years earnings, the *Price:Earnings* ratio of 6, multiplied by £40,000, would indicate a company valuation of £240,000. Apart from the arbitrary nature of the multiple, the value accorded to the business is at the time of choosing the earnings and this may be a bad guide when other assessment criteria are examined.

14.12 *Price:Earnings ('PE')* ratios are best used on a comparative basis; where a company having a share quotation and trading in the same line of business may be compared with the unquoted company. The unquoted company would have its *PE* multiple adjusted from that of the quoted company to allow for the disadvantages of having less marketability of its shares and probably its smaller size and therefore greater risk, but it may also have an advantage of faster growth due to trading from a smaller operating base.

14.13 A fourth method is to take the Net Worth employed (invested) in the business and appoint a suitable earnings yield figure to it, after accounting for the risks inherent in the type of business being conducted. The actual yield from trading is compared with the appointed yield and this adjusts the Net Worth amount into a required valuation. Averaging may be employed to allow for fluctuations in trading returns. The empirical appointed yield is the weakness in this calculation, although in practice if the prospective purchaser decided at outset that a certain yield for his investment was to be the main target, this method would be a useful comparative check.

For example, if government stocks yield 10% p.a. (having no earnings growth prospects since they are fixed interest investments); small quoted companies may yield 15% (to denote the greater risk to the investment); and a majority share in an unquoted company might be put on a yield rating somewhere between 20% p.a. and 25% p.a. If the Net Worth investment was £200,000 and the earnings £30,000; the target yields would be (20% x £200,000 =) £40,000 and (25% x £200,000 =) £50,000 and the valuation range on this basis would reduce to:

125

between   £200,000 × £30,000/£40,000 = £150,000

and   £200,000 × £30,000/£50,000 = £120,000.

14.14   The danger in using a Net Worth to Earnings calculation is in determining accurately the definition of Earnings. Where money in a general sense is employed long-term in the business, it should be classified as part of the Net Worth because it is 'permanently' being used to earn profit. Thus, long-term borrowings are so classified and, if they are a permanent feature, so should overdraft balances be (as adjusted for any non-representative 'rogue' figure at the singular date of the Balance Sheet). It is especially important to take borrowings into account where the credit lines have to be repaid on the transfer of ownership of the business. Bank borrowings and loans should be assessed for inclusion in the Net Worth figure on a case-by-case basis according to circumstances.

14.15   Yet another business valuation method may be adopted where the business shows little or no profit but is endowed with valuable assets. The value may be judged on the market worth of those assets in a sale. Some small premium might be added for the value attaching to the trading element of the business, but this may even be a negative factor if a large investment is required to make the business profitable again or costs will be incurred to cease trading, particularly redundancy liabilities.

14.16   Where the business being acquired is not being continued, its value to a purchaser may be the past tax losses that are available for the new owner to use to reduce the tax assessment on his own profits. Care must be taken to ensure that the rules of eligibility are met, i.e. that there is continuance of a like business.

What business valuation method to adopt

14.17   In short, there is no 'proper' method of valuing an unquoted business, but some guidelines can be advanced, as follows:

14.18   Where possible a business valuation should reflect the actual yield being offered out of distributable profits (earnings), since this is what will actually go into the shareholder(s) pocket. The valuation for a minority shareholder should be the actual dividends being declared annually and, where the dividend pay-out ratio has fluctuated significantly, then an average dividend yield should be adopted to iron out annual variations.

14.19   If the shareholder(s) can exercise majority control, the earnings yield should be adopted for valuing the business rather than the dividend yield. This will be the yield shown as represented by the full distributable profits of the business that are judged to be sustainable. Where the earnings have fluctuated a lot in the past, or are likely to do so in the future, an average yield should again be used to smooth out the annual variations.

14.20   Sole traders will take their remuneration as drawings and the valuation will be calculated on earnings before the deduction of drawings. Partnerships often have some salaries charged against profits before the residual earnings are distributed. If an incoming partner wishes to value the business on an earnings basis, the salaries (and pension payments) of the other partners should be allowed as a deduction against profits if it is laid down in the Partnership Agreement.

14.21   If the business is a private company the directors usually take their annual earnings in the form of remuneration, comprising a salary, pension payments and possibly benefits in kind, rather than as dividends. Where a valuation based on majority control is being considered and shareholder/director(s) participate in the running of the business, then fair, but not excessive, salaries should be allowed as a deduction against profits before any valuation calculation is done.

14.22   Where the previous majority owner worked in the business and charged a fair salary and pension, but the new majority owner is to be an investor only, the valuation should allow for the cost of a manager to be employed in place of the outgoing working director. If the new investor is to be a minority owner of the private company, the valuation of the minority interest will be in accordance with the earnings being distributed to the minority holder, which may be through dividends, or some directors' fees, or a mixture of both.

14.23   The valuation to an investor when the investment will have no set income rights, but will participate in a business winding up or sale after a set period of time, requires a calculation of the expected eventual return, discounted back to the present day at a chosen annual interest rate. The future value will be based on past track record and a projection of forward returns. The discounting rate to take may be the return the investor will be giving up elsewhere to invest in the business.

14.24   If there is the opportunity to invest as a minority shareholder in a private company, the investor may be asked simply to subscribe £x for y shares that would give him a $z\%$ share in the business earnings and assets. The valuation will be a matter of judgment and its calculation may be based on one of the methods previously described. The potential investor, however, may wish to reduce the risk of making a poor valuation by negotiating one or more of the following options as the means of investment:

Minority investment by	Valuation advantages	Valuation disadvantages
Ordinary shares	Full profits participation. Companies Acts regulation.	Sharing the full risk. No control over dividends.
Preferred shares	Gives right to a set dividend. Dividend may be cumulative. Prior right in repayment.	No sharing in profits. Limited share in assets. Risk of a liquidation.
Split rights holdings	Rights varied to suit investor.	Possible valuation dilution.
Debentures	Repayment secured on assets. Priority for interest payments	No sharing in profits. No management control.
Royalty Agreement	Full participation in trading. Tailored to income sources.	Rights of contract law. Difficult to monitor.

14.25 Any of the above investments may have special rights attaching that will change the advantages and disadvantages shown, or the investor may negotiate to add certain special rights to the type of investment chosen. Split rights holdings may take the form of '*B*' shares, where the '*A*' shares have preference as to an initial proportion of annual profit distributions and/or repayment. For the loss of preferences, the '*B*' shares would be eligible for the residual, larger, sharing of profit earned and/or the residual repayment on a dissolution or winding up of the business.

14.26 The investment through a Royalty Agreement can be suitable where the investor is only interested in, or has knowledge of, one aspect of the business. The Agreement may specify a percentage share of turnover or unit payment per sale, to be audited monthly or at less frequent intervals by an independent party at the investor(s) cost. What can be difficult to monitor is the effort the business owner will be expending to make that aspect of the business achieve the best return. A valuation, however, will be easier to accomplish since it will devolve on the turnover to be expected and the resulting income flow that is produced.

The purpose of the business valuation

14.27 Perhaps the most pertinent question to ask is: For what purpose is the valuation required? In this respect the business may be categorised as an 'embryo' concern, a 'going' concern or a 'dead' concern.

An embryo concern

14.28 The purpose of investing in an embryo business is to share in the reward of exploiting either a new product or service, or in the development of an existing market through a new, competitive, venture. An example of the former is a dot com internet service, and of the latter a mining venture having a latent mineral asset base requiring development.

Latent assets can be more readily valued by estimating the size of their trading (mineral) reserves; the cost and period of mining and then discounting back the resulting cash flow to the present. A non-developed asset is more nebulous to value and the easiest way is to judge it by market demand. This may fluctuate a lot until a more discernible base for valuation becomes apparent in the form of a future income flow, however uncertain, or a comparison with similar businesses already established.

14.29   When valuing an embryo business, one is effectively valuing risk. That is, the risk is of applying money to the venture, not receiving a subsequent return and losing the investment. Just as personal credit rating agencies calculate mathematically an overall profile of borrowers and assume that a certain proportion will fail, so the same principles might be adopted for different types of start-up businesses. Frequently, the easiest businesses to start up and invest in are the most risky: one can commence a used vehicle dealership with one car, but, as the business grows, more stock for resale will be required and these are wasting assets, with their value constantly reducing the longer they are not sold.

14.30   The risk can become evident in two main ways: through not achieving sufficient turnover and/or by not trading at sufficient profit. In turn, the type of venture that is to be commenced will influence this risk. Insufficient turnover may be due to competition or failure to promote the product or service. Insufficient profit may be due to inadequate trading margins, or bad debts, or poor management leading to an inferior quality of product/service or to contracts being completed at a loss.

14.31   There is a third risk that should be judged at inception of the new venture: whether there is a chance that the business will run out of money and have to be refinanced. A new dot com service is a good example how a shortage of capital may occur: as the initial finance is spent on marketing and development costs, the income return may be slower to materialise and there may come a time when the question of 'should more money be invested in the venture or should it be closed down (possibly preceded by a 'for sale' sign)?' has to be answered.

14.32   A proper judgment of the management will go a long way to achieve an accurate business valuation for the investor. There will be no track record to contemplate. One must ask the question: 'Is there a reasonable expectation that the entrepreneur will achieve the targets set?' A valuation based on lower targets may help to indicate whether the venture is viable but, in the end, it will be a case of survival is success.

A going concern

14.33   An entrepreneur that has started a business venture will look to value the money that has been spent to date on the project and call this the basic value. There will then be added an enhanced value calculated according to the expectation (size) of earnings. There are merits to this method, because as the investment grows the likelihood of success should improve and the forecast of future earnings becomes more pronounced. The same valuation principle can then be used as a guide if other parties later invest funds in the project:

Project cost	Investment by Entrepreneur £'000	Investment by Business Angel £'000	Earnings forecast p.a. £'000	Price: Earnings ratio
At start	25	0	200	8.0
At time of new capital invested	75	0	175	175/75 = 2.33
New capital invested	0	25	250	(250–175) /25 = 3.0
Share of the investment	75%	25%		
Earnings value per £ invested	*P:E* ratio 2.33 × 75= 175	*P:E* ratio 3.0 × 25= 75		
Share of the business %	70%	30%		

The example shown in the table indicates that the Business Angel has subscribed one-third the amount invested to date by the Entrepreneur and in simple terms the Angel's share in the investment is 25%. It is also shown that the additional funds invested are expected to raise earnings by £75,000. This is a higher proportionate return than that forecast for the Entrepreneur because fixed overheads remain the same, thereby boosting the earnings return on the Angel's investment. The Angel is due, therefore, a greater investment valuation and the share is calculated as 30% accordingly. Were the Angel to have invested the money at the outset, the sharing would likely to have been half each. By investing at a later date the Angel should obtain a lower share of the business. This type of valuation does depend on both parties agreeing to the principles involved.

The view of the purchaser

14.34 Taking a simple overview, without going into asset values, goodwill and such, the purchaser will require the business to give a certain income (profit) per year. Let us take two examples of this:

Case One	Year 1	Year 2	Year 3	Year 4	Year 5
Profit before tax & exceptional items	10,000	10,000	10,000	10,000	10,000
Return required by the purchaser	10% p.a.	10% p.a.	10% p.a.	10% p.a.	10% p.a.
Average Rate of Return over 5 yrs	10% p.a.				
Present Value of required return	9,091	8,264	7,513	6,830	6,209
Total Present Value	37,907				
Discounted Rate of Return	7.58%p.a.				

Case Two	Year 1	Year 2	Year 3	Year 4	Year 5
Profit before tax & exceptional items	10,000	7,692	8,333	9,090	12,500
Return required by the purchaser	10% p.a.	13% p.a.	12% p.a.	11% p.a.	8% p.a.
Average Rate of Return over 5yrs	10.8% p.a.				
Present Value of required return	9,091	6,024	5,931	5,988	8,507
Total Present Value	35,541				
Discounted Rate of Return*	7.11% p.a.				

Determined by calculating then totalling each year's Present Value as an annual return.
The Present Value for Year 1 is given by 10,000/1.10; Year 2 by 7,692/(1.13 × 1.13) etc.

It should be noticed that with *Case One*, because the profit is not increasing, the return on the original investment is diminishing each year. If the business is for sale at £100,000, the prospective purchaser will be paying, in advance, ten years purchase of the year one or just over 13 years profits taking a five year view (calculated by dividing the price by the discounted rate of return). This ratio is the *Price:Earnings* multiple. It is more difficult to visualise what the multiple will be for *Case Two*, but the calculation shows it as just over 14 years.

14.35 The prospective purchaser should evaluate the likely profit before tax of the business to be achieved over (in this case) the next five years.

131

14.36 *Valuation of a Business*

The trend in sales should be discussed with the vendor and account taken of how operating costs and margins might alter over this time period. Care should be taken to add in any expenditure on capital equipment needed to achieve the sales projections. A summary of the estimates will look as follows:

Purchase price	£100,000
Indicated *P:E* multiple (over 5 years)	13.2
Advised multiple after due diligence	14.1
Reduction in price suggested (100,000 × 13.2/14.1=)	£93,617
Less Equipment needed by year 3 £20,000	
Discounted value of equipment (5,931 × 20,000/10,000=)	£11,862
Adjusted purchase price	£81,755

Of course, whether the vendor will agree to this price reduction is another matter and the purchaser may also wish to amend the required income return aspirations from the acquisition.

14.36   The purpose behind investing in a business that is already trading will be set out by the prospective owner. It may be to accelerate growth; acquire assets; improve liquidity or rescue the business from failure. Each of these must be valued on the basis of whether the investment is worthwhile or not.

Purpose	*Questions to ask*
Accelerate growth	What additional turnover and profits will accrue?
	Will this be a sufficient investment to achieve all objectives?
	Is the reasoning behind the expansion sound?
	What is the trading outlook generally for this business?
Acquire assets	Are the assets pertinent to the need?
	Is there a risk of low utilisation?
	Are there new skills and training involved?
	Will more labour have to be employed?
Improve liquidity	Will this be the most efficient way to raise more finance?
	Can efficiencies be made to reduce the investment need?
	Will the new money go to replace any existing debt?
	Will the money be used for the purpose stated?
Rescue the business	Will it be good money likely to turn into a bad investment?
	Is the business worth rescuing?
	Are there better ways to rescue the business?
	Is it best financially to 'pick up the pieces' after liquidation?

The lending banker will value a going concern in other ways: calculations will be done to ensure that the borrowing requested can be serviced and repaid, followed by regular monitoring of the business to be satisfied that there has been no significant change in the situation.

A dead concern

14.37   The lending banker will also value the business on a break-up principle. Percentages of book value will be allotted to each asset that is not cash. Regular valuations of Land & Buildings will enable the bank to keep in touch with current market worth. There will be extra value in a long-term lease (over 20 years to run), particularly if the present rent is below market rates for that type of building. If the property has been fairly recently purchased, a quick sale value may be 70% of the book price. The same percentage may be taken where the property has been formally valued, to allow for the expenses and waiting time on a forced sale. Where property has a first charge thereon, a residual value may be no more than 45% of the net value after satisfying the first charge liability.

14.38   Non-specialist moveable Plant and Motor Vehicles may be worth 50% or more of their written down value, less the value of any outstanding hire purchase amount or other loan. There is the example of a fleet of lorries having nil value because they could not be used for other load carrying after being used to transport cheeses. Specialist moveable Plant may be worth 25% or less and immoveable Plant and Fixtures & Fittings worth 10% or less of their written down values.

14.39   Stocks generally may be valued at one-third their book values. In practice these assets should be more closely reviewed: The value of unused raw materials will depend on their age and condition and market prices. Partly completed goods will have little value but may be discounted drastically for possible resale to existing customers. Finished stocks may be 'remaindered' as having some value as replacements or spares for other stockists.

14.40   Trade Debtors generally may be valued at two-thirds their book values. Debts having provisions against their recoverability or being well overdue or in dispute should be classed as of no value and small debts may have to be treated likewise due to the cost of attempting a recovery. Other debts should be reviewed according to age with particularly large debts being individually assessed. Further influences as to break-up values are shown in the table on the next page.

Type of asset	Influences on a break-up valuation
Goodwill	Nil; except there may be some marketing value in selling the company name and any tax losses.
Patents & Brand names	The market value to a competitor depends on the continuation of the branded product and the life of the patents.
Land & Buildings	The value depends on the flexibility of layout of the buildings for other uses, the location and Planning Permission constraints. Short Leaseholds on frequent rent reviews will have limited value.
Plant & Machinery	Specialist 'immovable' plant will have limited value. Machinery having a long life may be worth above-book values.
Fixtures & Fittings	Very limited values. Equipment may have a small value if it is to remain on-site.
Stocks	Raw materials will have some wholesale value. Finished products will have a reduced wholesale value.
Debtors	Overdue and disputed debts may be expensive to recover.
Cash	Usually not seen. There may be bank set-off arrangements to consider.
Secured assets	There may be a residual value after repayment of the linked loans.

Valuing a future transfer of a business

14.41   Where a commercial value has to be ascribed either to a majority or a minority share of a business, as in the case of a disposal or acquisition, the contracted terms should allow for the possibility of future transfers of interest. Instances of future transfers that can arise are given below:

Safeguarding a continuing minority interest

14.42   Where a minority interest is initially acquired, the purchaser(s) will wish to safeguard the investment in case majority ownership changes or a future opportunity arises to increase the holding. This may arise due to death or other circumstances. The minority owner will not be in an advantageous position to dictate any future terms, but at the time of acquiring the minority holding it might be possible to agree also to have the right to make a first or last offer on any future sale of an interest in the business. The circumstances activating the right would have to be clearly stated and unambiguous as to their interpretation.

14.43 Where the minority holding has been inherited or has subsisted for some time it will be difficult to get the majority holder to amend the rights of minority holders. If the minority holders are working in the business a case may be raised that their input is valuable and should be recognised in a more tangible way. This may be in the form of a gradual purchase of the whole business, irrevocable as to the purchase price and the acquisition of the majority shares; or a contract may be agreed for the sale of the business to the minority holder when the present majority holder retires.

14.44 If the minority holder has cash to invest, this may be used to expand the business or to replace more expensive borrowings. In either situation there should be an improvement to the majority holder's income and it may be assumed that a smaller share of a larger business could be the reward for agreeing now to an eventual change in majority control.

Safeguarding a future minority interest

14.45 Where a majority interest is being acquired, so too will be the day-to-day running of the business. The, by now minority, owner will want to safeguard the remaining investment held. The terms of transfer of the majority holding should be drafted to allow for future dividend policy; significant disposals or acquisitions of assets; and circumstances where the earning power and net worth of the business is being eroded through mismanagement by the new majority owner.

14.46 If a company is involved, the setting up of control over future events affecting the business is much easier. For example, if the original owner wishes to retire but retain some control, he would retain at least a 25% shareholding. If all the shares are being sold but the income from the business is to pay a pension to the vendor, he may wish to accept a debenture or similar surety secured on the business assets and setting out the terms of regular payment of income to the holder. The terms may be for a fixed interest payment or variable payment according to a benchmark, e.g. the National Earnings Index or future profits earned (with the calculation to be clearly defined) by the business.

14.47 Where a minority interest company shareholding has attached income rights that are paid out regularly and there are clauses stating what will occur in the event of a default in payment, these rights are valuable and will largely determine the value of the shareholding except where transfer of ownership is blocked. In this case, the minority shares may instead be valuable as collateral for a commercial loan so long as the income rights will service both the loan interest and repayment of principal.

The timing of a future change of ownership

14.48   There is also the question what is the best timing for a future transfer of controlling ownership. The personal tax position(s) of the owners will be paramount, especially if retirement is close at hand and/or tax legislation is changing for the worse. A further important factor will be the future net worth of the business. The present owner(s) will wish to agree a sale price at the best time to maximise the value of the business.

14.49   The value of the business can be maximised partly by the owners through a beneficial reorganisation of the Balance Sheet in ensuring that all business assets are shown thereon; debts are more quickly collected and more expensive borrowings are replaced. There may be scope to emphasise greater trading in those products having the most beneficial profit margins. The level of staffing should also be examined for savings and greater productivity. Capital expenditure programmes should be attuned to preserve cash flow. The general aim will be to improve earnings. A change of ownership can also try to be timed after external cyclical trading patterns have accentuated product demand and increased turnover.

Chapter 15

Trading Overseas

15.1   Many small and medium-sized businesses starting their operations in the United Kingdom, unless their trading is largely dependent on cross-border deals, will try and keep things simple and conduct business within the sterling area. The occasional overseas sales order will be quoted in sterling and the purchase of stocks from abroad will necessitate a short visit to their bank to settle the payment details.

15.2   Complications ensue when the buyer or the seller, or both, demand security of release of the payment with successful receipt of the goods. There may or may not be a period of credit to take into account. One party may insist on trading in a different currency to that of the other party. The accounting systems of the parties may not be geared up to trading in multiple currencies. There may be a real risk of losing business in not being adaptable to overseas trading and the potential reward may be that much greater in achieving a higher profit margin and increased turnover compared with concentrating only on UK markets.

The general options met when trading overseas are:

- Individual closed-end deals;
- Individual account on-going deals;
- Multiple account dealing;
- Currency transactions.

Individual closed-end deals

15.3   The trader will be dealing with a single order and once settlement is made the deal is closed. For low value transactions with automatic translation of currencies the use of a credit or charge card account will ensure rapid transfer of the funds without credit acceptability problems. Payments through the banks' computerised SWIFT system (Society for Worldwide Interbank Financial Telecommunications) may be done for a modest payment charge. An alternative is a Telegraphic Transfer (T.T.) for a fee and there is, of course, the ordinary mail for cheque payments.

Method of payment/receipt	Advantages	Disadvantages
SWIFT	Rapid transfer; Good security.	Expensive for small sums.
T.T.	As per SWIFT; More flexible.	As per SWIFT; Less automated.
Mail	Very flexible if more data is to be sent.	Slower; Lower security.
Credit card	Good security; Ease of payment.	Time taken before receipt is known; Expensive for large sums.

Individual account on-going deals

15.4   As trade builds up and regular transactions are made with suppliers or customers the need for a simplified method of settlement will become more acute. Differentiation should be made here between postal goods deliveries and larger shipments, for the time to be taken in delivery and the security requirements to ensure that the selling party receives the cash and the buying party receives the goods.

15.5   The trader, to effect payments and receipts in sterling or other currencies, may wish to set up a bank account, either in the home country or with a branch of the bank abroad. Transfers of funds from these accounts may be by several methods:

Method of transmission	Advantages	Disadvantages
By telephone instructions to the bank branch.	Quick and relatively easy.	Poor security; Subject to human error; May need language skill.
By written instructions.	Slower but surer	As above.
By own bank giro transfer.	Any amount; Inexpensive.	Takes two working days to credit.
By bank draft (i.e. cheque).	Any amount or currency.	Costly for small sums. Difficult to cancel. Time delay to clear. Possible non-acceptance.
By bank CHAPS transfer of sterling in the UK.	Same day value. For any amounts.	Instructions to be lodged by early afternoon.

Using banks when making currency transfers

15.6   There may be considerable time delays and costs incurred where a money transfer is to be made between two 'local' (as opposed to international branches of) banks situated in different countries, each of whom conducts its international business through correspondent banks. The chain of instructions and payment may extend from the local (UK) branch to its international branch, say, in London (or to another bank that deals direct with banks situated in the country concerned) who will then transfer the funds to its own branch in the country concerned or directly to a correspondent bank that deals with its affairs in that country. This correspondent bank will then have to transfer the funds away to the local bank in that country that holds the account of the trading party completing the transaction. The trader will have to bear transaction fees to the UK bank(s) and the bank(s) situated in the overseas country unless part of the fees are agreed to be paid by the other party to the trade.

15.7   It will be far simpler and less costly for the trader to appoint a bank in the UK who also has a branch in the country concerned and for both trading parties to deal through these branches. This may be a British bank having the required overseas branch network or an international bank of the overseas country that has a (London) branch. The choice may be wide and dependent on their relative charging structures; their trade intelligence services; the Government regulations of the countries concerned; the currencies that are being dealt in; and whether or not credit is on offer to the trader.

Multiple account dealing

15.8   The trader may be more established in trading overseas by this time and will be requiring a more standardised method of overseas settlement. There are four principal types of payment in this situation:

15.9   *Open Account* is where the trading parties deal with each other on credit terms and complete deals by agreed settlement dates, the exporter/importer accepting the risk of non-receipt of funds for whatever reasons.

15.10   *A Documentary Collection* is where settlement is through a Bill of Exchange (or similar draft) that may be for payment immediately (on sight) or at some future date (term drafts). A Bill of Exchange may be useful to know and is legally defined as:

'An unconditional order in writing, addressed by one person to another, signed by the person giving it, requiring the person to whom it is addressed to pay on demand or at a fixed or future determinable time, a sum certain in money, to or to the order of, a specified person or to bearer.'

Thus, the Drawer signs the Bill, addresses and gives it to the Drawee, to pay the amount stated at a certain time either to the Payee or to the bearer of the Bill. The advantages of a Bill are that it may be able to be tendered for cash (discounted) early by the beneficiary and if it is guaranteed by a bank ('avalised') it may be discounted for cash at a lower interest rate cost than if its credit standing was subject to the Drawer's status. Some banks offer an Accelerated Bills Service, where the exporter deals directly with the collecting bank abroad rather than the bank branch in the UK. The Uniform Rules for Collections provides 26 Articles generally accepted by banks under which they transact collections for their customers to avoid misunderstandings. Special clauses may be inserted relating to the collection in case of need to ensure that the goods are securely collected and stored in the event of a dispute or problem. There may be disadvantages in certain countries to use Bills due to stamp duties being levied.

15.11 *A Documentary Credit* is a conditional (or it might be non-conditional) guarantee of payment that is issued by a bank to a named beneficiary, but guaranteeing payment only if the terms of the credit are met on presentation. They may be revocable or irrevocable and will involve an Issuing Bank of the trader raising the payment instruction; an Advising Bank of the beneficiary that is usually situated overseas; and a Confirming Bank that the Issuing bank chooses and instructs to raise the (ir)revocable undertaking.

A typical transaction would be where an overseas importer asks its own bank to guarantee payment and issue an irrevocable Documentary Credit pertaining to the goods and requests (the confirming) bank to contact the UK exporter (as its advising bank) to ensure that the sales contract terms and details are in order so that they can confirm the credit. The exporter will check the documentary details of the transaction, send them back to its advising bank and ship the goods to the importer. The advising bank then sends the documents stating the amount due to the overseas (confirming) bank, which sends them on to the importer. When the goods are delivered the exporter tenders the documents for the release of the goods.

The transaction does not necessarily require a Bill of Exchange if the overseas issuing bank will guarantee payment, when the deal will be known as a Deferred Payment Credit. There may be various types of paper transferring the right to the goods that are involved in the transaction apart from the documentary credit. For example, a Bill of Lading evidences a contract of carriage and is a receipt given by the shipping company to the shipper for goods that are accepted for shipment overseas and can transfer title to the goods. There is usually issued more than one identical Bill of Lading in case the original (and title to the goods) is lost. Any one copy will release title.

There is a Uniform Customs and Practice for Documentary Credits in issue that is updated every few years to take account of changes in banking practices. It provides internationally accepted rules and definitions governing the liabilities and duties of all parties to such credits. The URBBR consists of Uniform Rules for Bank-to-Bank Reimbursements under Documentary Credits and is a part of the overall Customs and Practice agreement.

15.12 *Payment in advance* is what it signifies, in that the trader is prepared to pay in advance for the goods and accepts the risk involved of non-delivery or deficient delivery. The main advantages and disadvantages of each method of payment are:

Payment methods	Advantages	Disadvantages
Open Account	Easy to operate; May be £ or currency.	No payment security; No control on goods.
Documentary Collection	Bill can be discounted; Avalised Bills; Direct collections; Insert collection clauses; Uniform Rules for Collections.	Fairly secure; Buyer risk; Country risk; Transit risk; Possible stamp duty.
Documentary Credit	Popular for shipments; Uniform Customs; URBBR.	More secure but exceptions; Credit risk from bank; Non-confirmation risk; Credit terms risk.
Payment in advance	Greatest acceptability.	Most risk for the trade.

15.13 The UK exporter, therefore, has to take account of the potential risks when dealing with the buyer of the goods; the country to which the goods are shipped; and the period of transit for the goods. A status search of the buyer's credit standing will help, but not go as far as gaining a bank-related guarantee of payment. The exporter's bank will be able to provide advice on the status of the country to which the exporter trades and any special regulatory controls that might prevent payment being made. The transit risk may be insured against and, again, the exporter's bank should provide suitable advice. There is various shortened terminology in use to denote when an exporter's responsibility for the goods ends and where the importer's begins in respect of the payment of freight charges and transit insurance. Broadly, there are different policies available to cover contracts and finance terms for periods of six months, one year and longer, each having their own special conditions. These conditions can change at very short notice.

Finance for exports

15.14 A loan or overdraft may be agreed with a bank to finance an export transaction. This can take the form of assignment of up to the value

141

of 95% of a credit insurance policy supporting the deal providing the bank can obtain good title. The bank may allow any credit facility to be repaid from the proceeds of the transaction, with or without any additional security. On the other hand, the bank may rely on the good credit standing of the importer and take direct control of the proceeds of the deal. For smaller value exports there may be insurance cover under a block scheme of the bank, granting up to 100% value of the transaction for up to six months duration before final settlement.

15.15 The exporter's bank may accept a Negotiation Facility giving it the right to deal with the trade documents. A Bill of Exchange issued to fulfil the transaction may be held or discounted by the bank to raise funds in the same or a foreign currency. This is the traditional Acceptance Credit, where the exporter draws a Bill of Exchange supporting the trade on its own bank, that the bank then accepts and thereby transforms it into a Bank Bill which can then be discounted in the money market at fine rates for immediate cash. The most eligible Bills are for three to six months maturity and for amounts in excess of £100,000, although sums as low as £15,000 may be accepted for discounting, for a higher cost. The exporter is free to ask the discounting charge to be borne by the importer.

15.16 Where Bills are required to be discounted for longer than six months and perhaps as long as seven to ten years depending on the type of deal, Forfaiting is prevalent. The importer obtains a bank to guarantee the debt (to 'avalise' the Bill(s) to meet the payment liability) that may extend over several Bills having successively longer maturity dates. The importer gains from having several years, say, to repay the debt. The exporter obtains immediate payment of the full debt, without recourse, with no exchange or buyer risk. The administration/collection costs and the fixed discounting interest rate charged may be for the account of either party as agreed. Not every deal or parties involved, however, will be an accepted risk for this form of financing.

15.17 Other general types of trade finance will include Supplier and Buyer Credit issued by a bank that may be attached to insurance guarantee policies and cross-border Factoring or Invoice Discounting arrangements similar to those available in the UK but having the advantage of dealing in other currencies. Performance and Warranty Bonds will also assist trade deals through a bank guaranteeing to the importer that the exporter's obligations will be fulfilled. In many cases the bank concerned will require a counter indemnity from the exporter against loss. Letters of Credit, analogous to Documentary Credits, may be issued to obtain credit not related to a specific trade. It is a negotiable paper that is presented to banks abroad enabling the beneficiary to draw funds in part or whole up to the full value of the credit in a number of different countries. As the funds are drawn under the terms of the Letter it is endorsed with the amount(s) withdrawn. This form of credit is not widely used due to the risks involved.

Currency risks

15.18 The most important consideration when trading in currencies is to account for the effects of changes in their relative values. Paying for supplies in another currency with a time differential between ordering, delivery and payment could result in a loss on the transaction if the sterling exchange value falls against the other currency (i.e. more sterling would be needed to buy the required amount of foreign currency). Similarly, exporting in sterling and waiting for the foreign currency equivalent before converting into pounds could also be less profitable if the foreign currency appreciated against sterling in the meantime.

15.19 If foreign currencies have to be held for any length of time, their asset value and any currency liabilities of the trader should always try to be matched in amount. In this way, any currency fluctuation against sterling would have no net effect. This is particularly true when investing in overseas assets and paying in the local currency, while having to borrow in the same currency to raise funds for the investment.

15.20 As with other currencies, so long as sterling remains outside the dollar and euro areas there will be a number of options for traders to consider when dealing in those currencies. A summary of the most likely options is given in the table following. The terminology is described thereafter.

Situation	*Problems*	*Result*	*Action*
Exporting in £	Currency appreciates	Increased profit	Repatriate or Hold overseas
	Currency depreciates	Lower profit	Cover forward
Importing and paying in currency	Currency appreciates	Lower profit	Buy forward
	Currency depreciates	Increased profit	Buy spot
Borrowing in £ to buy currency	Currency appreciates	Higher cost	Buy forward or Forward option
	Currency depreciates	Lower cost	Ignore option
Borrowing in currency	Currency appreciates	Increased repayment liability	Raise currency income
	Currency depreciates	Less repayment liability	Try to match with currency assets

Cover (Sell) Forward

15.21 The UK exporter will sell the amount of currency to be received from the trade based on the exchange rate prevalent now for delivery and receipt at the date set in the future when the currency will be received. The two potential disadvantages are that, for whatever reason, the currency is not received at that time, or the currency appreciates and the additional exchange benefit is lost. The advantage is that the UK exporter knows at outset how much sterling equivalent value will be received and, therefore, the profit margin on the deal will be achieved.

Buy Forward

15.22   This is the corollary to covering forward: the UK importer purchases the amount of currency needed for the trade now based on the prevailing exchange rate for delivery and payment at the date set in the future when the currency will be required. The disadvantage is that if the currency depreciates it could have been purchased 'spot' at the exchange rate prevailing and at less cost at the time it was required. The advantage is that the UK importer will only have to pay the amount originally agreed upon for the goods.

When buying or selling forward the bank will quote the deals based on the currency/sterling relative market rates as adjusted for the (interest rate) differential in time between today and when the trade matures. There is a cost, therefore, to take into account when dealing forward in currencies.

Forward Option

15.23   In this case the trader does not know what will be the relative exchange rate movement between sterling and the currency concerned, but does wish to trade on the basis of knowing exactly how much will be received or paid out in sterling. A Forward Option is purchased that may be taken up or ignored at the time of settlement. If the currency was being purchased and it appreciates by the time settlement arises, the Forward Purchase would be taken up. If the currency was being sold and it appreciates, the Forward Purchase would be abandoned. The reverse would apply if the currency depreciated. If the currency was being received and it appreciates or depreciates the opposite of the above would be done. This may be summarised as follows:

Trader	Situation	Exchange result	Action
Importer	Currency purchased	Currency appreciates	Take up option
		Currency depreciates	Abandon option
Exporter	Currency being sold	Currency appreciates	Abandon option
		Currency depreciates	Take up option

Mechanics of a foreign exchange deal

15.24   A Call Option gives the trader the right to purchase currency and a Put Option the right to sell the currency. When an option price is quoted it indicates a higher and a lower price; the trader will be buying currency at the lower price and selling the currency at the higher price. When a Forward deal is done there is a premium or discount to the 'spot' (immediate) quoted prices to take account of the time differential between the present day and when the deal matures. The spot price should be adjusted by this premium or discount.

15.25   When a trader decides to deal forward there is a credit risk to the bank involved. The potential liability may be swept up in the overall facility agreement between the bank and the trader, otherwise the bank will take a proportion (say, up to 20%) of the full amount of the forward deal into account as part of the trader's credit facility in use. What currency is being traded is also important in setting the parameters of the forward deal. If the currency is easily marketable and the value is a standard trading amount then the foreign exchange rates quoted will be 'fine' (preferential).

15.26   There are more esoteric options that the trader can consider to alleviate the foreign exchange risks involved on trading. A Cylinder Option will be a standard forward cover with the addition of set exchange rates to buy and sell the option. The spot rate at the time of maturity determines whether the option is to be taken up or abandoned at the favour of the trader depending whether the spot rate falls within the higher and lower limits set in the option (hence the 'cylinder' aspect of the deal). The trader benefits by setting limits to the exchange rates of the option and hence the cost of the option will be lower because the trader is accepting some of the currency risk and will not benefit as much were the option to be open-ended.

Living with foreign currency trading

15.27   Assuming that the trader has expanded the business from the occasional currency deal to more regular trading in currencies, it could be attractive to open a bank account in the main currency regularly being traded. If trips and expenses abroad were also on the agenda the use of a currency cheque account would be useful to meet day-to-day transactions. Joined with a credit card to cater for the more occasional trips and trades in other currencies, this set-up should be sufficient to meet immediate financial needs.

15.28   Invoicing in foreign currency is becoming more common, particularly as the euro currency area becomes fully established. Accounting for currencies with a currency bank account and for sterling through a UK bank account could be an ideal solution, leaving the trader to monitor balances with the help of the bank and to transfer and convert funds too and from currencies as required. Through having both currency and sterling accounts with the same bank, a set-off arrangement for balances could maximise interest receivable and minimise cross-border borrowing costs.

15.29 Translation of currency exposures into sterling for the small trader may not hold a significant problem. If it does, foreign exchange deals spanning the accounting year-end may be 'closed out' through taking up mirror deals to eliminate any imbalance between currency assets and liabilities. This may be reversed after the year-end.

15.30 Traders may be tempted to carry foreign currency risks in the hope of gaining additional profits. Quite often the economics of one country against another would suggest that to hold one currency in favour over another would lead to a profit. This may be so, but as always the timing when this view bears fruit will be difficult to attain since the daily currency rates are subject to so many variables. The trader should ask: what is my objective? To trade in goods profitably or to speculate in currencies? What the trader might do, is to set aside in the chosen currency a part of the profit earned from trading and to consider this a reserve for future use.

15.31 If the trader is wishing to set up a company overseas rather than just have a branch or trading relationship with that country, the overseas company Balance Sheet will be denominated in currency although the investment value will be held by the UK parent company in sterling. There will be the need to consolidate the currency and sterling Balance Sheets and to convert the Profit and Loss Accounts accordingly. An annual exchange gain or loss to be accounted for may ensue.

15.32 Should the trader have an active overseas depot or plant to manage, demanding frequent visits from senior employees and the management out of the UK, an examination of the internal set-up of the business should be made. Staff may be seconded overseas if this is less expensive than employing staff in the country concerned. Management may be employed both by the UK parent company and the overseas subsidiary company. Alternatively, a management charge annually may be raised to account for the cost of sharing of tasks. In these instances, the incidence of local personal and corporate taxation will be important in the planning process.

Loans and Currency Swaps

15.33 In the past, by and large, sterling interest rates have been higher than the rates of other major trading currencies. Borrowing in those currencies, therefore, has been attractive for their lower interest costs. Mention has already been made of the possible mismatch of currency assets and liabilities. If currency borrowings are to be raised, the trader always holds the option to 'swap' the debt from a variable interest cost into a fixed interest cost, and vice versa (i.e. an exchange of interest payments). There is also the option to exchange the loan (principal) itself.

15.34 A typical example might be where a UK company is able to raise longer term borrowings locally but requires it in a currency to expand the business. In this instance, it is not possible for the company to raise the currency loan overseas and to do so in the UK would give rise to a long-term currency liability. The company will first raise the longer term debt in sterling and immediately swap it into the required currency. When the debt matures it will be automatically reversed and the company will have its sterling liability at the original sum to repay or to rollover.

15.35 During the intervening years the company holds the potential option to reverse the swap early if exchange rates are beneficial to do so. Interest payments on the (now currency) debt are settled in currency while the debt is outstanding. There is the future option to swap back interest payments as well, but the deal assumes that the debt swap was to raise a currency interest scenario in the first place.

Other forms of hedging

15.36 Foreign exchange risk cover through currency options is one form of hedging currency exposure. Other forms of hedging risk are to use commodity and currency and investment derivatives. The financial instrument is derived (hence 'derivative') from the value and type of risk involved. The trader may have to buy a certain commodity to trade in future and may wish to hedge this exposure by entering into an option contract to sell, at today's price, the same quantity of commodity. If the price falls in the meantime, the buyer will purchase spot at the new lower price and exercise the hedge by selling at the old higher price, thereby making a monetary gain. Hedging is usually done over relatively short time scales (say, up to three months) but can be renewed at further cost and revised terms.

15.37 Companies may adopt a full, partial or no hedging rule for its exposures. If the company is trading with minimal resources to counteract the effect of adverse trading periods, or is sensitive to adverse changes in its profit margins or sales prices, it may not want to have the added risk of currency exposures and will try and offset any currency risk through hedging. Similarly, a trader having the opportunity to enter into a profitable and one-off large deal is likely to wish to retain the profit and will be looking to eliminate the currency risk. Otherwise, a trader may take the view to trade according to the currency rate of the day because the currency deals are small in value or infrequent or the business can afford, due to its size, to ignore currency fluctuations on the basis of 'swings and roundabouts'.

Chapter 16

Business Grants

16.1   There are initiatives constantly being raised both at national Government and at European levels to promote under-privileged geographic areas, working populations, advances in technology, training, research and development and to replace exhausted industries with new interests. These initiatives can be tapped through area offices of the Department of Trade and Industry, local offices of the Small Business Service through Business Links, local authorities, Chambers of Commerce, national Trade Organisations, Federations of Industry and Institutes each having their own branch representation. There is a representative list of websites drawn up in Appendix C to aid research.

16.2   Rather than duplicate the many opportunities for Grant aid that are available and the attendant regulations attached thereto, which is a continuously moving field of potential assistance, this chapter assumes that the business has been advised on the correct Grant programme to ask for financial help and concentrates on how the business may best approach the application.

The Grant programme

16.3   Each programme is allocated a set sum for dispensation under strict guidelines. Individual applications may stand on their own merits or may share a part of a larger-scale programme that is already running. Each programme will have cut-off points and these may be accelerated if the amount of applications exceeds the Grant sum that has been made available. Each programme will have a 'window' for applications to be processed. If an application is too late then there may be a delay of up to six months or so before another opportunity arises. The applicant should be advised at the time of receiving the application papers the target date for new proposals. There will be extensive guidelines given with the application papers and these should be read carefully.

The application

16.4   There are five very important aspects to any Grant application:

•   a Business Plan will be required;

- there may be a better chance of success if only a portion of the maximum Grant is applied for;

- the project will be monitored and the Grant payments will be subject to checks;

- all other sources of finance must have been tried and exhausted;

- the project must satisfy the assessors that there is a financial need while at the same time showing that the project will be viable.

It is usual for applications to be regularised on a set Business Plan format and a Cash Flow analysis will be the fundamental sheet to compile. Strict guidelines will be provided advising where each item of income and expenditure is to be placed and there are 'blank' entry places for any additional headings.

If a maximum Grant application is made then greater emphasis is likely to be placed on comparative judgments if the amount of applications exceeds the total Grant sum available. It also leaves open the inference that if, say, only 90% of the application is allocated, the project may not be viable because it was shown in the application that Grant support of 100% maximum was needed for the project to proceed. Where will the 10% shortfall come from?

Monitoring will be done to ensure that further tranches of Grant money can be authorised. The application, therefore, will have to be realistic in terms of achieving its income and expenditure targets.

Rather than assuming that a Grant application will act as a start ingredient for a project, it has to be looked at as a final topping-up to existing pledged finances after their money has been received or firmly pledged so that the project can proceed.

Finally, and possibly the most important aspect of all, the application has to meet a financial viability test while at the same time having the need of Grant assistance in order to be viable. This is an apparent non sequitur. The key lies in the Cash Flow of the project. In the early months of the project there will be an immediate need for finance. The applicant will have to provide own (and/or borrowed) funds to bridge the periods between receipt of each Grant interim payment. In this way the need for the full amount of the Grant support can be substantial. Viability will be apparent once the project starts generating earnings and the non-viability in the early stages is shown to be a temporary situation.

16.5   Two rather typical examples are provided of a project requesting Grant support. The first concerns eligibility for a Heritage Lottery Fund Grant. It is useful to show the interaction possible between a commercial profit-making business and a non-profit making heritage interest. The second example relates to research and development of a new product requesting funding under the innovation SMART support scheme from the DTI.

Heritage Lottery Fund

Eligibility

16.6   Grants are normally made to a public or not-for-profit organisation such as a voluntary association or charity. It can also be a training and educational institution, but in this case a lower grant priority and award may be accorded, particularly if the application comes from individuals or a commercial organisation and does not constitute part of a wider project. The not-for-profit organisation must buy and retain the asset permanently that is the subject of the application. The asset may be land, buildings or items to form a collection. If a lease is being acquired of less than 99 years, the freehold owner must also agree to be bound by the terms of the Grant in so far as it relates to matters within its control. The public benefits offered by the project must be sustained. The owner(s) of the asset(s) must be involved as a party to the Grant.

Types of project funded

16.7   These may include museum collections, historic collections and archives, including photographic, sound and film archives. Museum applicants must meet the minimum standards of the Museums & Galleries Commission registration scheme. Assistance is given with costs relating to conserving individual objects, restoring items to working order, improving the storage of items, buying individual items more than 20 years old, improving physical access to museums and cataloguing. Priority is given to existing museums, museums designated pre-eminent, regional considerations, collaboration with other heritage organisations and where benefits flow internally. Low priority is given to the establishment of new museums, unless based on strong heritage or collection importance or a strong case can be made on financial viability or regional grounds.

Education projects

16.8   A high priority is given to educational access, especially to young children. Details must be provided of the project's wider educational policy objectives, how these will be furthered by the project, the on-site activities, the use of communications technology, learning packages, staff expertise and training, and how the effect of the Grant will be monitored and evaluated. Projects with mainly educational objectives that involve non-capital expenditure will be assessed under the Revenue Grants Programme (see later).

Priority will be given to applications from heritage rather than educational institutions and which address young persons and build new audiences for the heritage. Applications are considered on the grounds of stated educational objectives, the quality of project planning, the expertise of education staff, the extent of teaching methods appropriate to the needs of those at whom it is aimed, how far standards will be raised, the quality and use of educational materials, the accessibility and suitability of the accommodation, the arrangements for assessing progress, and the procedures for evaluating the effectiveness of the project. Applications aimed solely at research, the establishment of a heritage education centre, or the development of heritage training courses will have a low Grant priority.

Capital Grants

16.9 Capital Grants are awarded under the Main Grants Programme where the main costs are for capital expenditure on physical works, their purchase, or aimed at preserving and enhancing access to items of importance to the heritage.

Criterion 1: Importance of the project to the heritage – described in local and national terms.

Criterion 2: Conservation benefits of the project – including better management, reducing/eliminating the risk of loss outside Statutory protection and whether or not replacement is possible.

Criterion 3: Access benefits of the project – including equality of opportunity and enhanced physical or intellectual access.

Criterion 4: Additional public benefits – including the support of the national/local community, their development plans and policies, the social/economic benefits, whether it is environmentally sustainable and its effect on existing heritage sites.

Criterion 5: Quality design of the project – the appropriate standards of conservation and other technical skills, visitor facilities and educational objectives must be met.

Criterion 6: Financial need and viability that
- Costs are realistic;
- Funding from other sources will be forthcoming and sufficient; there is a need for the Grant *or* whether
- The project could reasonably be expected to succeed using only funding from other sources;
- The applicant's organisation and current financial position is satisfactory;
- The applicant is likely to have the (financial) ability to continue the project in the longer term.
- The assumptions underlying income projections are acceptable and on-going running costs can be met out of the resources proposed;
- In terms of the relative level of Grant applied for and

the extent of conservation and public benefit obtained, it is 'value for money'.

Criterion 7: Strengths of the organisation – including whether there is the experience and capacity and commitment to manage the project now and in the future.

Costs not funded include day-to-day running costs (but see later), feasibility studies, financing costs, staff costs of existing employees, non-specialist furniture and fittings, and retrospective costs or costs incurred on works already commenced. These latter costs may be included in the element of expenditure financed out of other funds provided and may incorporate professional fees and in-kind voluntary labour costs.

Revenue Grants

16.10 Revenue Grants are awarded to widen and enhance popular access by encouraging projects that meet one or more of the following aims:

Criterion 1: Developing new audiences – by targeting new groups or significantly developing an already identified audience.

Criterion 2: Delivering educational benefits, especially to young persons – by improving the quality and effectiveness of educational provision including services, interpretation and programmes of activity.

Criterion 3: Increasing study, understanding and enjoyment of the heritage – including enhancing access by presenting information in new ways to increase knowledge for a wider audience.

Criterion 4: Encouraging active participation in heritage activities – through harnessing community and voluntary effort and involvement in the practical activities of conservation, maintenance and recording.

The proposal must be based on adequate research and analysis, showing:

- a commitment to equal opportunities;

- a successful track record in areas relevant to the application;

- plans to develop any necessary additional skills;

- how the success of the project will be measured;

- that the benefits extend beyond the period of Grant funding;

- that the project costs must be realistic and resources identified to maintain the benefits of the project in the longer term.

Costs funded are those shown to be essential to achieving the project's objectives. Costs not normally funded are those not relevant to the project and this will include specific core staff and running costs, but these are covered through allowing 20% of the total project costs instead. As with Capital Grants, retrospective costs are not allowed.

Grant limits

16.11   Capital Grants for under £500,000 can have a one-stage application and there is a fast-track decision process of within six weeks if there is an urgent need. Competitive tendering is necessary if the Grant requested exceeds one-half of the cost of a supplier or services contract worth a minimum £140,000.

Revenue Grants having a total project cost of up to £100,000 and up to three years duration require at least 10% external funding of which at least one-half must be in cash. Overheads and administration costs must not exceed 20% and capital equipment must not exceed 25% of project costs. A Grant decision may take up to six months. Normally 90% of the Grant is payable quarterly in advance on receipt of invoices with the remaining 10% payable after the completion report is lodged, indicating the success of the project. If projects last over one year, an annual report may be required.

Project Cash Flow example

16.12

Business Plan – Layout

- Introduction – scope of the project

- Background – track record and participants

- Management – structure and responsibilities

- Facilities – suitability of the premises

- Costs of the project – capital (equipment) and running costs (list)

- Equipment to be acquired – for which Grant aid is requested (list)

- Financing – how much and its sources

- Grant application – amount and description

- Cash Flow projections – e.g. heritage centre and commercial enterprise

16.13   The financing summary includes a number of assumptions: the commercial enterprise relates to a cafeteria and gift shop adjoining the heritage activity. This is formed as a company that has covenanted over a period to meet any shortfall in operating costs of the heritage centre until the centre can support itself fully financially. Both activities have commenced development and therefore have incurred expenditure that is not eligible for Grant assistance. Some heritage exhibits have been 'gifted' long-term to the Centre but it is hoped that other items may be purchased with the aid of the Grant. In the event, the first year profit from the commercial company is insufficient to meet all the expenditure (capital and revenue) of the Heritage Centre, but later years' projections provide good grounds for future financial viability. This includes forecast income from the Centre. The Grant request is to bridge the first year cash shortfall and ensure that the project proceeds. It has been assumed that the various costs have been correctly accounted for as to eligibility.

Project financials *Period: first year*	*Heritage Centre*	*Commercial*	*Combined*
Capital works	£×1	£×2	£×1 + £×2
Revenue costs	£×3	£×4	£×3 + £×4
Pre-application expenditure:	£×1 + £×3	£×2 + £×4	£×1...£×4
Capital works	£×5	£×6	£×5 + £×6
Revenue costs year 1	£×7	£×8	£×7 + £×8
Post application expenditure:	£×5 + £×7	£×6 + £×8	£×5...£×8
Total expenditure	£×1/3/5/7	£×2/4/6/8	£×1...£×8
Value/cost of exhibits	£e	–	£e
Total project value	£×1/3/5/7/e	£×2/4/6/8	£x1..×8 + £e
Financed by:			
Local community	£y1	£y2	£y1 + £y2
Own resources	£y3	£y4	£y3 + £y4
Other sources	£y5	£y6	£y5 + £y6
Exhibits value	£e	–	£e
Operating profit	–	£a	£a
Operating loss	–£b	–	–£b
Covenanted subsidy	£a	–£a	–
Total project income	£a – £b	nil	£a – £b
Shortfall: (Grant request)	Project value less income	nil	Project value less income

16.14 The financial summary would be supported by a detailed monthly cash flow. This would incorporate estimates of the number of visitors at the Centre multiplied by the average expected entry charges. Some educational income from groups of students may also arise. The expenditure would be apportioned between the Centre and the commercial company based on staff time spent on each activity and premises overheads would be apportioned according to floor areas if both activities used the same building. Prior approval of the (non)/profit-making split of interests would have been obtained to ensure Grant support.

SMART award – Innovation funding

Eligibility

16.15   The award aims to encourage innovation in technologies of interest to the DTI and includes ideas for the modernisation of traditional industries as well as for those industries already using high technology. Awards such as SMART are subject to guidelines and Grant ceilings laid down by the European Commission. They do not represent prior (public) disclosure of intellectual property that should be safeguarded by an application for a patent. The overall objective is to improve the competitiveness of businesses by developing new products and processes to the benefit of the national economy. Grants are won on a competitive basis to assist with a technical and commercial feasibility study and with the development of new products and processes involving a significant technological advance up to the pre-production stage.

16.16   The eligibility of a particular technology is subject to DTI approval. Awards are made depending on the level of innovation, the likelihood of technical success, the commercial prospects for the end product or process (which includes the proposed means of turning the project results into a commercially successful product or process), the managerial, technical and commercial expertise that is evident in or is available to the business, the business's track record, the financial health both of the business and the applicant, whether the Grant is necessary to proceed and wider aspects such as the environmental and design impacts of the project.

16.17   For a **Feasibility Study** the applicant must:

- be resident in England, intending to start a business in England or be an enterprise already operating in England;

- have fewer than 50 people in employment;

- have an annual turnover not exceeding Euro 7 million;

- have a Balance Sheet asset total excluding depreciation of Euro 5 million;

- have less than one-quarter of the capital or voting rights owned singly or jointly by another enterprise (other than non-controlling institutional investors); *or*

155

- where a substantial shareholder, being associated with other enterprises would not otherwise make the applicant ineligible for the Grant;

- show eligible costs of at least £30,000 and a project lasting between 6 and 18 months.

16.18   For a **Development Project** the applicant has similar constrictions except that the criteria are higher:

- 250 employees;

- turnover Euro 40 million;

- total assets Euro 27 million;

- eligible costs of at least £60,000 and a project lasting between 6 and 36 months.

The award maximum for a Feasibility Study is £45,000 (75%) and that for a development project is £150,000 (30%). These limits and the criteria are subject to change.

The Application

16.19   Apart from the specific forms to complete, there must be submitted a separate Project Proposal, Business Plan, audited Accounts (if available) and individual personnel information. The Project Proposal should be outlined in non-technical language (including diagrams if appropriate) covering no more than ten pages and have supporting documentation given in an annex. The format suggested is:

- The Project – an overall view.

- Objectives – technical and commercial to be achieved by the project end.

- Technical description – the approach done to date (in detail) and the major problems solved, how they were solved and the technical risk involved.

- Timetable – a chart to show the planned progress of the project.

- Level of innovation – will something new be produced and why this is a significant step for the industry or sector.

- Marketing and commercial exploitation – when the project has been completed, setting out the likely demand, market size, worldwide competition and their strengths and weaknesses, and to what extent the completed project will displace existing technologies.

- Business background/management – the track record, the applicant's experience and qualifications in the project area, and how the project is to be managed.

- Use of available funds – state how much money will be raised by the applicant and the financial constraints that were evident at the time of the application and, if a business, indicate the competing claims on the available funds and how much has been spent on research and development in the last two years.

- Need for Grant support – it must be essential to proceed with the project; explain why financial assistance is being applied for and how it will affect the project. Indicate how the project will be funded, listing the sources. Other public money received will reduce the Grant award.

- Project costs – estimate the costs (reasonable overheads are allowed). Explain why consultancy and sub-contracted work cannot be done in-house. Capital equipment costs necessary for the project are allowable but their residual value must be deducted.

- Non-eligible costs include interest, VAT, the purchase of land and buildings, consultancy work in making the application, and work done on the project in advance of an award.

The Business Plan should be written in the usual format and should include how the business is seen to develop over the next few years (sales, profit, employment projections) and how it will be financed.

16.20 Apart from the depth of information requested and the import of the project on the applicant, the technology and the competition, the key structure financially speaking will be to show separately and then consolidated any existing business operations within the project as it develops, so that proper judgment can be made on the viability and effect of the project. An example of the Cash Flow (the individual cost entries have been summarised) is shown on the next page:

16.21 Business Grants

Development Project	Month 1	Month 2	etc	Month 12	Year
Expected month	January	February		December	2001
Number of weeks	5	4		4	52
Expenditure:					
Materials	1,200	1,000		500	10,600
Wages (staff)	2,800	2,240		2,240	28,000
Consultants (R&D)	0	0		1,500	6,400
Utility costs	300	300		300	3,600
Laboratory costs	500	400		400	5,200
Office costs	600	500		500	6,600
Other running costs	500	500		500	7,400
TOTAL	5,900	4,940		5,440	67,800
Income:					
Sales	0	0		300	900
Own finance	10,000	0		0	25,000
Borrowings	0	10,000		0	10,000
Sub-Total	10,000	10,000		300	35,900
Grant application	15,000	0		0	35,000
TOTAL	25,000	5,000		300	70,900
Net Cash Flow	19,100	60		−5,140	3,100
Cumulative Cash Flow	19,100	19,160		3,100	

16.21 In the example the applicant's own funds are invested first, with subsequent top-ups, followed by a commercial borrowing. The Grant is assumed to be payable quarterly and the project development period 18 months. There is a school of thought not to show the Grant entry but to leave this to the assessors on the assumption that the application may have been shown to have been 'modelled' on achieving the amount of Grant applied for. After the first year the cash flow points to a small amount of funds in hand to ensure continuity of the project. The figures do not show that the applicant cannot provide more funds for investment; this must be attached separately or form a letter that is not a part of the element of the application open to public view. Sales are minimal and comprise test products for evaluation purposes.

16.22 The remaining six months of the project occurring in year two should reflect growing sales and cash flow in effect to take the place of the Grant money that enabled the project to reach the marketing stage. By this time the business will have implemented a strategic decision whether to commence production in-house or to sub-contract or to enter into a production and marketing agreement with a manufacturer. It is assumed that the product will have already been patented. Sales, therefore, in this latter respect would arise as royalty or commission receipts.

Although only two examples of Grant-aided project have been outlined, the general principles of the application will apply to other types of Grant as adjusted to specific circumstances.

Appendix A

Example of a Business Plan together with an Investment Proposal

NOTE: *The text contained within square brackets should be adjusted to specific case requirements.*
This example of a Business Plan and Investment Proposal is not related to any known publication or company or type of business described and any such similarity is purely coincidental.

BUSINESS PLAN
and
INVESTMENT PROPOSAL

NEW MAGAZINE LIMITED
Location
Date

[**Disclaimer:**

This Business Plan and Investment Proposal has been commissioned by and raised for the sole use of New Magazine Limited who have given instructions for its preparation from the information and explanations they have provided and no warranty expressed or implied is given to any other party for any actions taken or conclusions drawn therefrom. In particular this document does not constitute an offer of securities under The Public Offer of Securities Regulations 1995 by reason of paragraph 7 sub-section (2) (d): that any securities which constitute an offer will be made to a restricted circle of persons whom the offeror reasonably believes to be sufficiently knowledgeable to understand the risks involved in accepting the offer. Unquoted businesses carry a high risk of failure and such investments may be difficult to repay.]

Prepared by: Name

Address

160

New Magazine Limited

Contents   *Page*

Investment Proposal

New Magazine Limited

INVESTMENT PROPOSAL

The launch of a new nationally distributed magazine is proposed to be published to fill a gap in the market catering for young adults and families with an interest in **biking**. No other biking magazine currently being published is dedicated to the editorial content now proposed as its prime attraction. It will be called ['On Your Bike'] and issued monthly with a cover price of £2.50, available through the major chains and other national outlets.

An experienced management team has been put together by Twin Wheeler, an entrepreneur with a flair for business development and offering long-standing experience of the biking world. He will be ably assisted by recognised media advertising and distribution companies to ensure that the launch will be professionally managed from the outset.

Equity finance of £25,000 has already been raised and negotiations are in progress to obtain a bank loan of £60,000 for a period of two years to help finance production and trading. As with all new publications, the level of investment in start-up promotion costs will be crucial to the degree of success of the launch.

- It is estimated that a further **£100,000 equity (risk) capital** will be needed for this aspect of the operations, perhaps being contributed by up to four investors.

- For this cash investment **a 31.25% share of the business is offered**, with projected repayment of the whole investment **at the end of the third trading year**.

- Thereafter profits are forecast to expand further and **at least a dividend of similar amount should be possible to be declared annually** to shareholders.

The investment can be structured for approval under the Enterprise Investment Scheme if investors prefer. Otherwise, shares may be realised through an earlier trade sale or possible market flotation if the business expands sufficiently in the UK and overseas.

This Proposal should be read in conjunction with the Business Plan which has been formulated and the caveats stated therein that any money invested will be fully at risk of loss if assumptions about the market and the trading projections underlying the Business Plan do not materialise for whatever reason. Potential investors should be aware that all forecasts given in the Business Plan and the Investment Proposal have been put forward on the basis that any person relying on their accuracy and authenticity do so wholly at their own risk. The forecasts, comments and assumptions provided are the personal views of Twin Wheeler who has given and not withdrawn his consent for their publication.

1. Introduction

1.1 *The Project*

New Magazine Limited is a new company raised to publish a nationally distributed magazine to cater for young adults and families in the socio-economic A/B/C1 groups in the age range of 15 to 35 years old with an interest in biking. It will be a quality publication to be issued monthly through newsagents and by individual subscription with a cover price of £2.50. There is no direct competitor dedicated to bike news with special reference to the niche area of [put in the target theme].

1.2 *The Controlling Management and Business Background*

The entrepreneur and major shareholder is Mr Twin Wheeler, aged 50 years, who has had a life long interest in bikes. He has built up an extensive list of contacts in the industry and in 1998 spotted a gap in the magazine market for this type of publication. With the financial help of his family a 'pilot' publication was launched in 1999 named ['Off your Bike']. This was conceptually a success but was backed by limited financial resources, professional editorial and advertising staff and eventually was forced to fold after several issues due to insufficient advertising revenue being generated to spend on promoting the publication. A circulation of 20,000 copies was reached, offering readers 64 magazine pages for a cover price of £2.25. The experience gained from this foray into the market has proved invaluable for this proposed launch. Twin is now well supported by a skilled editorial, administrative and marketing team. A nucleus of equity investment has been raised and it is planned to have this augmented by risk capital from other interested parties. A modest amount of commercial funding is also to be raised.

1.3 *The Magazine Market*

There are four bike magazines currently on sale which are likely to be Twin's nearest competitors, the largest by circulation being ['Big Spokes'] (c.70,000 copies) but this is more a young men's lifestyle publication. ['Medium Rim'], the second largest by sales (c.50,000 copies) also focuses on young male readership and mainstream biking. The third publication is ['Small Wheel'], having the lowest circulation at c.30,000 per month and offering an emphasis on highbrow features but with little advertising content. Finally there is ['Tiny Saddle'] which is available free at garages and covers just news on all new bike products. These publications sell for between £2.50 and £3 per copy. An examination of a recent edition of ['Big Spokes'] disclosed that the magazine had 172 pages including 66 pages of advertisements, a proportion of just over 38% of the total page area.

2. Proposed Operations

2.1 *The Concept*

It is realised that to operate successfully there are three key aspects which must be correctly tackled: (a) targeted marketing to gain readership; (b) a sustained distribution network; and (c) a growing level of advertising revenue.

(a) Marketing

The marketing campaign is designed to create an awareness of and to stimulate interest in the magazine through strategies that will effectively drive the target readership into the retail environment so that they are induced to buy a copy through a combination of in-store and magazine promotions. The campaign initially will be promoted nationally through in-store displays and modest expenditure on external posters and 'flyer' advertisements in other publications in London & SE England, which houses about one-third of the UK population. Depending on the speed of success, further promotions will prioritise other urban centres.

(b) Distribution Network

The distribution network appointed is ['Wheeler Dealers'], a company related to Twin Wheeler's family. This company will take one half of the cover price (£1.25) in return for supplying the magazine to at least 8,000 outlets throughout the UK. An initial print run of 80,000 copies will be ordered, 50,000 for the full magazine and 30,000 for a free marketing issue of 24 pages. Cash sales will be received in instalments: 40% in the month after publication; 40% one month later and the balance one month after that, with deductions allowed for unsold copies.

(c) Advertising

It is aimed to sell an initial 14 pages of advertising per issue of circa 96 pages. This is close to a 15% advertising content, for which the standard charge will be pitched at a rate some 30% less than the established bike magazines currently offer. The advertising space will be heavily discounted initially and managed through an established agency ['Wheels in Print'] for a commission of 22.5%. National consumer goods companies and bike manufacturers and distributors will be approached for paying space. The terms of trade will be 30 days credit for the national companies and pro-forma invoicing to smaller firms. A classified section will be added in due course.

2.2 *Resources*

The editorial office, administration centre and marketing co-ordination base will be situated at Twin's premises at [Wheeler's Heights], The Fens, England. This location offers the added benefit of being situated in a Government assisted area and raises the possibility of start-up Grant assistance. Separate premises are likely to be required as the business grows. Printing and distribution, as has been indicated, will be sub-contracted out. Indirect overheads, therefore, during the crucial start-up trading period will be minimal, except for travel costs and the promotional budget. All staff requirements for the first two years are contained in the expenditure budget, with additional article writers being added on a self-employed basis as the publication expands.

2.3 *Administration*

A local book-keeper will be employed full-time to monitor the day-to-day accounting system and administer the office and a qualified accountant will serve part-time to control all finances and raise monthly management returns. A ['Venerable'] computer accounting system will be used with network access available by the management. A strict budgetary control of expenditure, particularly during the first years of operations, will be established.

2.4 *Promotion*

It was originally intended to concentrate the marketing effort in London and to aim for an intensive but short run expenditure period. After further research the advice given was to emphasise in-store promotions generally over a longer period as being better value for money. Apart from the initial launch budget, future advertising and promotion expenditure will be subject to available resources and revenue achievement.

2.5 *Pricing*

The newsstand price of £2.50 has been pitched slightly below the average retail price of existing biking publications. It was felt that a much lower price would detract from the quality of the publication and reduce the potential revenue to an unacceptable level.

2.6 *Royalty Fee*

A Royalty fee of 5% of the Net Profit before tax to be earned is proposed payable to Twin Wheeler in recognition of his past development services to the project, with a maximum aggregate payment of £50,000.

3. Funding

3.1 *An Overview*

With some 64% of income in the first trading year dependent on advertising revenue and some 27% of expenditure expected to be taken up on promotion of the magazine, the extent of its success or otherwise will depend significantly on attaining the former targets within the cost limitations of the latter. Advertising revenue has already been heavily discounted in the first months and, for financial prudence beyond the expectations of the advertising agency, this income projection has been further reduced assuming that not all of the advertising space will be filled. It will be up to the management and the investors how they react to the actual monthly trading results as they occur: whether more or less promotional expenditure is warranted and for what, in order to establish a viable publication circulation.

3.2 *Projected Cash Flow and Dividend Forecasts*

Based on the assumptions given in the various Appendices tables, there is projected a peak funding requirement of circa £160,000 by month three of trading, which is eliminated by month 30. It is proposed that investors provide equity capital of £100,000 and Twin Wheeler's family connections £25,000, which is topped up by a commercial bank loan of £60,000 repayable over two years. For the present possible Grant support has been ignored. Thereafter, monthly cash flow is forecast to be increasingly positive with a first dividend to investors being payable at the end of the third trading year. If all targets are attained, the first dividend can be 100% return, subject to retaining sufficient cash in the business and to Corporation Tax liability. Future annual dividends may be expected at a similar figure, unless it is decided by the shareholders to expand the magazine into other international markets for greater returns and retain part of the distributable profits for this purpose.

3.3 *Future Financial Requirement*

The financial projections have assumed that income will not vary significantly from month to month. In practice, if a range of advertisers can be persuaded to fill the pages of each issue, this will not be a problem. However, it will be prudent to have some financial resources ready to enable the publication to continue production should income temporarily drop for whatever reason. The cash flows show that the bank facility to be drawn is £60,000, of which no more than about £30,000 will be used and then only during the first six months of trading. This will leave the business with the flexibility of a contingency allowance to meet any unexpected temporary dip in income.

3.4 *The Risks and Rewards – a SWOT Analysis*

The critical period for operations will be the initial months of trading. Expenditure bills will have to be settled before advertising and retail receipts are received. For example, months two to six are scheduled to generate income of circa £255,000; any shortfall on this total will require further financing or a cutback in expenditure such as the promotion budget.

Strengths:

- Diligent agency work should attain adequate launch advertising revenue before the bulk of the proposed funding is invested or drawn down.

- Much advertising is related to new bike products, a necessary spend if each new model is to generate public awareness and future sales.

- Heavy discounting of advertising rates should prove attractive to potential advertisers.

- The magazine is aiming both for general and specialist bike readers.

Weaknesses:

- The saturation point for bike magazine readers is unknown.

- Circulation has to attain a critical mass to attract future advertisers.

- For the magazine to become established, further investment in promotion may be necessary.

Opportunities:

- The retail sales circulation figures forecast compared with the size of the overall market are very modest.

- The age range of readers targeted is a premium segment of the buying market.

- Most expenditure is known in advance, hence the gearing factor to expand profits at a greater rate than expenditure is high.

- The budgets set exclude distribution of the magazine in other World markets.

Threats:

- Existing magazines may try and duplicate the proposed editorial emphasis.

- The retail outlets for circulation may be curtailed due to unforeseen external reasons.

- Any future imposition of VAT on magazines would adversely affect cash flow.

3.5 *Investors' Potential Returns*

Subject to Corporation Tax due on profits from year three, over the first three years of trading investors are forecast to receive their original investment returned and thereafter similar annual dividends. Allowing for the risks involved, this average return is very generous. It should be possible for investor(s) to apply for immediate personal tax relief on their investment in the company under the Government's Enterprise Investment Scheme and also receive the benefit on disposal of their shares free of Capital Gains Tax. There are other developments in the offing from which investors may gain benefit: in particular, plans are at the formative stage to promote the magazine internationally and through the Internet. Investors will be given news of these opportunities at a later stage.

3.6 *The Funding Package Proposed*

The funding package example proposed is to increase the share capital in two stages:

No of shares	Twin Wheeler	Other Directors	New Investors	Total
Already in issue	2	0	0	2
Issue shares at par £1	4,718	280	0	4,998
Rights 3 for 5 @ £40	2,832	168	0	3,000
Rights waived	–2,452	– 48	+ 2,500	0
Revised shares in issue	**5,100**	**400**	**2,500**	**8,000**
Proportions owned	*63.75%*	*5.00%*	*31.25%*	
The shareholders pay:				
Shares @ £1	4,720	280	0	5,000
Shares @ £1 + premium £39	15,200	4,800	100,000	120,000
Total Investment	**£19,920**	**£5,080**	**£100,000**	**£125,000**

3.7 *Profit Sensitivities*

The preamble to Appendices d and e describes the assumptions made in the various Budgets on which the investment returns are based. They have been drawn up with the aim of showing a reasonably conservative trading outlook and the objective is to achieve a much higher profit return than that indicated. However, as with all new ventures which have to win a foothold in the market, no matter how careful the project plans are laid out and how experienced the management, the financing requirement in practice may or may not prove sufficient and this risk must be understood by potential investors. Appendix f provides a number of changed trading assumptions to the base model and how they could affect the profit to be earned.

Appendix a – The Management

Twin Wheeler – Managing Director, age 50

Twin is an entrepreneur with an aptitude for creative writing. He started his career in 1962 as an assistant editor for a local newspaper and was sent round on his bike to provide copy for each weekly issue. In 1968 Twin moved to a magazine publishers and boosted his earnings at the same time by selling bike parts. He was appointed Regional Development Manager of the sports section of the magazine by his publishers in 1975 and later this was to incorporate responsibility for the Group's chief overseas representative office in Asia in 1980. Meanwhile his bike parts business had flourished into a chain of six shops, all of them profitable. Early in 1990 Twin resigned from the publishing firm to concentrate on his bike shops. In 1996 he acquired a competitor ['Bikes Downhill'] when they had cash flow difficulties. This business was turned round into profitability within two years and a year later Twin sold his enterprise to an Asian conglomerate and put all the proceeds into Trust for his family. He now wishes to utilise his skills and experience in promoting a new magazine for biking enthusiasts.

Anno Domini   Creative Director   age 47

C.V. description ...

Justin Scribble   Graphics Editor   age 40

C.V. description ...

Opti Mystick   Marketing Manager   age 31

C.V. description ...

Count Ant   Accountant (part-time)   age 52

C.V. description ...

Miss Itout   Administrator   age 21

C.V. description ...

Freelance Writers to include ...

Appendix b – Outline of Marketing Programme

The marketing strategy to be adopted is to gain acceptance at a wide number and range of 'high street' retail outlets using 'point-of-sale' promotion within those shops to urge the purchase of the magazine itself. In this way, a rapid direct feedback of consumer acceptance at individual retail sources can be monitored and it is believed this will show a better reward on marketing expenditure than through indirect and more expensive static advertising spots. A breakdown of the marketing spend within the projected budget is as follows:

Week	*Outlet (codename)*	*Type*	*Month 1*	*Month 2*	*Month 3*	*Total*
One	Pound	Stand	7,000	0	0	7,000
	Pound	Posters	2,400	0	0	2,400
	Euro	Posters	0	600	3,000	3,600
	General	Leaflets etc	7,000	6,000	6,000	19,000
		Total	**16,400**	**6,600**	**9,000**	**32,000**
Two	Franc	Stand	5,000			5,000
	Mark	Posters	4,000			4,000
	Lira	Posters		1,500		1,500
	Peseta	Posters		1,000		1,000
	General	Leaflets etc	7,000	6,000	6,000	19,000
		Total	**16,000**	**8,500**	**6,000**	**30,500**
Three	Euro	Stand	3,000			3,000
	Dollar	Posters		4,000		4,000
	General	Leaflets etc	6,000	6,000	6,000	18,000
		Total	**9,000**	**10,000**	**6,000**	**25,000**
Four	Franc	Posters		4,000		4,000
	Rand	Posters	5,500			5,500
	Guilder	Posters	3,000			3,000
		Total	**8,500**	**4,000**	**0**	**12,500**
Month	Campaign budget	Total	**49,900**	**29,100**	**21,000**	**100,000**

The campaign continues at month four with refresher advertisements.

The free issues will be inserts in various existing publications.

APPENDIX d
Sheet One

Appendix d – Profit and Loss projections: Years One to Three

PROFIT AND LOSS ACCOUNT — BUDGET YEAR ONE

NEW MAGAZINE LIMITED	Month 1	Month 2	Month 3	Month 4	Month 5	Month 6	Month 7	Month 8	Month 9	Month 10	Month 11	Month 12	Year One
INCOME:													
Print run	50,000	40,000	30,000	30,000	30,000	30,000	30,000	30,000	30,000	30,000	30,000	30,000	390,000
Copies sold (%)	30.0	30.0	35.0	35.0	35.0	35.0	35.0	35.0	35.0	35.0	35.0	35.0	20.0
Retail sales	15,000	12,000	10,500	10,500	10,500	10,500	10,500	10,500	10,500	10,500	10,500	10,500	78,000
Promotion issue – free	30,000	0	0	0	0	0	0	0	0	0	0	0	
Retail income	1.25	1.25	1.25	1.25	1.25	1.25	1.25	1.25	1.25	1.25	1.25	1.25	
Retail sales revenue (£)	18,750	15,000	13,125	13,125	13,125	13,125	13,125	13,125	13,125	13,125	13,125	13,125	165,000
Copy pages	96	96	96	96	96	96	96	96	96	96	96	96	
Advert pages	14.0	14.0	14.5	14.5	15.0	15.0	15.5	15.5	16.0	16.0	16.0	16.0	
Advertising content (%)	14.6	14.6	15.1	15.1	15.6	15.6	16.1	16.1	16.7	16.7	16.7	16.7	
Advert revenue per page	3,250	3,250	3,250	3,250	3,250	3,250	3,250	3,250	3,250	3,250	3,250	3,250	
Percent of advertising space filled	100	90	80	70	60	60	60	60	60	60	60	60	
Advertising revenue (£)	45,500	40,950	37,700	32,988	29,250	29,250	30,225	30,225	31,200	31,200	31,200	31,200	369,688
Subscriptions (number)	0	75	60	53	53	53	53	53	53	53	53	53	
Subscription revenue (£)	0	1,875	1,500	1,313	1,313	1,313	1,313	1,313	1,313	1,313	1,313	1,313	15,188
TOTAL REVENUE (£)	64,250	57,825	52,325	47,425	43,688	43,688	44,663	44,663	45,638	45,638	45,638	45,638	581,075
EXPENDITURE:													
Direct costs:													
Advertising Commission	10,238	9,214	8,483	7,422	6,581	6,581	6,801	6,801	7,020	7,020	7,020	7,020	90,200
Subscriptions carried forward	0	1,719	2,938	3,859	4,672	5,375	5,969	6,453	6,828	7,094	7,250	7,297	59,453
Print costs	17,500	14,000	10,500	10,500	10,500	10,500	10,500	10,500	10,500	10,500	10,500	10,500	136,500
Print cost of promotion issue	15,000	0	0	0	0	0	0	0	0	0	0	0	15,000
Salaries & Employers NI:	5,114	5,114	5,476	5,114	5,114	5,476	5,114	5,114	5,476	5,114	5,114	5,476	62,822
Article Writers fees	3,000	3,000	3,000	3,000	3,000	3,000	3,000	3,000	3,000	3,000	3,000	3,000	36,000
Photographic Library	400	400	400	400	400	400	400	400	400	400	400	400	4,800
Sub-total	51,252	33,447	30,796	30,296	30,268	31,333	31,784	32,268	33,225	33,128	33,284	33,693	404,775
Indirect costs:													
Directors Salaries & NI	2,764	2,764	2,831	2,764	2,764	2,831	2,764	2,764	2,831	2,764	2,764	2,831	33,438
Administration Wages & NI	1,935	1,935	2,419	1,935	1,935	2,419	1,935	1,935	2,419	1,935	1,935	2,419	25,156
Accountancy fees	800	800	800	800	800	800	800	800	800	800	800	800	9,600
Travel & Sundry costs	600	600	600	600	600	600	600	600	600	600	600	600	7,200
ABC Circulation fees	1,006	785	0	0	0	0	0	785	0	0	0	0	2,576
Promotion budget	50,626	31,500	17,874	6,000	6,000	8,000	6,000	6,000	8,000	6,000	6,000	8,000	160,000
Finance costs	1,700	479	458	438	417	396	375	354	333	313	292	271	5,825
VAT recovery	0	0	0	-21,162	0	0	-13,320	0	0	-13,611	0	0	-48,093
Depreciation	250	250	250	250	250	250	250	250	250	250	250	250	3,000
Sub-total	59,682	39,114	25,232	-8,375	12,766	15,295	-595	13,489	15,233	-949	12,641	15,170	198,702
NET PROFIT BEFORE TAX	-46,684	-14,736	-3,703	25,504	654	-2,940	13,474	-1,094	-2,820	13,458	-288	-3,226	-22,402
Less Royalty fee	0	0	0	1,275	33	0	674	0	0	673	0	0	2,654
ADJUSTED NET PROFIT	-46,684	-14,736	-3,703	24,229	621	-2,940	12,800	-1,094	-2,820	12,785	-288	-3,226	-25,056

171

APPENDIX d
Sheet Two

NEW MAGAZINE LIMITED

PROFIT AND LOSS ACCOUNT — BUDGET YEAR TWO

	Month 1	Month 2	Month 3	Month 4	Month 5	Month 6	Month 7	Month 8	Month 9	Month 10	Month 11	Month 12	Year Two
INCOME:													
Print run	30,000	30,000	30,000	30,000	30,000	30,000	30,000	30,000	30,000	30,000	30,000	30,000	360,000
Copies sold (%)	35.0	35.0	35.0	35.0	35.0	35.0	35.0	35.0	35.0	35.0	35.0	35.0	20.0
Retail sales	10,500	10,500	10,500	10,500	10,500	10,500	10,500	10,500	10,500	10,500	10,500	10,500	72,000
Promotion issue – free	0	0	0	0	0	0	0	0	0	0	0	0	
Retail income	1.25	1.25	1.25	1.25	1.25	1.25	1.25	1.25	1.25	1.25	1.25	1.25	1.25
Retail sales revenue (£)	13,125	13,125	13,125	13,125	13,125	13,125	13,125	13,125	13,125	13,125	13,125	13,125	157,500
Copy pages	96	96	96	96	96	96	96	96	96	96	96	96	
Advert pages	16.0	16.0	16.0	16.0	16.0	16.0	16.5	16.5	16.5	16.5	16.5	16.5	
Advertising content (%)	16.7	16.7	16.7	16.7	16.7	16.7	17.2	17.2	17.2	17.2	17.2	17.2	
Advert revenue per page	3,500	3,500	3,500	3,500	3,500	3,500	3,500	3,500	3,500	3,500	3,500	3,500	
Percent of advertising space filled	65	65	65	65	65	65	70	70	70	70	70	70	
Advertising revenue (£)	36,400	36,400	36,400	36,400	36,400	36,400	40,425	40,425	40,425	40,425	40,425	40,425	420,525
Subscriptions (number)	53	53	53	53	53	53	53	53	53	53	53	53	
Subscription revenue (£)	1,313	1,313	1,313	1,313	1,313	1,313	1,313	1,313	1,313	1,313	1,313	1,313	15,750
TOTAL REVENUE (£)	50,838	50,838	50,838	50,838	50,838	50,838	54,863	54,863	54,863	54,863	54,863	54,863	634,200
EXPENDITURE:													
Direct costs:													
Advertising Commission	9,100	9,100	9,100	9,100	9,100	9,100	10,106	10,106	10,106	10,106	10,106	10,106	115,238
Subscriptions carried forward	7,203	7,203	7,203	7,203	7,203	7,203	7,203	7,203	7,203	7,203	7,203	7,203	86,436
Print costs	12,000	12,000	12,000	12,000	12,000	12,000	12,000	12,000	12,000	12,000	12,000	12,000	144,000
Print cost of promotion issue	0	0	0	0	0	0	0	0	0	0	0	0	0
Salaries & Employers NI:	5,330	5,330	5,709	5,330	5,330	5,709	5,330	5,330	5,709	5,330	5,330	5,709	65,475
Article Writers fees	4,500	4,500	4,500	4,500	4,500	4,500	4,500	4,500	4,500	4,500	4,500	4,500	54,000
Photographic Library	500	500	500	500	500	500	500	500	500	500	500	500	6,000
Sub-total	38,633	38,633	39,012	38,633	38,633	39,012	39,639	39,639	40,018	39,639	39,639	40,018	471,149
Indirect costs:													
Directors Salaries & NI	2,903	2,903	2,972	2,903	2,903	2,972	2,903	2,903	2,972	2,903	2,903	2,972	35,110
Administration Wages & NI	1,993	1,993	2,491	1,993	1,993	2,491	1,993	1,993	2,491	1,993	1,993	2,491	25,910
Accountancy fees	880	880	880	880	880	880	880	880	880	880	880	880	10,560
Travel & Sundry costs	700	700	700	700	700	700	700	700	700	700	700	700	8,400
ABC Circulation fees	900	900	0	0	0	0	0	900	0	0	0	0	1,800
Promotion budget	24,000	6,000	8,000	6,000	6,000	8,000	6,000	6,000	8,000	6,000	6,000	8,000	98,000
Finance costs	250	229	208	188	167	146	125	104	83	63	42	21	1,625
VAT recovery	-8,432	0	0	-16,352	0	0	-16,371	0	0	-16,880	0	0	-58,034
Depreciation	188	188	188	188	188	188	188	188	188	188	188	188	2,250
Sub-total	22,482	13,792	15,439	-3,501	12,830	15,377	-3,582	13,667	15,314	-4,154	12,705	15,252	125,621
NET PROFIT BEFORE TAX	-10,277	-1,588	-3,614	15,706	-625	-3,551	18,806	1,556	-470	19,378	2,518	-408	37,430
Less Royalty fee	0	0	0	785	0	0	940	78	0	969	126	0	2,898
ADJUSTED NET PROFIT	-10,277	-1,588	-3,614	14,920	-625	-3,551	17,865	1,478	-470	18,409	2,392	-408	34,532

172

New Magazine Limited

NEW MAGAZINE LIMITED

PROFIT AND LOSS ACCOUNT — BUDGET YEAR THREE

	Month 1	Month 2	Month 3	Month 4	Month 5	Month 6	Month 7	Month 8	Month 9	Month 10	Month 11	Month 12	Year Three
INCOME:													
Print run	30,000	30,000	30,000	30,000	30,000	30,000	30,000	30,000	30,000	30,000	30,000	30,000	360,000
Copies sold (%)	35.0	35.0	35.0	35.0	35.0	35.0	35.0	35.0	35.0	35.0	35.0	35.0	20.0
Retails sales	10,500	10,500	10,500	10,500	10,500	10,500	10,500	10,500	10,500	10,500	10,500	10,500	72,000
Promotion issue – free	0	0	0	0	0	0	0	0	0	0	0	0	0
Retail income	1.25	1.25	1.25	1.25	1.25	1.25	1.25	1.25	1.25	1.25	1.25	1.25	1.25
Retail sales revenue (£)	13,125	13,125	13,125	13,125	13,125	13,125	13,125	13,125	13,125	13,125	13,125	13,125	157,500
Copy pages	96	96	96	96	96	96	96	96	96	96	96	96	
Advert pages	17.0	17.0	17.0	17.0	17.0	17.0	17.5	17.5	17.5	17.5	17.5	17.5	
Advertising content (%)	17.7	17.7	17.7	17.7	17.7	17.7	18.2	18.2	18.2	18.2	18.2	18.2	
Advert revenue per page	3,750	3,750	3,750	3,750	3,750	3,750	4,000	4,000	4,000	4,000	4,000	4,000	
Percent of advertising space filled	75	75	75	75	75	75	80	80	80	80	80	80	
Advertising revenue (£)	47,813	47,813	47,813	47,813	47,813	47,813	56,000	56,000	56,000	56,000	56,000	56,000	566,875
Subscriptions (number)	53	53	53	53	53	53	53	53	53	53	53	53	
Subscription revenue (£)	1,313	1,313	1,313	1,313	1,313	1,313	1,313	1,313	1,313	1,313	1,313	1,313	15,750
TOTAL REVENUE (£)	62,250	62,250	62,250	62,250	62,250	62,250	70,438	70,438	70,438	70,438	70,438	70,438	796,125
EXPENDITURE:													
Direct costs:													
Advertising Commission	11,953	11,953	11,953	11,953	11,953	11,953	14,000	14,000	14,000	14,000	14,000	14,000	155,719
Subscriptions carried forward	7,203	7,203	7,203	7,203	7,203	7,203	7,203	7,203	7,203	7,203	7,203	7,203	86,436
Print costs	13,500	13,500	13,500	13,500	13,500	13,500	13,500	13,500	13,500	13,500	13,500	13,500	162,000
Print cost of promotion issue	0	0	0	0	0	0	0	0	0	0	0	0	0
Salaries & Employers NI	5,498	5,498	5,881	5,498	5,498	5,881	5,498	5,498	5,881	5,498	5,498	5,881	67,504
Article Writers fees	4,500	4,500	4,500	4,500	4,500	4,500	4,500	4,500	4,500	4,500	4,500	4,500	54,000
Photographic Library	500	500	500	500	500	500	500	500	500	500	500	500	6,000
Sub-total	43,154	43,154	43,537	43,154	43,154	43,537	45,201	45,201	45,584	45,201	45,201	45,584	531,658
Indirect costs:													
Directors Salaries & NI	3,048	3,048	3,121	3,048	3,048	3,121	3,048	3,048	3,121	3,048	3,048	3,121	36,866
Administration Wages & NI	1,993	1,993	2,491	1,993	1,993	2,491	1,993	1,993	2,491	1,993	1,993	2,491	25,910
Accountancy fees	880	880	880	880	880	880	880	880	880	880	880	880	10,560
Travel & Sundry costs	700	700	700	700	700	700	700	700	700	700	700	700	8,400
ABC Circulation fees	0	900	0	0	0	0	0	900	0	0	0	0	1,800
Promotion budget	16,000	6,000	8,000	6,000	6,000	8,000	6,000	6,000	8,000	6,000	6,000	8,000	90,000
Finance costs (leased equipment)	3,000	1,000	0	1,000	1,000	1,000	1,000	1,000	1,000	1,000	1,000	1,000	12,000
VAT recovery	-7,750	0	0	-18,506	0	0	-18,663	0	0	-19,450	0	0	-64,368
Depreciation	188	188	188	188	188	188	188	188	188	188	188	188	2,250
Sub-total	18,059	13,708	15,380	-4,698	13,808	16,380	-4,855	14,708	16,380	-5,641	13,808	16,380	123,418
NET PROFIT BEFORE TAX	1,037	5,388	3,334	23,794	5,288	2,334	30,091	10,528	8,474	30,878	11,428	8,474	141,049
Less Royalty fee	52	269	167	1,190	264	117	1,505	526	424	1,544	571	424	7,052
ADJUSTED NET PROFIT	985	5,118	3,167	22,604	5,023	2,217	28,587	10,002	8,051	29,334	10,857	8,051	133,996

173

Appendix e – Cash flow, project financing and balance sheet projections: Years One to Three

APPENDIX e Sheet One

CASH FLOW   **BUDGET YEAR ONE**

NEW MAGAZINE LIMITED

	Month 1	Month 2	Month 3	Month 4	Month 5	Month 6	Month 7	Month 8	Month 9	Month 10	Month 11	Month 12	Year One
REVENUE:													
Retail sales	0	7,500	13,500	15,000	13,500	13,125	13,125	13,125	13,125	13,125	13,125	13,125	141,375
Advertising sales	0	0	53,463	48,116	44,298	38,760	34,369	34,369	35,514	35,514	36,660	36,660	397,723
Subscriptions	0	1,875	1,500	1,313	1,313	1,313	1,313	1,313	1,313	1,313	1,313	1,313	15,188
REVENUE CASH FLOW	0	9,375	68,463	64,429	59,110	53,198	48,806	48,806	49,952	49,952	51,098	51,098	554,285
EXPENDITURE:													
Advertising commission	0	0	12,029	10,826	9,967	8,721	7,733	7,733	7,991	7,991	8,249	8,249	97,736
Printing costs	0	0	38,188	16,450	12,338	12,338	12,338	12,338	12,338	12,338	12,338	12,338	165,675
Salaries	5,114	5,114	5,476	5,114	5,114	5,476	5,114	5,114	5,476	5,114	5,114	5,476	62,822
Article fees etc	0	3,995	3,995	3,995	3,995	3,995	3,995	3,995	3,995	3,995	3,995	3,995	43,945
DIRECT COSTS	5,114	59,326	36,748	31,414	30,168	29,542	29,180	29,438	29,800	29,695	29,695	30,057	370,178
Salary & Wages	4,700	4,700	5,249	4,700	4,700	4,700	4,700	4,700	5,249	4,700	4,700	5,249	58,594
Other indirect office costs	2,827	2,567	1,645	1,645	1,645	1,645	1,645	1,645	1,645	1,645	1,645	1,645	22,767
Promotion budget	0	59,486	37,013	21,002	7,050	7,050	9,400	7,050	7,050	9,400	7,050	7,050	178,600
INDIRECT COSTS	7,527	66,752	43,907	27,347	13,395	13,944	15,745	14,317	13,944	15,745	13,395	13,944	259,961
Royalty fee				1,498	38		791			791			3,119
EXPENDITURE CASH FLOW	12,641	126,079	80,655	60,259	43,601	43,486	45,716	43,755	43,744	46,231	43,090	44,002	633,258
NET OPERATING CASH FLOW	−12,641	−116,704	−12,192	4,170	15,509	9,711	3,090	5,052	6,208	3,721	8,007	7,096	−78,973
Equipment expenditure	14,100												14,100
Bank Loan repayments		2,500	2,500	2,500	2,500	2,500	2,500	2,500	2,500	2,500	2,500	2,500	27,500
TOTAL NET CASH FLOW per month	−26,741	−119,204	−14,692	1,670	13,009	7,211	590	2,552	3,708	1,221	5,507	4,596	−120,573
Cumulative Cash Flow	−26,741	−145,945	−160,637	−158,967	−145,958	−138,746	−138,156	−135,605	−131,897	−130,676	−125,168	−120,573	
FINANCING:													
Investors cash advanced	125,000	0	0	0	0	0	0	0	0	0	0	0	125,000
Bank Loan	60,000	0	0	0	0	0	0	0	0	0	0	0	60,000
Net Cash Flow cumulative	158,259	39,055	24,363	26,033	39,042	46,254	46,844	49,395	53,103	54,324	59,832	64,427	
Bank facility outstanding	60,000	57,500	55,000	52,500	50,000	47,500	45,000	42,500	40,000	37,500	35,000	32,500	
Net borrowing (−)/Funds in hand (+)	98,259	−18,445	−30,637	−26,467	−10,958	−1,246	−1,844	6,895	13,103	16,824	24,832	31,927	
BALANCE SHEET													
Fixed Assets: Office/other Equipment	12,000	12,000	12,000	12,000	12,000	12,000	12,000	12,000	12,000	12,000	12,000	12,000	12,000
Less Depreciation @ 25%	250	500	750	1,000	1,250	1,500	1,750	2,000	2,250	2,500	2,750	3,000	3,000
Net Book Value	11,750	11,500	11,250	11,000	10,750	10,500	10,250	10,000	9,750	9,500	9,250	9,000	9,000
Current Assets: Debtors	65,071	128,639	119,522	126,896	111,416	101,015	109,194	103,298	96,741	104,055	96,009	87,938	64,427
Cash at Bank	158,259	39,055	24,363	26,033	39,042	46,254	46,844	49,395	53,103	54,324	59,832	64,427	64,427
Less Current Liabilities: Creditors	−96,764	−58,114	−40,257	−27,322	−26,481	−28,481	−26,701	−26,701	−28,920	−26,920	−26,920	−28,920	−28,920
Net Current Assets	126,566	109,581	103,628	125,607	123,977	118,787	129,337	125,993	120,924	131,459	128,921	123,445	123,445
EMPLOYMENT OF CAPITAL	138,316	121,081	114,878	136,607	134,727	129,287	139,587	135,993	130,674	140,959	138,171	132,445	132,445
Bank Loan	60,000	57,500	55,000	52,500	50,000	47,500	45,000	42,500	40,000	37,500	35,000	32,500	32,500
Shareholders Funds	125,000	125,000	125,000	125,000	125,000	125,000	125,000	125,000	125,000	125,000	125,000	125,000	125,000
Profit and Loss Account	−46,684	−61,419	−65,122	−40,893	−40,273	−43,213	−30,413	−31,507	−34,326	−21,541	−21,829	−25,055	−25,055
CAPITAL EMPLOYED	138,316	121,081	114,878	136,607	134,727	129,287	139,587	135,993	130,674	140,959	138,171	132,445	132,445
Creative Director	2,203	2,203	2,254	2,203	2,203	2,203	2,203	2,203	2,254	2,203	2,203	2,254	26,645
Graphics Editor	1,829	1,829	1,870	1,829	1,829	1,829	1,829	1,829	1,870	1,829	1,829	1,870	22,117
Marketing Manager	1,081	1,081	1,352	1,081	1,081	1,081	1,081	1,081	1,352	1,081	1,081	1,352	14,059

APPENDIX e
Sheet Two

CASH FLOW — BUDGET YEAR TWO

NEW MAGAZINE LIMITED	Month 1	Month 2	Month 3	Month 4	Month 5	Month 6	Month 7	Month 8	Month 9	Month 10	Month 11	Month 12	Year Two
REVENUE:													
Retail sales	13,125	13,125	13,125	13,125	13,125	13,125	13,125	13,125	13,125	13,125	13,125	13,125	157,500
Advertising sales	36,660	36,660	42,770	42,770	42,770	42,770	42,770	42,770	47,499	47,499	47,499	47,499	519,938
Subscriptions	1,313	1,313	1,313	1,313	1,313	1,313	1,313	1,313	1,313	1,313	1,313	1,313	15,750
REVENUE CASH FLOW	51,098	51,098	57,208	57,208	57,208	57,208	57,208	57,208	61,937	61,937	61,937	61,937	693,188
EXPENDITURE:													
Advertising commission	8,249	10,693	10,693	10,693	10,693	10,693	10,693	11,875	11,875	11,875	11,875	11,875	131,778
Printing costs	12,338	14,100	14,100	14,100	14,100	14,100	14,100	14,100	14,100	14,100	14,100	14,100	167,438
Salaries	5,330	5,330	5,709	5,330	5,330	5,709	5,330	5,330	5,709	5,330	5,330	5,709	65,475
Article fees etc	3,995	5,875	5,875	5,875	5,875	5,875	5,875	5,875	5,875	5,875	5,875	5,875	68,620
DIRECT COSTS	29,911	35,997	36,377	35,997	35,997	36,377	35,997	37,180	37,559	37,180	37,180	37,559	433,310
Salary & Wages	4,896	4,896	5,464	4,896	4,896	5,464	4,896	4,896	5,464	4,896	4,896	5,464	61,021
Other indirect office costs	1,857	2,914	1,857	1,857	1,857	1,857	1,857	2,914	1,857	1,857	1,857	1,857	24,393
Promotion budget	9,400	28,200	7,050	9,400	7,050	7,050	9,400	7,050	7,050	9,400	7,050	7,050	115,150
INDIRECT COSTS	16,152	36,010	14,370	16,152	13,802	14,370	16,152	14,860	14,370	16,152	13,802	14,370	200,564
Royalty fee	0	0	0	923	0	0	1,105	91	0	1,138	148	0	3,405
EXPENDITURE CASH FLOW	46,063	72,007	50,747	53,072	49,800	50,747	53,255	52,131	51,929	54,471	51,130	51,929	637,280
NET OPERATING CASH FLOW	5,034	-20,910	6,461	4,135	7,408	6,461	3,953	5,077	10,008	7,466	10,807	10,008	55,908
Equipment expenditure	0	0	0	0	0	0	0	0	0	0	0	0	0
Bank Loan repayments	2,500	2,500	2,500	2,500	2,500	2,500	2,500	2,500	2,500	2,500	2,500	2,500	30,000
TOTAL NET CASH FLOW per month	2,534	-23,410	3,961	1,635	4,908	3,961	1,453	2,577	7,508	4,966	8,307	7,508	25,908
Cumulative Cash Flow	-118,038	-141,448	-137,487	-135,852	-130,944	-126,983	-125,530	-122,954	-115,446	-110,479	-102,173	-94,665	
DISTRIBUTIONS:													
Investors Dividend	0	0	0	0	0	0	0	0	0	0	0	0	0
Bank Loan	0	0	0	0	0	0	0	0	0	0	0	0	0
Net Cash Flow cumulative	66,962	43,552	47,513	49,148	54,056	58,017	59,470	62,046	69,554	74,521	82,827	90,335	
Bank facility outstanding	30,000	27,500	25,000	22,500	20,000	17,500	15,000	12,500	10,000	7,500	5,000	2,500	
Net borrowing (-)/Funds in hand (+)	36,962	16,052	22,513	26,648	34,056	40,517	44,470	49,546	59,554	67,021	77,827	87,835	
BALANCE SHEET													
Fixed Assets: Office/other Equipment	12,000	12,000	12,000	12,000	12,000	12,000	12,000	12,000	12,000	12,000	12,000	12,000	12,000
Less Depreciation @ 25%	3,188	3,375	3,563	3,750	3,938	4,125	4,313	4,500	4,688	4,875	5,063	5,250	6,750
Net Book Value	8,813	8,625	8,438	8,250	8,063	7,875	7,688	7,500	7,313	7,125	6,938	6,750	6,750
Current Assets: Debtors	93,994	95,504	87,617	96,590	88,745	80,920	94,026	90,615	82,324	91,455	83,228	74,999	74,999
Cash at Bank	66,962	43,552	47,513	49,148	54,056	58,017	59,470	62,046	69,554	74,521	82,827	90,335	90,335
Less Current Liabilities: Creditors	-50,100	-32,100	-34,100	-32,100	-32,100	-34,100	-33,106	-35,106	-35,106	-33,106	-33,106	-35,106	-35,106
Net Current Assets	110,855	106,956	101,030	113,638	110,701	104,836	120,389	119,555	116,772	132,869	132,949	130,228	130,228
EMPLOYMENT OF CAPITAL	119,668	115,581	109,467	121,888	118,763	112,711	128,077	127,055	124,085	139,994	139,886	136,978	136,978
Bank Loan	30,000	27,500	25,000	22,500	20,000	17,500	15,000	12,500	10,000	7,500	5,000	2,500	2,500
Shareholders Funds	125,000	125,000	125,000	125,000	125,000	125,000	125,000	125,000	125,000	125,000	125,000	125,000	125,000
Profit and Loss Account	-35,332	-36,919	-40,533	-25,612	-26,237	-29,789	-11,923	-10,445	-10,915	7,494	9,886	9,478	9,478
CAPITAL EMPLOYED	119,668	115,581	109,467	121,888	118,763	112,711	128,077	127,055	124,085	139,994	139,886	136,978	136,978
Creative Director	2,292	2,292	2,345	2,292	2,292	2,345	2,292	2,292	2,345	2,292	2,292	2,345	27,711
Graphics Editor	1,903	1,903	1,945	1,903	1,903	1,945	1,903	1,903	1,945	1,903	1,903	1,945	23,001
Marketing Manager	1,136	1,136	1,419	1,136	1,136	1,419	1,136	1,136	1,419	1,136	1,136	1,419	14,762

175

APPENDIX e
Sheet Three

NEW MAGAZINE LIMITED

CASH FLOW / BUDGET YEAR THREE

	Month 1	Month 2	Month 3	Month 4	Month 5	Month 6	Month 7	Month 8	Month 9	Month 10	Month 11	Month 12	Year Three
REVENUE:													
Retail sales	13,125	13,125	13,125	13,125	13,125	13,125	13,125	13,125	13,125	13,125	13,125	13,125	157,500
Advertising sales	47,499	47,499	56,180	56,180	56,180	56,180	56,180	56,180	65,800	65,800	65,800	65,800	695,277
Subscriptions	1,313	1,313	1,313	1,313	1,313	1,313	1,313	1,313	1,313	1,313	1,313	1,313	15,750
REVENUE CASH FLOW	61,937	61,937	70,617	70,617	70,617	70,617	70,617	70,617	80,238	80,238	80,238	80,238	868,527
EXPENDITURE:													
Advertising commission	11,875	14,045	14,045	14,045	14,045	14,045	14,045	16,450	16,450	16,450	16,450	16,450	178,394
Printing costs	14,100	15,863	15,863	15,863	15,863	15,863	15,863	15,863	15,863	15,863	15,863	15,863	188,588
Salaries	5,498	5,498	5,881	5,498	5,498	5,881	5,498	5,498	5,881	5,498	5,498	5,881	67,504
Article fees etc	5,875	5,875	5,875	5,875	5,875	5,875	5,875	5,875	5,875	5,875	5,875	5,875	70,500
DIRECT COSTS	37,348	41,280	41,663	41,280	41,280	41,663	41,280	43,685	44,068	43,685	43,685	44,068	504,986
Salary & Wages	5,041	5,041	5,612	5,041	5,041	5,612	5,041	5,041	5,612	5,041	5,041	5,612	62,776
Other indirect office costs	1,857	2,914	1,857	1,857	1,857	1,857	1,857	2,914	1,857	1,857	1,857	1,857	24,393
Promotion budget	9,400	18,800	7,050	9,400	7,050	7,050	9,400	7,050	7,050	9,400	7,050	7,050	105,750
INDIRECT COSTS	16,297	26,755	14,519	16,297	13,947	14,519	16,297	15,005	14,519	16,297	13,947	14,519	192,919
Royalty fee	61	317	196	1,398	311	137	1,768	619	498	1,814	671	498	8,287
EXPENDITURE CASH FLOW	53,706	68,352	56,378	58,975	55,538	56,319	59,345	59,309	59,085	61,797	58,304	59,085	706,191
NET OPERATING CASH FLOW	8,231	-6,415	14,240	11,642	15,079	14,298	11,272	11,309	21,153	18,441	21,933	21,153	162,335
Equipment expenditure	0	0	0	0	0	0	0	0	0	0	0	0	0
Bank Loan repayments	2,500	2,500	2,500	2,500	2,500	2,500	2,500	2,500	2,500	2,500	2,500	2,500	30,000
TOTAL NET CASH FLOW per month	5,731	-8,915	11,740	9,142	12,579	11,798	8,772	8,809	18,653	15,941	19,433	18,653	132,335
Cumulative Cash Flow	-88,934	-97,848	-86,109	-76,967	-64,388	-52,589	-43,818	-35,009	-16,356	-416	19,018	37,671	
DISTRIBUTIONS:													
Investors Dividend	0	0	0	0	0	0	0	0	0	0	0	-125,000	
Bank Loan	0	0	0	0	0	0	0	0	0	0	0	0	
Net Cash Flow cumulative	96,066	87,152	98,891	108,033	120,612	132,411	141,182	149,991	168,644	184,584	204,018	97,671	
Bank facility outstanding	0	0	0	0	0	0	0	0	0	0	0	0	
Net borrowing (-)/Funds in hand (+)	96,066	87,152	98,891	108,033	120,612	132,411	141,182	149,991	168,644	184,584	204,018	97,671	
BALANCE SHEET													
Fixed Assets: Office/other Equipment	12,000	12,000	12,000	12,000	12,000	12,000	12,000	12,000	12,000	12,000	12,000	12,000	
Less Depreciation @ 25%	3,188	3,375	3,563	3,750	3,938	4,125	4,313	4,500	4,688	4,875	5,063	5,250	
Net Book Value	8,813	8,625	8,438	8,250	8,063	7,875	7,688	7,500	7,313	7,125	6,938	6,750	
Current Assets: Debtors	77,038	81,258	74,873	86,523	79,156	71,763	91,812	93,192	84,777	96,358	87,969	79,555	
Cash at Bank	96,066	87,152	98,891	108,033	120,612	132,411	141,182	149,991	168,644	184,584	204,018	97,671	
Less Current Liabilities: Creditors	-46,453	-38,453	-36,453	-36,453	-38,453	-38,453	-38,500	-38,500	-40,500	-38,500	-38,500	-40,500	
Net Current Assets	126,652	131,957	135,311	158,103	163,315	165,720	194,494	204,683	212,921	242,443	253,487	136,726	
EMPLOYMENT OF CAPITAL	135,464	140,582	143,749	166,353	171,377	173,595	202,182	212,183	220,234	249,568	260,425	143,476	
Bank Loan	0	0	0	0	0	0	0	0	0	0	0	0	
Shareholders Funds	125,000	125,000	125,000	125,000	125,000	125,000	125,000	125,000	125,000	125,000	125,000	125,000	
Profit and Loss Account	10,464	15,582	18,749	41,353	46,377	48,595	77,182	87,183	95,234	124,568	135,425	18,476	
CAPITAL EMPLOYED	135,464	140,582	143,749	166,353	171,377	173,595	202,182	212,183	220,234	249,568	260,425	143,476	
Creative Director	2,383	2,383	2,438	2,383	2,383	2,438	2,383	2,383	2,438	2,383	2,383	2,438	28,820
Graphics Editor	1,979	1,979	2,023	1,979	1,979	2,023	1,979	1,979	2,023	1,979	1,979	2,023	23,922
Marketing Manager	1,136	1,136	1,419	1,136	1,136	1,419	1,136	1,136	1,419	1,136	1,136	1,419	14,762

Appendix f – Profit Sensitivities

A number of different operating scenarios have been calculated from the base model (Example 1) after month 3, together with their effect on trading results. These are:

Examples	Print run	Retail sales	Advert pages	Advert space filled	Promotion budget: Weekly	Mths 13–25
1 (base)	30,000	10,500	14.5 – 17.5	60–80%	£1,500	£40,000
2	30,000	10,500	14.5 – 17.5	100%	£1,500	£40,000
3	30,000	10,500	14.5 – 17.5	80%	£1,500	£40,000
4	30,000	8,000	14.5	80%	£1,500	£40,000
5	30,000	8,000	14.5	60%	£1,500	£40,000
6	20,000	8,000	14.5	60%	£1,500	£40,000
7	20,000	8,000	14.0	60%	£1,500	£40,000
8	20,000	8,000	14.0	60%	£1,000	Nil

Profit (+) or Loss (-) projections before tax

Example	Year One £'000	Year Two £'000	Year Three £'000
1 (base)	– 25	+ 34	+ 134
2	+ 125	+ 205	+ 268
3	+ 42	+ 100	+ 148
4	+ 18	+ 60	+ 109
5	– 60	– 45	– 10
6	– 30	– 5	+ 33
7	– 52	– 48	– 34
8	– 34	– 10	– 4

The first major assumption has been to write down the projections of advertising space filled by the percentages shown. This is a conservative contingency in case the forecast advertising response proves to be optimistic in any way. Were the agency selling the advertising space to be proved correct, the profits would be shown as in Example 2. Example 3 gives a mid-way drop in advertising revenue expectations, and is then modified in Example 4 for (24%) lower retail copies sold.

Example 5 takes the assumptions given in the previous example but drops the advertising space back to a more conservative 60% figure. In practice, if retail sales drop, then the print run would be lowered, as is shown by Example 6, and possibly the number of advertised pages may be curtailed as well (Example 7). Finally, if these very much lowered trading scenarios did occur, the management would be expected to reduce the future promotion budget to conserve expenditure and an idea of this result is projected in Example 8, which shows that even on this extreme case a near break-even position by Year Three. Twin Wheeler wishes to emphasise that it is very unlikely that all the forecast returns will be missed to the degree shown and he is confident the business can ride out any temporary difficulty.

Appendix B

Spreadsheet Example

A BUSINESS A manufacturing concern that, for simplification, has one staple product and is about to increase production by purchasing new equipment (the project). **Sheet 1**

General Guidelines:

Sheet 1 provides the underlying assumptions of the model.
Sheet 2 displays on a monthly basis the results for the previous year 2000.
Sheet 3 displays the trading projections for the ensuing year 2001 based on the monthly seasonality indicated by Sheet 1.
Sheet 4 displays the actual results for the year 2001 (it is assumed that the present time is January 2002).
Sheet 5 displays the Balance Sheets of the business at the beginning and end of year 2001.

NOTES TO SHEET 2: CASH FLOW

1 Sales are those invoiced two months earlier based on the principle that January invoicing will be done in February and the cash received in March (credit allowed being at least 30 days after the month end).
2 VAT on sales relates to sales invoiced in the month.
3 Labour costs are the wages of the month in question.
4 Other costs from March 2000 comprise materials costs of the month in question with no supplier credit and Fixed Other Costs of two months earlier (assumed when the bills were paid).
5 VAT has been assumed as averaging 80% of standard rate on the costs of that month (refer note 4).
6 The Net VAT payable is the amount irrecoverable from sales for the preceding three months (on Outputs less Inputs) and paid one month after each quarter's end.
7 The capital expenditure figure for new plant has been assumed. Note that the VAT payment in October 2000 has accounted for the VAT incurred in July on the equipment.
8 The loan repayments comprise a total of interest and principal each month.
9 The Corporation tax liability has been assumed as stated and paid in the months shown.
10 The profit distribution (dividend) figure has been assumed as stated.

NOTES TO SHEET 3: PROFIT AND LOSS ACCOUNT

11 Seasonal variations in monthly sales (and thus production) have been allowed by allocating the projected total annual production monthly in proportion to that achieved from the old plant in the previous year.
12 The unit output per month is the projected annual total from both the old and new plant that is required by the sales budget multiplied by the monthly percentage production.
13 A new price has been set for the year 2001 and, for simplicity, has been taken at the same value per unit for items produced by both the old and new plants.
14 The variable labour cost is calculated by multiplying estimated employee numbers by their average annual cost to the business (including Employer's NI and pension) and spread monthly in 4 or 5 weekly periods.
15 The number of employees includes additional labour to work the new plant.
16 Employee costs include a 3% wage rise at the beginning of the year based on the wage bill for December 2000.
17 Materials costs have been calculated by multiplying the forecast quantity of output by the expected average cost per item of components per unit produced.
18 Fixed labour costs have also allowed for the number of weeks in each month that wages will be paid.
19 Other fixed costs have been assumed and in practice will be separately estimated for each cost centre.
20 For cash flow assumptions refer to Notes 1 through to 10 above.

NOTES TO SHEET 4: PROFIT AND LOSS ACCOUNT/CASH FLOW

21 The example has assumed that sales did not materialise as well as expected from April 2001 and the business accordingly cut its selling prices and started to reduce output from June 2001.
When sales did not recover to the original levels expected the business started to lay off workers until December.
The variable materials average cost per item has changed according to the (assumed) ruling market prices.
Because of the projected strong cash flow the business had scheduled to repay the loan early in August 2001. When the cash position started to deteriorate the early repayment idea was abandoned.
The business found it possible to reduce slightly its fixed labour costs but underestimated its other fixed overheads.
Note the differences between the monthly Operating Results and Net Cash In/Outflows. For the year as a whole the Pretax Profit was double the Net Cash Inflow.

179

Sheet 2

A BUSINESS — PROFIT AND LOSS ACCOUNT — Year 2000

All columns are "Actual".

PROFIT AND LOSS ACCOUNT	January	February	March	April	May	June	July	August	September	October	November	December	YEAR
OUTPUT (quantity)	114,985	113,031	98,640	87,120	109,890	99,000	107,250	125,400	125,400	125,400	125,400	125,400	1,356,916
PRICE (per item)	1.65	1.65	1.65	1.65	1.65	1.65	1.73	1.73	1.73	1.73	1.73	1.73	1.69
New Plant Output (quantity)	0	0	0	0	0	0	9,200	14,600	19,300	24,600	24,600	24,600	116,900
Price (per item)	0	0	0	0	0	0	1.50	1.50	1.50	1.50	1.50	1.50	1.50
Total TURNOVER (£)	189,725	186,501	162,756	143,748	181,319	163,350	199,611	239,156	246,206	254,156	254,156	254,156	2,474,837
COSTS													
Variable Labour	57,810	61,880	63,427	54,177	55,532	56,920	61,844	65,782	67,426	69,112	70,840	72,611	757,361
number employed	50	50	50	50	50	50	50	53	55	60	60	60	54
average cost per capita	13,874	14,851	15,222	13,002	13,328	13,661	14,002	14,352	13,485	13,822	14,168	14,522	14,025
Materials etc	59,680	48,940	46,880	47,574	49,708	50,499	56,527	63,246	69,761	76,951	76,647	76,311	722,725
average per item produced	0.52	0.43	0.48	0.55	0.45	0.49	0.49	0.48	0.45	0.51	0.51	0.51	0.49
Total	117,490	110,820	110,307	101,751	105,240	107,419	118,371	129,028	137,187	146,063	147,487	148,922	1,480,086
Fixed Labour	5,920	5,920	5,920	5,920	5,920	5,920	5,920	5,920	5,920	5,920	5,920	5,920	71,040
Other	36,240	35,670	36,562	30,000	30,750	31,519	32,307	33,114	33,942	34,791	35,661	36,552	407,107
Depreciation	5,354	5,354	5,354	5,354	5,354	5,354	5,884	5,884	5,884	5,884	5,884	5,884	67,428
Total	47,514	46,944	47,836	41,274	42,024	42,793	44,111	44,918	45,746	46,595	47,465	48,356	545,575
Combined Total costs	165,004	157,764	158,143	143,025	147,264	150,212	162,482	173,947	182,933	192,658	194,951	197,278	2,025,661
OPERATING RESULT before tax	24,721	28,737	4,613	723	34,055	13,138	37,129	65,209	63,272	61,497	59,204	56,877	449,176

CASH FLOW

CASH FLOW	Notes	January	February	March	April	May	June	July	August	September	October	November	December	YEAR
SALES (Outputs)	1	180,000	180,000	189,725	186,501	162,756	143,748	181,319	163,350	199,611	239,156	246,206	254,156	2,326,526
VAT @ 17.5%	2	33,202	32,638	33,202	32,638	28,482	25,156	31,731	28,586	34,932	41,852	43,086	44,477	465,305
TURNOVER INFLOW		213,202	212,638	222,927	219,139	191,238	168,904	213,049	191,936	234,542	281,008	289,291	298,633	2,791,831
COSTS: Labour	3	63,730	67,800	69,347	60,097	61,452	62,840	67,764	71,702	73,346	75,032	76,760	78,531	828,401
Other	4	95,680	83,940	83,120	83,244	86,270	80,499	87,277	94,765	102,068	110,066	110,589	111,102	1,128,619
Add VAT @ 17.5% on costs	5	15,540	15,484	13,638	13,198	13,444	12,899	13,142	14,305	15,591	16,844	18,218	18,284	180,588
net VAT payable	6				50,644		45,590				63,054			159,288
EXPENDITURE OUTFLOW		174,950	167,224	166,105	207,183	161,166	156,238	213,773	180,772	191,005	264,996	205,567	207,917	2,296,896
GROSS OPERATING INFLOW		38,252	45,414	56,822	11,956	30,073	12,666	-724	11,164	43,538	16,012	83,724	90,716	439,612
CAPITAL EXPENDITURE (incl VAT)	7	0	0	0	0	0	0	57,400	0	0	0	0	0	57,400
LOAN repayments	8	8,000	8,000	8,000	8,000	8,000	8,000	8,000	8,000	8,000	8,000	8,000	8,000	96,000
TAXATION payable	9	0	0	0	0	0	0	0	0	80,000	0	0	0	80,000
DISTRIBUTION of profit	10	0	0	120,000	0	0	0	0	0	0	0	0	0	120,000
NET CASH INFLOW		30,252	37,414	-71,178	3,956	22,073	4,666	-66,124	3,164	-44,462	8,012	75,724	82,716	86,212
CASH in hand brought forward		25,000	55,252	92,666	21,488	25,443	47,516	52,182	-13,942	-10,777	-55,240	-47,228	28,496	
CASH in hand carried forward		55,252	92,666	21,488	25,443	47,516	52,182	-13,942	-10,777	-55,240	-47,228	28,496	111,212	

A BUSINESS
PROFIT AND LOSS ACCOUNT

Year 2001	Notes	Projected January	Projected February	Projected March	Projected April	Projected May	Projected June	Projected July	Projected August	Projected September	Projected October	Projected November	Projected December	Projected YEAR
percent of production (quantity)	11	8.47	8.33	7.27	6.42	8.10	7.30	7.90	9.24	9.24	9.24	9.24	9.24	100.00
OUTPUT	12	152,532	149,940	130,850	115,568	145,773	131,327	142,271	166,348	166,348	166,348	166,348	166,348	1,800,000
PRICE (per item)	13	1.75	1.75	1.75	1.75	1.75	1.75	1.75	1.75	1.75	1.75	1.75	1.75	1.75
														150,000
Total TURNOVER (£)		266,931	262,395	228,987	202,244	255,103	229,823	248,975	291,109	291,109	291,109	291,109	291,109	3,150,000
Wages weeks in month		5	4	4	5	4	4	5	4	4	5	4	4	
COSTS (£)														
Variable Labour	14	86,295	69,036	69,036	86,295	69,036	69,036	86,295	69,036	69,036	86,295	69,036	69,036	897,472
number employed	15	60	60	60	60	60	60	60	60	60	60	60	60	60
average cost per capita	16	14,958	14,958	14,958	14,958	14,958	14,958	14,958	14,958	14,958	14,958	14,958	14,958	14,958
Materials etc	17	83,893	82,467	71,967	63,562	80,175	72,230	78,249	91,491	91,491	91,491	91,491	91,491	990,000
average cost per item		0.55	0.55	0.55	0.55	0.55	0.55	0.55	0.55	0.55	0.55	0.55	0.55	0.55
Total		170,188	151,503	141,004	149,858	149,212	141,266	164,545	160,528	160,528	177,787	160,528	160,528	1,887,472
Fixed Labour	18	6,098	6,098	6,098	6,098	6,098	6,098	6,098	6,098	6,098	6,098	6,098	6,098	73,176
Other – per Budget	19	42,000	37,000	40,000	39,000	41,000	38,000	39,000	35,000	39,000	40,000	37,000	35,000	462,000
Depreciation		5,884	5,884	5,884	5,884	5,884	5,884	5,884	5,884	5,884	5,884	5,884	5,884	70,608
Total		53,982	48,982	51,982	50,982	52,982	49,982	50,982	46,982	50,982	51,982	48,982	46,982	605,784
Combined Total costs		224,170	200,485	192,986	200,840	202,194	191,248	215,527	207,510	211,510	229,769	209,510	207,510	2,493,256
OPERATING RESULT before tax		42,761	61,910	36,001	1,404	52,910	38,574	33,448	83,599	79,599	61,340	81,599	83,599	656,744

CASH FLOW

	Notes 20	Projected January	Projected February	Projected March	Projected April	Projected May	Projected June	Projected July	Projected August	Projected September	Projected October	Projected November	Projected December	Projected YEAR
SALES (Outputs)		254,156	254,156	266,931	262,395	228,987	202,244	255,103	229,823	248,975	291,109	291,109	291,109	3,076,094
VAT @ 17.5%		44,477	44,477	46,713	45,919	40,073	35,393	44,643	40,219	43,571	50,944	50,944	50,944	615,219
TURNOVER INFLOW		298,633	298,633	313,644	308,314	269,060	237,637	299,746	270,042	292,545	342,053	342,053	342,053	3,691,312
COSTS: Labour		92,393	75,134	75,134	92,393	75,134	75,134	92,393	75,134	75,134	92,393	75,134	75,134	970,648
Other		119,553	119,019	113,967	100,562	120,175	111,230	119,249	129,491	130,491	126,491	130,491	131,491	1,452,213
Add VAT @ 17.5% on costs		18,347	19,798	20,312	17,774	16,723	19,491	18,380	19,014	21,471	20,911	21,471	21,611	235,303
net VAT payable		76,938	0	0	72,938	0	0	64,610	0	0	82,558	0	0	297,044
EXPENDITURE OUTFLOW		307,231	213,952	209,413	283,668	212,033	208,855	294,633	223,639	227,097	322,354	227,097	228,237	2,955,208
GROSS OPERATING INFLOW		-8,599	84,681	104,230	24,646	57,027	31,782	5,113	46,402	65,448	19,699	114,956	113,816	659,202

		Projected January	Projected February	Projected March	Projected April	Projected May	Projected June	Projected July	Projected August	Projected September	Projected October	Projected November	Projected December	Projected YEAR
CAPITAL EXPENDITURE (incl VAT)		0	0	0	0	0	0	0	0	0	0	0	0	0
LOAN repayments		8,000	8,000	8,000	8,000	8,000	8,000	8,000	96,000	0	0	0	0	152,000
TAXATION payable		0	0	0	0	0	0	0	0	89,835	0	0	0	89,835
DISTRIBUTION of profit		0	0	180,000	0	0	0	0	0	0	0	0	0	180,000
NET CASH INFLOW		-16,599	76,681	-83,770	16,646	49,027	23,782	-2,887	-49,598	-24,387	19,699	114,956	113,816	237,367
CASH in hand brought forward		111,212	94,613	171,294	87,524	104,170	153,197	176,978	174,092	124,494	100,108	119,807	234,763	
CASH in hand carried forward		94,613	171,294	87,524	104,170	153,197	176,978	174,092	124,494	100,108	119,807	234,763	348,579	

A BUSINESS

PROFIT AND LOSS ACCOUNT

Year 2001

	Notes	Actual January	Actual February	Actual March	Actual April	Actual May	Actual June	Actual July	Actual August	Actual September	Actual October	Actual November	Actual December	Actual YEAR
BUDGETED SALES (£)	21	266,931	262,395	228,987	202,244	255,103	229,823	248,975	291,109	291,109	291,109	291,109	291,109	3,150,000
PRICE (per item)		1.75	1.75	1.75	1.75	1.75	1.65	1.65	1.65	1.65	1.65	1.65	1.65	1.69
Units sold (number)		122,857	125,714	114,286	102,857	114,286	115,152	133,333	127,273	133,333	139,394	127,273	124,242	1,480,000
OUTPUT (quantity)		150,000	150,000	150,000	150,000	150,000	140,000	140,000	130,000	120,000	100,000	100,000	90,000	1,570,000
ACTUAL SALES (£)		**215,000**	**220,000**	**200,000**	**180,000**	**200,000**	**190,000**	**220,000**	**210,000**	**220,000**	**230,000**	**210,000**	**205,000**	**2,500,000**
COSTS														
Variable Labour		74,789	74,789	74,789	74,789	74,789	74,789	74,789	74,789	74,789	74,789	74,789	62,324	885,007
number employed		60	60	60	60	60	60	60	60	60	60	60	50	59
average cost per capita		14,958	14,958	14,958	14,958	14,958	14,958	14,958	14,958	14,958	14,958	14,958	14,958	15,450
Materials etc		82,500	82,500	84,000	84,000	84,000	77,000	75,600	78,000	72,000	60,000	60,000	54,000	893,600
average cost per item		0.55	0.55	0.56	0.56	0.56	0.55	0.54	0.60	0.60	0.60	0.60	0.60	0.57
Total		157,289	157,289	158,789	158,789	158,789	151,789	150,389	152,789	146,789	134,789	134,789	116,324	1,778,607
Fixed Labour		7,036	5,628	5,628	7,036	5,628	5,628	6,267	5,013	5,013	6,267	5,013	5,013	69,170
Other – per Budget		42,000	37,000	40,000	39,000	41,000	38,000	42,000	39,000	41,000	40,000	38,000	38,000	475,000
Depreciation		5,884	5,884	5,884	5,884	5,884	5,884	5,884	5,884	5,884	5,884	5,884	5,884	70,608
Total		54,920	48,512	51,512	51,920	52,512	49,512	54,151	49,897	51,897	52,151	48,897	48,897	614,778
Combined Total costs		212,209	205,801	210,301	210,709	211,301	201,301	204,540	202,686	198,686	186,940	183,686	165,221	2,393,385
OPERATING RESULT before tax		**2,791**	**14,199**	**-10,301**	**-30,709**	**-11,301**	**-11,301**	**15,460**	**7,314**	**21,314**	**43,060**	**26,314**	**39,779**	**106,615**

CASH FLOW

Year 2001

	Actual January	Actual February	Actual March	Actual April	Actual May	Actual June	Actual July	Actual August	Actual September	Actual October	Actual November	Actual December	Actual YEAR
SALES (Outputs)	291,109	291,109	215,000	220,000	200,000	180,000	200,000	190,000	220,000	210,000	220,000	230,000	2,667,217
VAT @ 17.5%	50,944	50,944	37,625	38,500	35,000	31,500	35,000	33,250	38,500	36,750	38,500	40,250	533,443
TURNOVER INFLOW	**342,053**	**342,053**	**252,625**	**258,500**	**235,000**	**211,500**	**235,000**	**223,250**	**258,500**	**246,750**	**258,500**	**270,250**	**3,200,661**
COSTS: Labour	81,825	80,417	80,417	81,825	80,417	80,417	81,056	79,802	79,802	81,056	79,802	67,337	954,177
Other	128,491	117,500	124,500	121,000	124,000	123,000	118,000	113,600	120,000	111,000	101,000	100,000	1,402,091
Add VAT @ 17.5% on costs	21,191	19,338	20,318	19,880	20,300	20,160	19,215	18,550	19,530	18,060	16,240	16,100	228,881
net VAT payable	87,894	0	0	49,490	0	0	39,025	0	0	55,755	0	0	232,164
EXPENDITURE OUTFLOW	**319,402**	**217,255**	**225,235**	**272,195**	**224,717**	**223,577**	**257,296**	**211,952**	**219,332**	**265,871**	**197,042**	**183,437**	**2,817,313**
GROSS OPERATING INFLOW	**22,651**	**124,798**	**27,390**	**-13,695**	**10,283**	**-12,077**	**-22,296**	**11,298**	**39,168**	**-19,121**	**61,458**	**86,813**	**316,667**

	Actual January	Actual February	Actual March	Actual April	Actual May	Actual June	Actual July	Actual August	Actual September	Actual October	Actual November	Actual December	Actual YEAR
CAPITAL EXPENDITURE (incl VAT)	0	0	0	0	0	0	0	0	0	0	0	0	0
LOAN repayments	8,000	8,000	8,000	8,000	8,000	8,000	8,000	8,000	8,000	8,000	8,000	8,000	96,000
TAXATION payable	0	0	0	0	0	0	0	0	89,835	0	0	0	89,835
DISTRIBUTION of profit	0	0	80,000	0	0	0	0	0	0	0	0	0	80,000
NET CASH INFLOW	**14,651**	**116,798**	**-60,610**	**-21,695**	**2,283**	**-20,077**	**-30,296**	**3,298**	**-58,667**	**-27,121**	**53,458**	**78,813**	**50,832**
CASH in hand brought forward	111,212	125,863	242,661	182,051	160,356	162,638	142,561	112,265	115,562	56,895	29,774	83,231	111,212
CASH in hand carried forward	125,863	242,661	182,051	160,356	162,638	142,561	112,265	115,562	56,895	29,774	83,231	162,044	162,044

A BUSINESS
BALANCE SHEETS
Year 2001

	Opening Position	Actual January	Actual February	Actual March	Actual April	Actual May	Actual June	Actual July	Actual August	Actual September	Actual October	Actual November	Actual December	Notes
FIXED ASSETS	150,000	150,000	150,000	150,000	150,000	150,000	150,000	150,000	150,000	150,000	150,000	150,000	150,000	1
Less Depreciation	50,000	55,884	61,768	67,652	73,536	79,420	85,304	91,188	97,072	102,956	108,840	114,724	120,608	
Net book value	100,000	94,116	88,232	82,348	76,464	70,580	64,696	58,812	52,928	47,044	41,160	35,276	29,392	
NET CURRENT ASSETS														
Stocks	100,483	91,491	82,500	82.5000	84,000	84,000	84,000	77,000	75,600	78,000	72,000	60,000	60,000	2
Trade Debtors (2 mths)	582,217	506,109	435,000	420,000	380,000	380,000	390,000	410,000	430,000	430,000	450,000	440,000	415,000	3
Cash at bank	111,212	125,863	242,661	182,051	160,356	162,638	142,561	112,265	115,562	56,895	29,774	83,231	162,044	4
	793,912	723,463	760,161	684,557	624,356	626,638	616,561	599,265	621,162	564,895	551,774	583,231	637,044	
Less:														
Trade Creditors (1 mth)	91,491	82,500	82,500	84,000	84,000	84,000	77,000	75,600	78,000	72,000	60,000	60,000	54,000	5
Other Creditors	152,000	160,454	166,187	88,195	98,974	100,115	97,330	87,724	83,018	76,970	67,319	54,849	57,330	6
VAT Creditor	87,894	17,308	36,190	49,490	11,340	25,900	39,025	19,390	37,030	55,755	24,150	45,080	64,855	7
Tax Creditor	89,835	90,393	93,233	91,173	85,031	82,770	80,510	83,602	85,065	-507	8,105	13,367	21,323	8
Bank Loan	152,000	144,000	136,000	128,000	120,000	112,000	104,000	96,000	88,000	80,000	72,000	64,000	56,000	9
Net Current Assets	220,691	228,808	246,051	243,693	225,011	221,853	218,696	236,948	250,049	280,677	320,200	345,935	383,536	
Employment of Capital	320,691	322,924	334,283	326,041	301,475	292,433	283,392	295,760	302,977	327,721	361,360	381,211	412,928	
SHARE CAPITAL	200,000	200,000	200,000	200,000	200,000	200,000	200,000	200,000	200,000	200,000	200,000	200,000	200,000	
RETAINED EARNINGS	120,691	122,924	134,283	46,042	21,474	12,433	3,392	15,760	21,611	38,662	73,110	94,161	125,983	10
Capital Employed	320,691	322,924	334,283	246,042	221,474	212,433	203,392	215,760	221,611	238,662	273,110	294,161	325,983	

NOTES TO SHEET 5: BALANCE SHEET

1 The opening fixed asset figure has been assumed.
2 Stocks have been calculated as the quantity purchased in the two previous trading months less the quantity utilised in the current trading month. The opening stocks have been assumed.
3 Trade Debtors have been taken as the sales achieved in the previous trading month and the current trading month.
4 Cash in hand accords with the cash flow shown as at end of each month.
5 Trade Creditors have been taken as the purchases made in the current trading month.
6 Other Creditors comprise Other Costs outstanding for the previous and current trading months together with other costs accrued due to cash flow timing differences in the model.
7 The VAT creditor is accumulated over each successive three months trading period before it is paid.
8 The Corporation Tax Creditor comprises the previous year's annual liability until paid and the cumulative monthly amounts accrued due at the rate of 20% on profits or losses.
9 The bank loan monthly repayments include interest but for simplicity these amounts have not been allowed for in the tax payable calculation.
10 Retained Earnings comprise the amount accrued to date together with the profit for each month less the Corporation tax due thereon.

check: The Operating Result for the year gave a profit before tax of £106,615   After deducting Corporation tax at 20%, retained earnings total £85,292   leaves a balance in
Retained earnings at the beginning of the year were £120,691   Adding retained earnings for the year and deducting the profit £80,000   hand at year end of   £125,983
distribution made in March of £162,044

check: The cash in hand carried forward as at the end of the year is £162,044   This is the same as the Net Cash Inflow for the year £50,832   plus cash in hand at the start   £111,212
of the year

183

Appendix C

Website References

The representative list following gives a number of references of Web addresses which the reader may access for further business information. No responsibility is taken for changes in the site address or content and the list is not exhaustive.

Government/National

For Grants/Awards/Assistance

www.dti.gov.uk	Department of Trade and Industry
www.patent.gov.uk	The Patent Office
www.nao.gov.uk	National Audit Office
www.parliament.uk/commons/selcom/pachome.htm	
	Public Accounts Committee
www.businessadviceonline.org.uk	Small Business Service
www.cec.org.uk	European Commission
www.euro.gov.uk	Euro information
www.oft.gov.uk	Office of Fair Trading (consumer credit)
www.londonstockexchange.com/aim	Alternative Investment Market (for smaller companies)
www.benchmarkindex.com	Performance benchmarking
www.princes-trust.org.uk	Charity assisting 18–30 year olds

For Taxation/Information

www.hm-treasury.gov.uk	The Treasury
www.inlandrevenue.gov.uk	Inland Revenue
www.payontime.co.uk	The Better Payment Practice Group

Commercial

For Finance/Investment/Advice/Information

www.bvca.co.uk	British Venture Capital Association

www.bnr.plc.uk	Business Names Register
www.britishchambers.org.uk	British Chambers of Commerce
www.fsb.org.uk	Federation of Small Businesses
www.british-franchise.org.uk	The British Franchise Association
www.cbi.org.uk	Confederation of British Industry
www.r3.org.co.uk	Society of Practitioners of Insolvency
www.icaew.co.uk	Institute of Chartered Accountants in England & Wales
www.cib.org.uk	Chartered Institute of Bankers
www.iba.org.uk	Institute of Business Advisers
www.inst-mgt.org.uk	Institute of Management
www.iod.co.uk	Institute of Directors

Taxation Checklist – How it will affect small businesses

The following references indicate pending legislation relating to small company and personal businesses that the Chancellor of the Exchequer has proposed in the recent March 2001 Budget. In all cases the references are general and specific reading of the legislation should be made. The proposals outlined are not an exhaustive list of all the Budget details.

From 1 April 2002 (companies) and **2002/03** year (non-corporates)

- **Company Corporation tax** rates are indicated to remain at 10% (starting rate up to £10,000 with marginal relief up to £50,000); 20% (small company rate from £50,000 up to £300,000 with marginal relief up to £1.5 million) and 30% (full company rate thereafter).

- **Personal income tax** rates are indicated to remain at 10% (lower rate up to £1,880); 22% (basic rate from £1,880 up to £29,400) and 40% (higher rate thereafter) with a 20% rate on certain interest income.

- **Capital Gains tax** rates generally are indicated to remain at 10%/20%/40% with taper relief. The personal exemption limit is indicated at £7,500.

- Car and van authorised mileage rates to be 40p per mile on first 10,000 miles and 25p thereafter. This may apply to holdings of at least 20% on reinvestment of the proceeds (rollover relief).

- Possible relief to apply on company gains on sale of substantial holdings.

- Subject to consultation, small businesses with a turnover of up to £100,000 will pay VAT at a (optional) lower flat rate as a percentage of turnover.

- A new Aggregates levy will be introduced of £1.60 per tonne.

From 1 December 2001

- A new scheme of vehicle excise duties for lorries will be introduced.

From October 2001

- National minimum wage to rise to £4.10 per hour (previously £3.70).

From 1 August 2001

- Zero VAT rate to apply on renovated houses empty for previous 10 years.

From the Royal Assent in 2001

- Capital Allowances on energy saving plant and machinery will be eligible for 100% First Year allowance. Property owners and occupiers will be eligible for 100% First Year allowance on unused space for conversion into flats for rent. Detailed rules of eligibility apply.

- Equipment lessors and lessees will not both be able to claim capital allowances on the same expenditure.

- Enhanced tax relief of 150% of the cost of cleaning up acquired contaminated land and to offset a remedial loss by a payment in lieu.

- VAT rate cut to 5% on renovating dwellings empty for 3 years or converting property into multiple dwelling accommodation or care home.

- Small Business Service to offer up to £2,000 to assist start-up businesses draw up a Business Plan.

- Small business borrowing costs to be cut through introduction of a new community investment tax credit and community development venture capital fund.

- Business and family relocation to selected urban areas will be exempt from property stamp duty.

From 6 April 2001

- Limited Liability Partnerships will be allowed. Detailed regulations will be raised.

- Companies may ask for advance qualifying clearance to administer an employee Enterprise Management Incentive Scheme. Details of the Scheme have been extended.

- Car fuel scale charges are slightly reduced for private motoring.

- Inheritance tax threshold rises to £242,000 (previously £234,000).

From 1 April 2001 (companies) and/or **2001/02** year (non-corporates)

- **Company Corporation tax** rates will remain at 10% (starting rate up to £10,000 with marginal relief up to £50,000); 20% (small company rate from £50,000 up to £300,000 with marginal relief up to £1.5 million) and 30% (full company rate thereafter).

- **Personal income tax** rates will remain at 10% (lower rate up to £1,520); 22% (basic rate from £1,520 up to £28,400) and 40% (higher rate thereafter) with a 20% rate on certain interest income.

- **Capital Gains tax** rates generally remain at 10%/20%/40% with taper relief. The personal exemption limit is £7,200.

- **VAT standard rate** remains at 17.5% with the registration limit £54,000 (previously £52,000).

- Withholding tax on UK-derived interest, royalties and other annual payments is abolished only where received by companies that are charged Corporation tax on that income.

- Allowable business gifts exemption to tax is raised from £10 to £50.

- Business assets capital gains taper relief to be allowed to employees holding up to 10% share of non-trading company.

- Employers may reimburse employees for use of own vehicle free of tax and national insurance up to the level of the authorised mileage rates.

- Amendments are made to the calculation of credit (on double taxation) relief under the onshore pooling rules.

- A consultation period is proposed to examine how small businesses might be allowed to align their profits calculated for tax purposes to those shown by their annual accounts.

- VAT zero rate to apply to transport seating 10 (previously 12) persons.

- VAT Cash Accounting scheme will be available to businesses with a turnover of up to £600,000 and where it is in use and the subsequent turnover of the business increases but does not exceed £750,000 annually.

From 8 March 2001

- VAT exemption limit on business gifts is raised from £15 to £50.

From 7 March 2001

- The Enterprise Investment Scheme rules are amended to allow companies to utilise 80% (previously 100%) of funds in the first year and for investors to receive investment benefits after one year (previously two years) and not to lose their tax benefit if the EIS company obtains a quotation at any time after their investment is made.

- Capital gains will not apply on investments by UK residents arising from interests of up to 10% in non-resident close companies (i.e. companies controlled by five or fewer contributors) or on assets used overseas in a trade overseas or gains from exempt approved pension schemes. There is an extended relief period available on any tax paid.

• Non-commercial transactions by controlled foreign companies to avoid tax on their acceptable distribution policy will not be allowed.

COMPANIES						
Fuel scale charges	Petrol/LPG To 1,400cc	Petrol/LPG 1,401– 2,000ccc	Petrol/LPG Over 2,000cc	Diesel To 2,000cc	Diesel Over 2,000cc	Cars without ccs
2001/02	£1,930	£2,460	£3,620	£2,460	£3,620	£3,620
2000/01	£1,700	£2,170	£3,200	£2,170	£3,200	£3,200
Authorised mileage rates	**First 4,000 miles**			**Over 4,000 miles**		
	To 1500cc	1501 to 2000cc	Over 2000cc	To 1500cc	1501 to 2000cc	Over 2000cc
2001/02	40p	45p	63p	25p	25p	36p
2000/01	35p*	45p	63p	20p +	25p	36p
	*28p up to 1000cc			+ 17p up to 1000cc		
From 6 April 2002	Cars/vans First 10,000 miles	Cars/vans Over 10,000 miles	Motorcycles	Bicycles		
Per mile	40p	25p	24p	20p		

NATIONAL INSURANCE	On Earnings		Class 1 Per week	Class 1A/1B	Class 2	Class 3	Class 4
Not contracted out	Employee contribs	2001/02	10% from £87 to £575				
		2000/01	10% from £76 to £535				
	Employer contribs	2001/02	11.9% from £87 to £575				
		2000/01	12.2% from £84 to £535				
Contracted out	Employee contribs	2001/02	8.4% ** from £87 to £575				
		2000/01	8.4% ** from £76 to £535				
	Employer contribs	2001/02	8.9% # from £87 to £575	11.9%	£2 per wk over £3,955	£6.75 per week	7% from £4,535 to £29,900
		2000/01	8.9% # from £84 to £535	12.2%	£2 per wk over £3,825	£6.55 per week	7% from £4,385 to £27,820

** *Also Employer rebate of 3% on earnings for salary related schemes (0.6% for money purchase schemes) from £72 to £87 (2000/01 from £67 to £76).*

Also Employee rebate of 1.6% on earnings from £72 to £87 (2000/01 from £67 to £76)

From 6 April 2000

- Capital gains taper relief on business assets will apply to employees (and trustees) holding not more than a 10% share in the company.

- Capital gains taper relief on the disposal of business assets will be allowed on shareholdings held by employees (limited to a 10% shareholding in respect of non-trading companies).

From 1 April 2000

- Authors and artists may average their profits over two years if profits of the lower year are less than 75% of profits of the higher year.

Small Firms Loan Guarantee Scheme

The Department of Trade and Industry for many years has been success-fully supporting small businesses through promoting, in conjunction with a number of banks, a loan guarantee scheme. Not all banks are involved and businesses that wish to avail themselves of this support may have to approach several banks before achieving success.

The Scheme

The Government through the DTI provides a guarantee to the commercial lender against default by the small business borrower. The guarantee cover is 70% of the amount outstanding for start-ups and 85% for estab-lished businesses. For this service the borrower generally pays a premium to the DTI annually of between 0.5% (for fixed interest rate loans) and 1.5% (for variable rate loans) on the whole loan amount. Previously this was 2.5% on the guaranteed element of the loan balance outstanding. If the loan does not exceed £30,000 the premiums are paid in advance and may be included in the loan amount borrowed. The premium on larger loans is paid quarterly in advance.

Eligibility

The business must have a **viable, new** (i.e. not a refinancing of existing debt) project for financing that has **failed to obtain conventional commercial support** by way of a loan or overdraft, either because there is a **lack of security** available for the lender, or the borrower's **past track record** has not been acceptable.

The loan must be used for business purposes for **starting up** or **develop-ing** a project, **expanding** a business or **improving its efficiency.** The business may be a **company, partnership, sole trader, franchise** or a co-**operative.** The borrower must be a small business with no more than 200 employees and related groups of businesses will be classified as one entity for eligibility. Its turnover, maximum £3 million for manufacturers and £1.5 million otherwise, will also be taken into account to determine the size criteria of the business. Owners holding more than a 20% interest in the business are not eligible for further loans in excess of the present loan maximum.

There is an extensive list of eligible and non-eligible activities conducted by the business and this is subject to change at any time by the DTI. Broadly speaking, manufacturing, construction and service industries are eligible but the following **services are not eligible** (subject to some concessions): financial services, gambling, intermediary agencies, non-vocational education, forestry, agriculture, fisheries, coal, shipbuilding, steel, transport, estate agents, hairdressers and saunas, insurance and brokers, museums and galleries, health care, motor vehicle maintenance, clubs, property, sporting organisations, railways, all retailing, catering, taxi hire, non-free public houses, travel agents.

Obligations of the borrower

The borrower will remain liable to repay the borrowing in full in the event of default, notwithstanding that the loan guarantee and all amounts owing may be pursued for restitution through legal channels up to liquidation of all security held and closure of the business. The lender holds the right to obtain repayment first from the borrower rather than through the guarantee.

The borrower is advised to raise a Business Plan for the business including the project. This should show the lender the viability of the business proposal and the personal commitment the borrower will bring to the project. The Business Plan will incorporate the usual headings: the management; the product or service offered; the markets involved; track record of the business; strategic objectives and long-term plans for the business; monthly financial projections preferably for at least two years ahead (Profit and Loss, Cash Flow, Balance Sheet, Capital expenditure); how much finance is required; what security is available; what management monitoring systems are in place; and the principal risks that have been discerned with the remedies to adopt.

The borrower must facilitate the monitoring of the loan, including providing a comparative statement on a quarterly basis of actual cash flow and trading profit achieved with the original project forecasts.

Terms of the lender

The lender will determine the terms and conditions of the loan, although this is negotiable with the borrower. The size of loan may be from £5,000 up to £250,000 and the period may not extend beyond ten years. The lender may allow the borrower to take capital repayment 'holidays'. The loan may be issued in stages but must be drawn within six months of the issue of the guarantee. It will be the choice of the lender to demand that the borrower provide additional security for the loan.

When to invoke the Scheme

Banks will prefer to evaluate a new project, whether for a start-up enterprise or for an existing business, on a regular commercial basis and only consider the Scheme as the final necessary (top-up) element for approval of the advance. This is because the costs of adopting and monitoring the Scheme are greater than for a programmed loan off-the-shelf that probably holds more profit for them than the DTI derivative. In essence, if the commercial risk is acceptable then the additional guarantee will not be necessary.

The borrower should concentrate on proving the viability of the business and the project, obviously given the commercial trading risks involved. If the lender accepts the risks then a more generalised loan facility can be agreed and should be less costly to negotiate than the DTI guarantee add-on. The potential sticking point may arise when the lender asks the borrower for additional personal security, say, such as a charge on the family home. (If the business is a sole trader then the borrower will already be personally liable in case of default, including putting the family home at risk dependent on who has ownership and who is in partial/whole possession). It is at this stage that the DTI guarantee may prove useful.

Consider the following example of a start-up venture:

	Investment
New Company.	
Proprietor's share capital invested	£50,000
'Soft' loan from family subordinated as to repayment	£20,000
Equity/pseudo equity investment	£70,000
Borrowing requested	£50,000
Net Worth of the business at outset	£120,000

The bank has requested additional security.
The borrower states that no other security is available.
The bank considers that the project is soundly based and should be viable.
The request is for DTI Loan Scheme Guarantee support.
The Guarantee will be to cover 70% of the debt, i.e.   £ 35,000

The bank's exposure is reduced from £50,000 (42% of Net Worth) to £15,000 (12.5% of the initial Net Worth).

It is suggested that the borrower should request the bank to approve the loan on this basis without the requirement for additional security in view of its reduced risk.

How to read a Balance Sheet

Entrepreneurs and business owners with limited time at their disposal to examine the financial implications in depth of the Profit and Loss Account and Balance Sheet of a company or firm may find the following guidelines of help. They will not take the place of a full 'due diligence' exercise, but they should enable a quick assessment of the business to be made from the figures so that any further in-depth appraisal can be channelled more appropriately. The order of the assessment is recommended as that shown but can be a matter of individual choice. The thirteen steps of 'wisdom' are as follows:

The Balance Sheet

1. Book Net Worth

- Sum the Share Capital in issue and the Retained Earnings figures;

- Add to this any 'pseudo capital' e.g. (interest-free) Loans and any pension balances due to the Proprietors/their families;

- Deduct any Intangible Assets e.g. Goodwill or Deferred Assets in the form of expenditure not yet represented by completed assets;

- (Optional) Deduct the stated value of Brand Names and similar items;

- The result will show the book value of the Net Worth of the business.

Analyse how the Net Worth is made up.
i.e. it will consist of so much Fixed Assets, so much Net Current Assets (or Liabilities) and so much other long-term items. Consider how much of Net Current Assets relates to Stock (and Work-in-Progress). This is what one would be taking on were the business to change ownership.

2. Borrowings

- Sum the external short-term and long-term debt outstanding in the form of Bank overdrafts, loans and other third party loans;

- Add hire purchase and leasing balances where they are 'on-Balance Sheet', ignoring any Notes showing future leasing commitments.

View the Borrowings as a percentage of Net Worth.
Is it high (over 100%), low (less than 50%) or middling bearing in mind the type of business being transacted and the need or otherwise for finance?
If the business is a company, consider whether any entries in Notes to the Accounts will affect the level of future borrowings (refer to item 12 hereafter).

3. Total long-term Assets compared with total long-term Debt

- Long-term Assets are taken as Tangible Fixed Assets and Investments held not being classified as short-term holdings;

- Long-term Debt is external third party Borrowings not being classified as Current Liabilities.

Do long-term Assets exceed long-term Debt? If not, by how much is the business 'imbalanced' and is this risky? (i.e. if long-term Assets exceed long-term Debt this means that some long-term Assets are being financed by short-term Debt, and the business is 'borrowing short to invest long-term' with the potential risk of not being able to renew short-term Debt thereby creating a future cash flow problem).

4. The mix of Fixed Assets

- Does the asset base comprise mostly of Freeholds and Leaseholds?

- Are the Leaseholds short or long-term?

- Is the asset base mainly written down Plant and Machinery?

Freehold assets may hold a current value in excess of their book value.
If so, is the Net Worth of the business properly shown by the Balance Sheet?
Is it good financial management to invest in Freeholds and/or Leaseholds?
Does much Plant and Machinery have to be expensively replaced soon?

5. Trade Debtors compared with Trade Creditors

- By how much does one total exceed the other total?

- Is the business accepting more credit than it is giving (to its suppliers)?

A business will be better placed if it accepts more credit since this will be part of its operating (working) capital from which to earn more profit.

(Note: by converting the annual Turnover into a daily amount one can calculate how many days are represented by outstanding Trade Debtors. If the standard terms of trade are to give 30 days credit after the month end, this approximates to 45 days outstandings on average. A higher figure shown than this suggests poor credit control).

6. Stocks and Work-in-Progress

- Compare the total Stock figure with that for Purchases made in the year.

- How are Stocks made up between raw materials and finished products?

- Divide the Stocks total into the Turnover figure to show stock turnover.

If Stocks are high relative to Purchases in the year, are excess stocks held?
If the finished products value is high it may mean that sales are sluggish. The number of times stock is turned over will indicate the business activity. A quick turnover and high activity will indicate good sales demand when the selling price of the goods being sold, relatively speaking, is not high.

7. Current Assets exceeding Current Liabilities (or vice versa)

- The higher the Net Current Asset total then the more financially strong will be the business, providing long-term Debt is more modest.

- Similarly, a Net Current Liabilities position will indicate the opposite.

To hold Net Current Assets, providing it is not principally invested in stocks and the year-end figure is not affected by seasonal influences, will denote a good cash position and augur well for future expenditure plans.

The Profit and Loss Account

8. Turnover and the Gross Profit margin earned thereon (after deducting the Direct Costs of running the business).

- Is the mix of Turnover (if made available) acceptable?
- Is the level of Turnover acceptable?
- Is the Gross Profit margin acceptable for the type of business?

These should be evaluated in accordance with the reasons for viewing the business.

9. Net Profit earned before Tax and Exceptional items

- Taxation is not directly controllable by the business and may be left out;

- Exceptional items should not be accounted as part of on-going trading.

- Is the Net Profit sufficient reward earned by the business?

The actual Taxation borne may be compared with the standard rate applicable in the Notes to the Balance Sheet, as it will indicate in conjunction with the amount of tax deferred what tax planning has been effected by the business. The reason for Exceptional items should be studied for the information given as to earlier activities. The Net Profit should be evaluated in accordance with the reasons for viewing the business.

10. Retained Earnings after tax compared with the Dividend and/or Drawings declared

- Is the reward acceptable?

- What is the percentage yield on the Net Worth invested in the business?

The dividend declared (or owners' drawings) may be insufficient for the investment. Can these returns be improved to a satisfactory level?
(Note: if the Net Worth at the beginning and end of the year has changed perceptibly other than through organic growth, it should be averaged, and possibly even weighted, to obtain a more representative figure).

Other factors

11. Operational Cash Flow

- Take the Retained Earnings from the Profit and Loss Account;

- Add to this the Depreciation/Amortisation deducted from the profit;

- Eliminate any profit or loss on sale of assets;

- The resulting figure will be the Operational Cash Flow for the year;

- Add any cash invested in the business during the year;

- Deduct any loan repayments made in the year;

- Deduct the total of Capital Expenditure on assets less sales proceeds;

- The resulting figure will be the overall Cash Flow for the year.

The business may show a profit being earned but a negative generation of cash due to other payments exceeding receipts. This important factor must be evaluated. It should be assessed whether the cash flow is sufficient to pay dividends/drawings at the level expected and to finance the future plans for the business.

12. Notes to the Accounts

- Examine each Note to see whether it portrays a better or worse scenario;

- There may be some expenses or receipts not otherwise indicated;

- They will include future liabilities to take account of.

It will be important to assess the effect on cash flow of any future liabilities. These will include the cost of future leasing and committed capital expenditure.

13. Trends

- A single Profit and Loss Account and Balance Sheet must be augmented by an assessment of trends shown by comparative figures for earlier years.

Funds for temporary investment

From time to time small businesses earn money in excess of their immediate spending needs and the Proprietor or Shareholder does not wish to
withdraw the surplus funds. There may still be borrowings not yet repaid
but locked into fixed rate loans or other conditions preventing their early
repayment. This leaves several options for the business to consider how
to manage the excess liquidity:

- Put the excess money on temporary deposit at short notice of withdrawal.

- Negotiate an account setoff with the bank at a fixed margin.

- Pay outstanding bills from suppliers early to obtain cash discounts.

- Order additional trading stocks early, negotiated at advantageous
  prices.

- Repay existing loans early.

- Match any fixed rate remaining term loans with fixed rate term
  deposits.

- Replace capital equipment earlier than planned to achieve cost
  savings.

- Embark on an additional marketing programme to boost sales.

- Consider buying currency early to gain an advantageous exchange
  rate.

Money on **temporary deposit** is probably the least beneficial method to
adopt given the poor relative rates of interest for short-term deposits. If
the business is likely to incur large swings in cash balances into and out
of overdraft, the bank may agree to accept a set margin on the daily net
balance (**setoff**) over successive trading periods. This can be particularly
advantageous if the period in overdraft is lengthy or the amount overdrawn can be large. **Suppliers' discounts** usually offered are up to 5%
and not very generous. If a particular supplier is short of cash and is
deemed a good credit risk, then a special rate may be negotiated. Special
deals may also be arranged for the **supply of stocks** prior to their required
date for production purposes.

If the business has a variable rate loan with several years remaining and since it was negotiated interest rates generally have risen, the loan may beneficially be **repaid early**. If the loan was taken out at a variable rate and early repayment could only be done by incurring penalties, and if the fixed rate currently available in the market for deposits of a term matching the remaining period of the loan at least equals the loan rate because interest rates in the meantime have risen, the future cost of the loan could be negated by **matching the loan** amount with an equal deposit. If the loan was at a fixed rate and interest rates generally have since fallen, it may be beneficial to repay the loan early even if interest penalties arise. Conversely, if interest rates have risen, the cost of continuing the (by now cheap) fixed rate loan will have to be weighed against using the surplus funds in other ways to gain a greater financial reward.

Replacing equipment early may lead to greater efficiency of working at lower (maintenance) costs and increased production. If a **marketing programme** is decided upon, the potential benefits should be carefully assessed beforehand. Where the business trades overseas and has an on-going currency requisite, rather than dealing in forward foreign exchange contracts the currency may be purchased in advance to benefit not only from accruing some deposit interest but also to hold the opportunity for gain should favourable currency exchange rate movements occur in future. It must be noted, however, that an incorrect reading of currency movements will lead to a loss.

Perhaps the key decisions to consider are whether or not to use the surplus funds in the business to improve performance and, above all, to ensure before the funds are spent that the projected needs of the business in terms of future cash flow requirements are not jeopardised.

The choice of becoming a corporate entity

Many businesses start as a sole trader or partnership and at a later stage reach the point of considering whether to convert into a company. There are disposal and Capital Gains tax considerations to consider where a previously unincorporated concern is being incorporated. The position is more straightforward if a company is being set up to trade as such from the outset. There are advantages and disadvantages in trading as a company and the principal aspects are listed below.

Advantages

- The company takes over responsibility of liability for the business.

- Divestment of a share of the business can easily be arranged.

- There are advantageous tax rates on the profits earned each year. (i.e. for the tax year 2001/02 the tax rate is 10% on the first £10,000 earned; 20% up to £300,000 and 30% above £1.5 million with marginal rates in between, whereas the personal tax rates are 10% on the first £1,880; 22% up to £29,400 and 40% thereafter).

- Company dividends are not liable to National Insurance contributions.

- A proportion of profits may be retained in the business and be taxed only at the time of withdrawal.

- The operating regulations of the company can be adopted (e.g. Table A under the Companies Acts) or made specific to the requirements of the directors. They do not have to be amended when a new shareholder/director is appointed.

- As a separate entity, there may be discretion to apportion business between a sole trader and a company on a VAT and non-VAT basis subject to the registration regulations.

- Companies may be eligible for special grants and reliefs that are not available to sole traders.

Disadvantages

- There are on-going regulatory returns to adhere to with penalties for non or late compliance.

- Company financial results have to be filed annually at Companies House and be subject to varying degrees of disclosure.

- A formal statutory audit may be required depending on the turnover of the business.

- Employer's National Insurance is levied on Directors' pay.

- Assets held in the company's name are owned by the company.

- Directors have personal responsibilities and may incur personal liabilities in the (negligent) performance of their corporate duties.

- Minority shareholders holding 25% or more of the issued share capital may exercise constraints on the majority owner over the disposal of company assets.

- Certain management decisions or changes of the operating regulations of a company will have to be approved by Special Resolution in General or Special meetings.

Index